COUNSELS AND THOUGHTS

FOR THE

SPIRITUAL LIFE OF BELIEVERS.

COUNSELS AND THOUGHTS.

COUNSELS AND THOUGHTS

FOR THE

SPIRITUAL LIFE OF BELIEVERS

IN RELATION TO—

I. FULL SALVATION IN CHRIST.

II. THE SPIRITUAL CONFLICT.

III. THE LIFE OF FAITH AND FELLOWSHIP.

IV. JUSTIFICATION, SANCTIFICATION, &c.

TOGETHER WITH

V. BRIEFER THOUGHTS AND COUNSELS FOR DAILY HELP IN
THE SPIRITUAL LIFE.

By THOMAS MOOR.

" As ye have therefore received Christ Jesus the Lord, so walk
ye in Him; rooted and built up in Him, and stablished in the
faith, as ye have been taught, abounding therein with thanksgiving." —COL. ii. 6, 7.

Second Edition.

SOLID GROUND CHRISTIAN BOOKS
PORT ST LUCIE FL USA

SOLID GROUND CHRISTIAN BOOKS
1682 SW Pancoast Street
Port St Lucie FL 34987
(205) 587-4480
mike.sgcb@gmail.com
http://www.solid-ground-books.com

COUNSELS AND THOUGHTS
FOR THE SPIRITUAL LIFE OF THE BELIEVER

by Thomas Moor

First Edition in London—1882
First Solid Ground Edition—October 2019

Cover Image from the studio of Ric Ergenbright

Cover Design by Borgo Design, Tuscaloosa, Alabama

ISBN: 978-159925-5125

****
SPECIAL DEDICATION OF THIS NEW EDITION
Solid Ground is delighted to dedicate this printing of
Counsels & Thoughts for the Spiritual Life of Believers
to
BOB HART
Simpsonville, South Carolina
Long-time customer and friend,
who first told us about this book!

PREFACE.

—◆—

THIS book is published, as its title indicates, for
the use of believers—that is, for the use of all
those who, through grace, have been effectually
led to see, in some measure, their position as
sinners before God, and their deep need of salvation through the atoning death of the Lord
Jesus Christ.

Its aim, through the gracious influence of the
Holy Spirit, is to be helpful to them for their
establishment in the full assurance of faith, in
relation to their perfected and unchanging salvation in Christ; also to be useful to them in their
conflict with indwelling sin; and to assist them
in their endeavour to live a life of faith on the
Lord Jesus, to walk in daily fellowship with Him,
and to be at all times His faithful witnesses.

It purposely contains repetitions of Gospel statements; for, although the spiritual needs of believers are many and varied, there is but one great fountain of fulness for all, even the Lord Jesus Christ Himself; for "the sum of all spiritual progress and spiritual life is—more of Christ in the mind, better to know Him—more of Christ in the heart, better to love Him, and to be more influenced by Him—more of Christ in the life, better to serve Him" (page 166).

Moreover, those who have been privileged to have much intercourse with believers in relation to their spiritual experience in all its varied stages, and in relation to the many mistakes and heart troubles they fall into, are well aware that spiritual truths which the believer had often thought about, without any apparent spiritual benefit, have, when presented to the mind in a different form, or in a different relationship, or at a different time, often been made instrumental of much blessing through the gracious influence of the Holy Spirit.

The fifth part of this book contains three divisions of briefer thoughts and counsels. Each division contains thirty-one; so that those who find them helpful in their spiritual life, may use them daily for three months.

One paper in the second part, two in the third, the last two in the fourth, and about one-third of the fifth part, were published separately some years ago. They have been revised, and are now included in this volume.

May our gracious Father—the Father also of our Lord and Saviour Jesus Christ—grant that this attempt to be useful to His eternally-loved, but often much-tried children, may result in much glory to the name of Jesus, in their hearts and lives, through the effectual blessing of the Holy Spirit.

July 1881.

CONTENTS.

FIRST PART.

COUNSELS AND THOUGHTS CONCERNING THE BELIEVER'S STANDING IN FULL SALVATION.

SECOND PART.

THIRD PART.

FOURTH PART.

COUNSELS AND THOUGHTS CONCERNING JUSTIFICATION, SANCTIFICATION, &c.

FIFTH PART.

BRIEF THOUGHTS AND COUNSELS, WITH SPECIAL PORTIONS OF SCRIPTURE FOR THE SPIRITUAL LIFE IN THE DAILY PATH.

COUNSELS AND THOUGHTS.

First Part.

CONCERNING THE BELIEVER'S STANDING IN FULL SALVATION.

I.

To the Believer—on living in the unclouded enjoyment of covenant blessings.

THE Lord Jesus did not die merely to make salvation possible for sinners, if they would but truly repent, and trust in Him, and persevere in faithfulness to the end of life. He died, not to make salvation possible, but to make it certain, for all that the Father gave Him. His death ensures that all such shall receive grace to repent and believe, and persevere to the end.

Covenant engagements include the gift of everything necessary for full, final, and complete

salvation; and place all the power in the hands
of the Lord Jesus, for carrying out these engagements, according to His own words: "Thou hast
given Him power over all flesh, that He should
give eternal life to as many as Thou hast given
Him."

It is written, "He hath made Him who knew
no sin, to be sin for us; that we might be made
the righteousness of God in Him." It is not
written that the Father made His Son to be sin
for us, that we might have an opportunity
of making ourselves the righteousness of God.
No: He who made His Son to be sin for us,
also made us to be the righteousness of God in
Him.

It is essential for your spiritual comfort, that
the certainty of your salvation should be with
you a matter of abiding and uninterrupted
consciousness in mind and heart. Many things
will tend to surround this consciousness with
clouds of darkness and doubt, and will succeed
in doing so, unless you are firmly built upon the
true foundation—Christ crucified; and unless
your mind so continually refers to it, on the first
approach of questioning doubts, as to make it
a refuge always at hand, and easily reached.
Indeed it is well very frequently to refer to
this, even when no questioning doubts arise, so

that what is true concerning you in God's purposes and work of grace, may become at all times a clear and vivid consciousness to yourself.

One of the greatest hindrances to the spiritual life of the child of God, is a state of continued doubt about his salvation. Such a state has a tendency to weaken the soul for everything good, and to lay it more open to the ensnaring influences of its spiritual enemies. It prevents the soul laying hold on eternal life, and laying claim to the promises of grace for time of need, and robs it of the enjoyment of all those spiritual blessings in Christ Jesus, which are its rightful portion. It makes trial harder to bear, and all the cares of life a heavier burden. It casts a gloom over every earthly good, making the present joyless, and the future hopeless.

Being spiritually enlightened to see its danger and need, the soul can find no true source of comfort or hope in anything earthly; yet it has no abiding comfort, no assured hope, no rest in anything heavenly. No joy in the world. No joy in spiritual things. Thick clouds above; deep waters beneath; storm and tempest all around; tossed to and fro like a ship without a helm, and ready to sink at any moment.

Nothing can remove you from the safety of the refuge provided by the perfect work of

Christ on your behalf. God Himself will take care of that. Let it be yours to take care that nothing prevents you from fully enjoying the comfort and peace of that refuge.

Remember that you have altogether done with the law as the covenant of works. One failure takes you out of that covenant for ever. You are now dealt with according to the covenant of grace, in which covenant you for ever abide. No failure can remove you from that; for in its arrangements every failure, every sin to the end of your life, is taken into account, and fully arranged for, and completely put away by the death of Christ. By His death you are for ever delivered. "The blood of Jesus Christ cleanseth us from all sin."

You cannot lay up a store of grace for future use. The Lord Jesus will have you to be a continual receiver from Himself, and, therefore, keeps your store of grace in His own hands, where it was first placed by your Heavenly Father for your use (2 Tim. i. 9). It is well, however, to be laying up a store of sound doctrine and spiritual experience; so that when the time of more pressing need may come, the soul so well knows its standing and refuge in Christ, that this special need is at once met and satisfied.

Look upon your salvation as a thing accomplished once and for ever; and live in accordance with this fact. The Lord Jesus never changes; but if it were possible that He could change, the work of salvation which He completed for you can never be altered. If a friend clears off the debts of a penniless debtor by paying all freely and fully; however much that friend might change in after-years, it would not alter the fact that the debtor is cleared and stands free. It is, however, your joy to know that the Lord Jesus is not like unto sinful men. What He has done for you is the result of a love without beginning and without end. Whom He loves He loves always; notwithstanding all the changes, and perverseness, and unworthiness of the object loved.

Furthermore, ever remember that, as a believer, you are already fit for the heavenly inheritance, and made so by One who never fails in any work to which He puts His hand, even by God the Father Himself, as it is written: "Giving thanks unto the Father, which hath made us meet to be partakers of the inheritance of the saints in light" (Col. i. 12). "Which hath made us meet." Then it is already done. You are already and always meet or fit to be a partaker of the heavenly inheritance, however much you may each day have cause to mourn over your want of conformity to the image of your Lord.

You have a twofold meetness or fitness for that inheritance : a legal meetness, and an experimental or spiritual meetness. A legal meetness, because the claims of the Divine law against you have been satisfied, and a perfect legal righteousness has been provided for you ; and an experimental meetness, because of a spiritual capacity implanted within you, enabling you to enjoy spiritual things.

You have neither meetness of yourself naturally ; inasmuch as you could never yourself satisfy the claims which Divine justice had against you because of your transgressions, nor work out for yourself a perfect legal righteousness ; and you have naturally no spiritual life whereby spiritual things and spiritual joys become desirable.

Your legal meetness is by the substitutionary work of Christ ; whereby through His obedience you are made righteous, and through His atoning death on the cross, you are redeemed from the curse of the law. Your spiritual or experimental fitness or meetness is by the quickening work of the Holy Spirit in your heart, whereby you become a possessor of a spiritual life, with spiritual capacities, enabling you to appreciate and enjoy the holiness of your heavenly inheritance.

Without the legal meetness, you could not enter heaven. Without the spiritual meetness, you could not enjoy heaven.

This twofold meetness is God the Father's gift to you. He gave for you His only-begotten Son to work out your legal meetness. He gave unto you the Holy Spirit, through whom you have your experimental meetness in being born again unto newness of life.

Let us then, evermore, out of the depths of our heart, give "thanks unto the Father which hath made us meet to be partakers of the inheritance of the saints in light."

II.

To the Believer—concerning legal and filial reconciliation to God; and concerning the forgiveness of sins.

As a believer you are not only a saved sinner, but a reconciled child of God, and it is your privilege to walk daily in the consciousness and enjoyment of that relationship.

You cannot, however, rejoice in the consciousness of your complete reconciliation to your Heavenly Father, and walk in unreserved communion with Him as His child, unless as a sinner you have the full consciousness that your reconciliation unto Him, as the holy and just God, against whom you have sinned, has been already completed for you by God Himself, through the death of His beloved Son.

If you think that your reconciliation to God's justice depends in the least degree upon your faith, or upon anything you can do, you will never know true comfort, because increasing knowledge of yourself will but show how utterly unable you are of yourself to do anything pleasing to God ; and that even when grace is imparted and grace assists, the best actions or thoughts, and even faith itself, are rendered so imperfect by the evil within that it is only through the merits of Christ they can be accepted of God, and pleasing in His sight.

Your consciousness of reconciliation unto your Heavenly Father must, however, rest upon the consciousness of your complete reconciliation unto Him as the just and holy God. The latter is ever the foundation of the former. Where there is any doubt about your reconciliation to Him as the just and holy God whose laws you have dishonoured, such doubt will hinder your walk of conscious reconciliation with Him as your Father.

Your reconciliation with God as God, is distinct from your reconciliation to God as a Father. Reconciliation to God has to do with your position as a sinner. Reconciliation to your Father has to do with your position as a child. Reconciliation to God must necessarily be in the way of strict justice, and is altogether independent of your experience whether of conviction or of faith. Your reconciliation to your Heavenly Father is different, and is the result of gracious operations in your heart.

As God, His justice must be satisfied. As a Father, His love must be satisfied. The former He Himself accomplished by the gift of His beloved Son, who satisfied Divine justice for the sins of the transgressors by laying down His life for them. The latter He accomplishes through the gift of the Holy Spirit, by whose quickening power the sinner is awakened to see his natural state of guilt and condemnation ; and is led to flee for refuge and salvation to the full provision made in the death of Christ for sinners. By this he learns his full reconciliation as a sinner to Divine justice ; and looks to God as a God of grace and mercy, without any fear of wrath or judgment to come. Taught by the word of God, and influenced by the spirit of adoption, he soon learns that the provision thus made for him as a sinner by the God of grace is also a provision made for him as a child by his Heavenly Father; and in this consciousness he looks as a reconciled child to God, calling Him " Abba, Father."

All the children of God considered as sinners under law condemnation were, once for all, reconciled by the death of Jesus Christ as their law surety (Rom. v. 10). This legal reconciliation was complete and can never be altered. Before multitudes of them were born, all their sins were beforehand known to God, and reconciliation was made and satisfaction rendered for all by Jesus Christ, as the Father's covenant servant on their behalf.

On the completeness of this legal reconciliation of the sinner rests the filial reconciliation of the child; and that filial reconciliation is the sure result of such legal reconciliation. Therefore, when, by the quickening grace of the Holy Spirit, a sinner is made anxious about his soul and longs to be reconciled to God : it is not only that he may receive the consciousness of full reconciliation as a sinner to God through the atoning death of Christ, but also that he may enjoy the privilege of sonship, and the consciousness of full reconciliation as a child to his Heavenly Father.

According to the order of God's word, legal
reconciliation is first provided, then proclaimed,
and afterwards received. Provided in Christ by
God Himself (Rom. v. 10). Proclaimed in the
ministry of the Gospel (2 Cor. v. 18). Received
through faith by the awakened sinner (Rom. v.
11, *margin*), resulting in conscious peace with God,
and in joy in Him as the God of grace and salvation ; followed by the consciousness of sonship,
which results in a loving and trusting walk with
God as his own Father, towards whom he looks
with a heart conscious of peace and rest and
reconciliation (Rom. viii. 14–16; Gal. iii. 26,
iv. 4–7 ; 1 John iii. 1, 2). Many saved sinners
do not, however, enjoy this latter privilege of
sonship and filial reconciliation, but stop short
at salvation.

It is indeed a great blessing to live in the
consciousness of being saved through the atoning death of the Lord Jesus ; but that privilege
should be the step to the further privilege of
assured sonship.

There was no antagonism between God as
God, and God as a Father ; but His love as a
Father moved Him to make every arrangement
for the satisfaction of His justice on behalf of His
loved ones, and to make every arrangement for
their eternal well-being ; so that the yearning of

His heart as their Father might be fully satisfied in having them evermore with Him as His happy children in their bright home above (Heb. ii. 10; John xvii. 2 ; Heb. ii. 13).

As the question of the forgiveness of sins is closely related to this subject, a few words in explanation of that question will not, therefore, be out of place.

Law and justice make no provision for reconciliation or forgiveness. It is a question beyond their domain altogether. All that law and justice require is full satisfaction—satisfaction either in the perfect obedience of the subject, or satisfaction in the payment of a suitable penalty for disobedience. In either way the law is satisfied. It thus reigns supreme in its own domain. Reward for obedience, or forgiveness for disobedience, pertains to the domain of grace and merey. This is altogether distinct from that of law and justice, but is, nevertheless, subordinate thereto, and founded thereon ; so that grace and mercy cannot have their full outflow until they have first found out a way to satisfy the claims of law and justice. Indeed, to suppose the contrary would be to overturn all true and just government. If grace and mercy reigned supreme over law, it would show that the arm of law and justice was too weak to assert its right ; for th strength of the law consists in its power to obtain satisfaction if transgressed. Failing this, it lies prostrate in the dust, eternally dishonoured.

Law and justice, however, reigning supreme, they require that grace and mercy should manifest their love of justice by first providing for the full satisfaction of their claims against the transgressors, before they wrought any further good for the objects of their favour. If grace and mercy would place the prisoners of the law amongst the most highly favoured subjects, or give them the place and privileges of the children of the king in the king's palace, they must first release the prisoners, not by lawless force, but by providing a full satisfaction of the law's just claims against them. After that, the way is open for grace and mercy to work out their fullest desires.

There are two kinds of forgiveness spoken of in Scripture. The one concerning the sinner as related to the royal law of Divine justice. The other concerning the child as related to the commands of his Father. The former forgiveness is alluded to in Acts xiii. 38: "Be it known unto you, men and brethren, that through this man is preached unto you the forgiveness of sins." This forgiveness is from the God of grace and mercy, for transgressions as regards an aveng-

ing law ; for which transgressions, satisfaction to
that law has been rendered by the atoning death
of the Lord Jesus. This forgiveness embraces
the whole of the sins throughout the whole life,
and is complete at once, and received by the
sinner when he first trusts in the Lord Jesus for
salvation.

The other kind of forgiveness is alluded to in
1 John i. 9 : " If we confess our sins, He is
faithful and just to forgive us our sins." This
forgiveness is from God as our Heavenly Father,
through the repentant confession of our sins to
Him as we are conscious of having acted contrary
to His will in our daily path. As regards Divine
justice, no repentance, no confession, however
sincere, will procure forgiveness. That comes to
believers, from the God of grace, solely through
the full satisfaction to Divine justice rendered by
Jesus Christ (Acts xiii. 38, 39 ; Eph. i. 7 ; Col.
i. 14). Divine justice being thus satisfied, and
grace having pronounced a full and free and
unconditional forgiveness, the way is fully opened
for the display of Fatherly pity and mercy, in
forgiving the child his daily transgressions.

God as judge gives an acquittance for the
whole of life's transgressions, even before many
of the transgressions have been actually committed, when justice has been beforehand fully

satisfied for all. But the Father only grants His Fatherly forgiveness after His child has actually sinned. It is only then the child consciously needs the forgiveness, and the Father is ready to grant it at once, on the confession of His child.

The eye of God, as a judge, sees no sin upon those sinners who truly trust in the Lord Jesus for salvation; for their sins and guilt were alike judicially taken away by Jesus through His death on the cross, when the iniquities and the resulting condemnation were laid upon Him (Isa. liii. 6, 11 ; Heb. i. 3). Their sins could not, judicially and in law, be upon both the sinners and their Surety at the same time. Therefore, by the death of Christ for those sins, both the sinners and their Surety are free.

Thus it is that God, as the Head of law and justice, beholds no sins on those who trust in the Lord Jesus. When, however, we consider the relation of God as a Father to His already redeemed and reconciled children, the question is completely different. God, as a Father, does behold the transgressions of His children whenever they disobey His commands ; and He will visit such with Fatherly chastisement, unless they confess their sins and seek His forgiveness.

The child of God in confessing to His Father,

should not ask forgiveness as if he were a sinner
in danger of eternal condemnation for his sins;
for there is no such condemnation for him now;
that being completely removed by the Lord
Jesus: but he should ask forgiveness as a
penitent child who is grieved for having dis-
pleased his loving and gracious Father.

The forgiveness sought in the Lord's prayer
is a Father's forgiveness, and is not in any
relation whatever to eternal judgment and condemnation.

III.

Concerning the distinctive character of the faith of God's elect.

THERE is a faith which is the faith of the
unregenerate; the faith of those who are still
dead in sin.   There is also a faith which is the
faith of the true believer; the faith of those
quickened by the Holy Spirit; the "faith of
God's elect."

Each may have the same general object—that
is, God, in the Trinity of the glorious persons,
Father, Son, and Holy Spirit—and the same
general subject—that is, the inspired word of
God,—but the faith of the unregenerate man

will influence him to come before God in the
plenitude of his religious rites and ceremonies,
his prayers and doings ; whereas the faith of the
true believer, the "faith of God's elect," will
influence its possessor to come before God in the
living consciousness of his inner life ; the consciousness of one possessing new, and spiritual,
and most pressing needs, which no religious
rites or ceremonies, no religious activities of
his own, can satisfy.

The one brings his religion before God, and
hopes for God's favour because of it. The other
brings before God his emptiness, his sinfulness,
and need, and casts himself upon God's mercy
as revealed in Christ. The former has no real
intercourse with God on his most religious day ;
when his attention is wholly given to his religious
observances, and when most surrounded by outward religious influences. But the latter, by a
mere thought heavenward, or by a few whispered
words of prayer or praise, will have real intercourse with God, even though his energies be
fully engaged in the duties of his calling, and
he be surrounded by circumstances apparently
unfavourable to the spiritual life.

Another distinctive feature in the "faith of
God's elect" is in the fact that, although its
object is the Eternal God in the Trinity of the

Persons, Father, Son, and Holy Spirit, it looks especially and continually to the Lord Jesus.

It not only credits the whole record of God concerning His Son Jesus Christ ; but because of the special need of salvation, a consciousness of which has been aroused by the Holy Spirit's quickening work in the heart, it has special regard to the Lord Jesus Himself, as made known in that record as the gift of God, that whosoever believeth in Him should not perish, but have everlasting life.

The " faith of God's elect " centres in the cross of Christ ; for it there beholds, in the death of Christ for sinners, the way of full salvation. The force of mere religiousness with its natural convictions will lead a man to do much, but it never makes him thoroughly out of conceit with the power of man. It never brings him solely to rely upon the " power of God " as made manifest in the cross of Christ. The natural man will be doing in some way or other ; and hence is the power of man, but it never brings salvation.

He who possesses spiritual life, and who, is guided by the word of God under the gracious influence of the Holy Spirit, ceases from his own doing in every way as regards the question of his salvation, and relies solely on the doing of God by the cross of Christ ; and thus the preach-

ing of the cross is to him the power of God unto
salvation (1 Cor. i. 18). It is God's way, and he
turns to it. Man's way, man's power, man's
wisdom, he no longer inquires about. He is
now content.

To the cross of Christ; to the atonement
there made for sin, and to the salvation thereby
accomplished for every needy sinner, must the
mind of the believer ever turn when he desires
to have his evidences of salvation brightened,
and his hopes of eternal life revived. It is the
one and only way, both for the newly-awakened
sinner and for the advanced believer.

In making progress in the spiritual life, the
" faith of God's elect " is fixed also on Christ
Himself, now in heaven at the right hand of
God; knowing that all fulness is in Him for the
supply of every need in the daily walk (Col. iii.
1–4 ; Eph. i. 22, 23).

IV.

*To the Believer—concerning sinnership and
salvation.*

Infinite wisdom, as well as infinite love, guides
the Lord Jesus in all His doings; and thus it
is He sees it best for His own glory and our

good, that His doings should at times be so
adverse to our own desires for ourselves.   All
things, the bitter and the sweet, are from the
hands of Him who makes all work together for
our good.   There is no cause to fear that He
will ever forsake you ; neither is there any cause
to fear that you will lose the consciousness of
your hope in His salvation, so long as you take
your stand upon your need as a sinner, and do
not go off that to self-doings or feelings, whereby
to recommend yourself to Him, or encourage
your hope in Him.

The worse a sinner is in his own sight, the
more is he welcome to Christ, and the more is
he suited to Christ's office as a Saviour.   The
better a sinner tries to be, in hope thereby of
coming with more confidence to Christ for salvation, the further off will he be, and the more
will doubt and darkness fill his mind, if he be a
truly awakened sinner.

When God the Father works for the salvation
of men, He is spoken of as "Him that justifieth
the ungodly."   When God the Son is spoken of
as working for the salvation of men, it is as
dying for sinners ; for the lost ; for enemies.
There is no warrant in Scripture for any one to
come to Christ but as a sinner.   He, therefore,
who would ignore his sinnership, will find no

welcome from Him, neither will he who tries to patch his sinnership with good works.

When Paul said to the gaoler, "Believe on the Lord Jesus Christ and thou shalt be saved," the only character the gaoler presented was that of a sinner trembling in view of the future. It is the same now. It is not the sinner trying to be religious or trying to be better, but the trembling sinner, that is suited to Christ and finds salvation in Him. Such a sinner has nothing to give—with him it is all need—and so Christ has all the glory of his salvation ; for God's salvation in Christ is all of grace, without works, lest any man should boast.

The question of growth in grace does not touch the question of salvation, for that is settled before grace begins to grow. The day of God's power for salvation over any soul, is when He makes that soul willing to look to Christ only for salvation, and to accept it without money and without price. That salvation is always unchangeable, and the believer's experience of it should be unchangeable also. It would be, if he were always content to rest only on God's testimony concerning it.

The day of God's fatherly care, and discipline, and leading homeward through much tribulation, is altogether distinct from His day of power for salvation; and witnesses much variety, and many changes in the believer, and in his path.

All the trials and afflictions the believer meets with in this life, are for the promotion of growth in grace, and in the true knowledge of self, and of Christ, and of our covenant God and Father; but this growth is much hindered if anything be allowed to dim the assurance of that salvation, which is God's free gift to awakened sinners.

Salvation is a certainty, and therefore we offer praise for that. The future incidents of our path on earth are, to us, all uncertainty, and, therefore, we trust—concerning them—to the wisdom and love of Him who, having given for our salvation His only-begotten Son, will, with Him, give also every needful thing.

V.

Concerning some of the causes of soul bondage.

There is no safety from spiritual bondage but in a clear and continued remembrance of the full liberty which we have in Christ. Believers in all ages have much need to bear in mind the exhortation of the Apostle to the Galatians: "Stand fast therefore in the liberty wherewith Christ hath made us free."

Some are in bondage to the law of God, under self-condemnation, because they see that they are not perfect in righteousness, according to that law, in its spiritual meaning. From this bondage Christ makes us free ; for He Himself is the end of the law for righteousness to every one who trusts in Him. He is its end as to its penal demands, for He died to satisfy them. He is its end as to the perfect righteousness it requires for full acceptance before God, for by His perfect obedience all His believing ones are made righteous with an everlasting righteousness. In this liberty we need to stand fast.

Others are in bondage to religious ordinances. They know that there is no salvation apart from Christ. They know that His death is necessary for their salvation ; but they think that ordinances also are necessary. With them salvation is thus partly by the death of Christ, and partly by the due observance of religious ordinances. This was the bondage into which the Galatians had been brought by false teachers, greatly to the dishonour of the finished work of Christ. They did not reject Christ and seek to be saved by works only. They would indeed rely upon Christ, but they would also rely upon their observance of religious rites and ordinances. This the Apostle told them would ruin all. Christ would profit them nothing. They would still remain under the condemnation of the law of God. Alas! this is what many are doing now, to the great bondage of their souls. From this bondage the way of deliverance is to make Christ all. The soul looking to Him and knowing that He is God's only way of salvation, and that God's way is sure, and His work perfect, and His word true, ceases altogether from any reliance whatever upon religious rites and ordinances, and is satisfied to rest its security on that way, and word, and work alone.

Others again are in bondage, not because they hope to do anything themselves to honour the law, or to make their salvation more secure by ordinances, for they know that Christ alone is sufficient both for perfect deliverance and for their standing in perfect righteousness before God; but they are in bondage because they look to their doings to find an evidence that they have an interest in this complete work of Christ. This may seem a very humble and God-honouring mode of action, but it is really neither; and besides, it is sure to bring upon the soul increased and grievous bondage. It is not humble, for there is a looking out for self-goodness. It is not

God-honouring, for there is dissatisfaction with the sure word of God. It engenders soul bondage, for it can never give a satisfactory evidence to warrant the appropriation of such infinite blessings. Out of this bondage right thoughts of Christ and His salvation will deliver the soul ; for in our thoughts of Himself is found our true evidence of having an interest in His finished salvation, His own word being witness : for if our need leads us to Him alone for help ; if our sin-sick state leads us to Him alone for healing ; if our lost condition leads us to trust in His atoning death alone for salvation ; we have the sure evidence that we are His. To all such, how assuring are His words : " Him that cometh unto me, I will in no wise cast out."

Some are in bondage from wrong views of faith. Their cry is, " I want faith. I know that salvation is free, and that it is all in Christ ; but I want faith. I am wretched because I have no faith ; and my salvation all depends upon my faith. I know it is the gift of God ; and I am continually praying to God to give it to me, and I shall never be happy until I have got it." This also is sore bondage, from which full deliverance is found in looking only to Christ, and thinking only of Him. So many look for faith instead of looking only to Christ. They do not see that in doing this the primary object of their desire is not Christ, but faith. If such an one be conscious that he is guilty before God, and utterly unable to do anything to save himself—if he knows that God's only way of saving sinners is through Jesus Christ His Son, whom He sent to be the Saviour by suffering and dying in their stead ; and who also was raised again from the dead, and ascended into heaven—if he has no other hope for the salvation of his soul but in the Lord Jesus thus dying, he already possesses faith, the faith for which he has been so long seeking and praying ; and he would have had the full consciousness of this, had not his seeking for faith, and looking for faith, instead of looking only to Christ, brought him into such bondage that his eyes were blinded to his real condition as already possessing faith, and already possessing salvation.

Soul bondage is also caused by relying upon faith as a kind of qualification by which to find acceptance with Christ ; whereas the consciousness of sinnership and need is the only true and scriptural qualification for acceptance by Him, and the only personal claim to His salvation. To those under this soul bondage how welcome should be the words of the Lord Jesus : " Come unto me, all ye that labour and are heavy laden, and I will give you rest." Yes ! it is our burdened, guilty soul that brings us to Jesus for salvation, and it is that only which brings us a hearty welcome from Him.

VI.

To the Believer—concerning the attainment of the full assurance of salvation.

Assurance of personal salvation comes only through trusting and believing—that is, through trusting to the death of Christ, as the only way of salvation, and believing God's word when He says that all who so do have eternal life. This, and this only, is the sure ground of assurance. God cannot lie. Christ has not died in vain. His death is the finished salvation of all who trust in Him.

You may, however, say : " Are there no after-experiences ? " Yes ; the first after-experience is satisfaction that you have found the sure way of peace, of deliverance, of salvation. You rest there. You want nothing more to make your salvation more secure. You have God's own word to rest upon, God's own salvation provided for you, and you are content.

But you may again say: " Am I not to be better ? " No ; not before salvation ; but after

salvation you will be both better and worse in
your own consciousness. You are sure to be
worse, because you will be sure to learn more
clearly, and more constantly, how far short you
come of all spiritual goodness, and how much
greater is the power of indwelling sin, and how
much deeper is the corrupt principle of your
natural heart, than you had ever imagined could
be possible. All your discovered badness does
not, however, alter your salvation in Christ. It
is only clearer evidence that your salvation must
be, as indeed it is, all of grace.

You will also be better in your own consciousness, inasmuch as you will be conscious that you
have a more healthy appetite ; for you will be
sure to hunger after Christ. You will want to
hear more about Christ, and think more about
Him. You will want to rejoice in Him, and to
please Him in your daily walk.

You will also find that sin, however it may
strive within, has not that mastery over you it
once had, because of your relationship to Christ,
who gives you strength against it; and because
of the new nature you possess, through the Holy
Spirit's gracious work, which gives you an increasing dislike to it.

All this, however, does not in the least make
your salvation from the wrath to come in any

way more perfect. It is perfect to start with, else your salvation would be of works, and not of grace alone.

Carefully consider the following statements of the Gospel of God's grace concerning all sinners who truly trust in the Lord Jesus for salvation.

It states that such sinners are already "justified by His blood " (Rom. v. 9) ; " justified from all things" (Acts xiii. 39), and that their salvation is already accomplished by His death in their stead (Eph. i. 7, ii. 8 ; Col. i. 12–14 ; 2 Tim. i. 9) ; and therefore there is now no condemnation to them (Rom. viii. 1) ; and that before Christ ascended, their sins were removed and judicially purged by His blood (Heb. i. 3 ; Rev. i. 5) ; and that they shall never perish, neither shall any pluck them out of the hands of Christ, nor out of the hands of His Father (John x. 28, 29) ; and that they already possess everlasting life (John iii. 36), and are already complete in Christ (Col. ii. 12), and fully accepted in the beloved (Eph. i. 6) ; and that it is their privilege now to rejoice as God's reconciled children, and in the assurance that they shall one day be with Him in glory (Rom. viii. 15–17, 30 to the end ; 1 John iii. 1).

VII.

Concerning the difference between the religion of the natural and the spiritual man.

To the natural man, even when religiously inclined, the most important teachings of the Gospel are but the dogmas of a creed in which he professes his belief. But he that is spiritual is never satisfied unless these teachings become to him the channel of heavenly blessing.

How differently the two look upon the Lord Jesus! The one is content with the acknowledgment that Christ is all He professes to be, and that His teachings are true, and to be fully received. The other acknowledges all this, but cannot be content unless Christ becomes the salvation, the strength, and the joy of his soul.

In everything outward, the two may appear alike; both professors of religion, and both active in religious duties. But what a difference in God's sight! What a difference in their condition in view of eternity! The one is in a state of death, ending in a more dreadful realisation of death hereafter. The other possesses a new and spiritual life, ending in a more glorious realisation of life in the world to come.

A correct creed, however well expressed or

firmly maintained, does not constitute a man a true believer; for he may possess a perfect creed without possessing that spiritual life, the gift of the Holy Spirit, which is peculiar to the true believer. This spiritual life is one of self-consciousness, apart from all rites, ceremonies, or creeds. True, the believer has a creed, but he has behind that creed a new life. His creed may be very imperfect, but the new life is still there. An imperfect creed may hinder its full manifestation, but can never cause its destruction.

It is written, "Ye are all children of God by faith in Christ Jesus." This faith is the faith of the spiritual man, of the true believer, and is not the mere believing a fact, but is the consciousness of a real life, which finds its deepest affinities in Christ Jesus. It is the consciousness of a need which is only met and satisfied in Him. It is a need so deepened by a truer and fuller view of Divine justice; that nothing but the substitutionary death and righteousness of the Lord Jesus will fully satisfy it. This is very different from a mere intellectual comprehension of, and satisfaction with, certain doctrines about Christ and His salvation, which are only influential in leading to an habitual engagement in religious services, leaving their possessor still an unsaved sinner.

The more excellent a mere natural man is, the less of evil is he conscious of possessing. Not so the child of God ; for the more spiritually-minded he becomes, the more conscious is he of his imperfections, and of his utter inability of himself for anything good before God. This is the only feature in the child of God which has no natural imitation. There may be a natural faith in Christ; a natural love for Christ; a natural following of Christ, and even a natural conviction of sin ; all without salvation : but never is there a continued natural conviction of utter inability for anything good before God. This is entirely and always the result of a spiritual nature previously given. The more a mere natural man has of natural religious regard for the Lord Jesus, the more satisfied is he with himself ; whereas the more there is of spiritual regard for the Lord Jesus, the more is there of increased dissatisfaction with self.

It is written, "But he that is spiritual judgeth (discerneth) all things" (1 Cor. ii. 15). One of the first results of this spiritual discernment is in his discernment of himself ; as it is again written, "In me (that is, in my flesh) dwelleth no good thing" (Rom. vii. 18).

The natural man has no new spiritual nature, with its spiritual principle, whereby to judge the natural, and therefore the natural judging the natural, he is right well pleased. The child of God, however, possesses a new spiritual nature whereby, with its spiritual principles, he can judge the natural that is in him. He only is able to have a right understanding of the natural; and the more healthy the manifestation of the spiritual nature, the more deep and vivid is the consciousness of the evil of the mere natural.

VIII.

Concerning the Father's indication of those sinners who are the objects of His love and salvation.

IT is evident from the teaching of Scripture, that although it is the Lord Jesus who alone saves by His atoning death, yet it is the Father who not only has charged the Lord Jesus whom to save, but who Himself, by the quickening power of the Holy Spirit, first begins that work of grace in the heart of the sinner which distinguishes him as the special object of salvation.

Those sinners whom Jesus came to save are spoken of in the word of God under certain terms and phrases; and although some of these terms and phrases do in other relationships pertain in a general sense to all mankind, yet in this relationship they are used in a particular sense to indicate the particular persons who are the objects of Divine love and salvation, even before such persons realise that love or that salvation. These phrases indicate a special and particular consciousness in the objects of salvation, which truly distinguishes them from the mass of mankind, and infallibly marks them as those for whom Christ was specially sent.

Such terms as " the broken-hearted—the captives—the blind—the bruised " (Luke iv. 18) clearly indicate the special persons who were the objects of our Lord's mission. But terms of more general signification are used with a like limitation. As, for instance, when the Lord Jesus says He came to save " that which was lost " (Matt. xviii. 10). The word " lost " in a general sense indicates the condition of all mankind, but our Lord does not use it in that general sense, but in a particular sense, as indicative only of those who are the special objects of His coming, and who will most assuredly be saved by Him ; otherwise His errand would be in vain and His labour lost. This term also no less clearly indicates the awakened consciousness of those whom He came to save. Such know themselves to be lost ones because of their sins—that is, they are

conscious that they have not only gone astray
from God and true holiness and eternal happiness, but so gone astray that, left to themselves,
there is for them no way of deliverance, and no
other portion hereafter but eternal misery. Now
it is the Father who causes this particular consciousness to arise in the heart; for He by the
Holy Spirit awakens the soul from its natural
unconsciousness, to understand in some measure
its position in relation to Divine law and justice,
and the eternity to come.

Many readily acknowledge the general position
that mankind are lost because of sin, who nevertheless show, by their utter indifference and care-
lessness, that they have not the least heart-
consciousness of their own individual danger.
The general acknowledgment never truly leads
the sinner to Christ, because there is no particular sense of personal need : but the soul that is
made conscious by the Father has a particular
sense of need, which nothing but Christ and His
salvation can fully satisfy ; and thus, even before
there is any consciousness of peace through Christ,
there is the mark (the Father's own mark) which
indicates those for whom Christ was specially
sent, and whose sins He bore on Calvary.

Sometimes a phrase is used which marks the
inner consciousness of those for whom the Lord

Jesus was *not* sent; and with it a contrasted
phrase which shows the consciousness of those for
whom He was sent; as, for instance, where He
says He "came not to call the righteous but
sinners to repentance" (Matt. ix. 13). The call
to repentance means eventually and effectually to
Himself, as their Lord and Saviour. This phraseology alludes to the difference of consciousness
in His hearers, some of whom were conscious of
being righteous in themselves (Luke xviii. 9),
whilst others, though probably but very few,
were truly conscious of being sinners before God.
The former were those for whom He did not
come. The latter were those for whom He was
specially sent.

It is true that some of the most determined
in their self-righteousness might ultimately be
brought by the Father, through the teaching of
the Holy Spirit, to the consciousness of their sinfulness; but until they were, they had not the
Father's mark upon them. Indeed, all those
whom Christ came to call effectually to repentance, are naturally more or less self-righteous;
but when the Holy Spirit opens their eyes to see
their true character in the sight of God's most
holy law, all their fancied self-righteousness is
seen in its true light, and they understand that
even at their very best they are sinners indeed.

Similar is the teaching in the words of our
Lord : "They that are whole need not a physician, but they that are sick" (Matt. ix. 12).
The "whole" are they who are unconscious of
any soul-malady. In their own view they need
not the Physician, and they never come to Him,
therefore His office is not for them. "They that
are sick"—these are they who, on the contrary,
are truly conscious of their soul's malady, and of
their need of the Physician, and it is for these
He is specially sent by the Father.

Again, it is written, "Christ died for the
ungodly." The word "ungodly" in this relationship does not designate those who live and die
in their ungodliness, but those to whom the
Father, by the Holy Spirit, eventually and
effectually shows their natural ungodliness and
consequent danger. For them Christ was specially sent. For them He specially died. And
His death becomes to them their only hope of
salvation.

"Come unto me, all ye that labour and are
heavy laden, and I will give you rest." These
terms show the particular characters for whom
Jesus was sent, that in Him they might have
rest ; and it is the Father who causes them,
through the Holy Spirit's gracious influence, to
be burdened with a sense of guilt.

Again, " Thy people shall be. willing ; " " Who-soever will;" " He that is athirst ; " " Whosoever believeth." These terms likewise show the particular people for whom the Gospel provision is made, and they indicate that the Father's special mark is upon them. It is the Father who, by the Holy Spirit, makes willing. It is the Father who, by the Holy Spirit, creates the heavenly thirst. It is the Father who, by the Holy Spirit, draws sinners to Jesus (John vi. 44, 45 ; Eph. ii. 8).

Blessed indeed are those whom the Father has marked as His own, and who are walking in the consciousness and under the influence of this wonderful, this eternal relationship.

IX.

To the Believer—concerning the experimental results of being in Christ.

LET your attention be directed chiefly to the provision made for you in Christ, and not to the work of the Holy Spirit within you, except-ing so far as He has fitted you for that provision, by showing you your great need of it, and its all-sufficiency to meet that need.

God's work for sinners is all of grace from first to last. He does not provide salvation for His needy ones, and then require at their hands certain conditions of action, or conditions of experience, before they can enjoy the rich salvation provided.

You do well to be always very clear on the point that salvation is unconditional to the undeserving. Unconditionally provided, and unconditionally bestowed, or else it could not be all of free grace. God Himself bestows the blessing of salvation upon His chosen ones in His own time and way. The first effect of the bestowal is not realised by the recipient as a blessing—at least not immediately, because the first effect is usually a very humbling, and often a very distressing one; for it is the awakening of the soul to a sense of guilt before God such as it never realised before; and eventually to a sense of utter hopelessness of deliverance through self-effort.

Although this is one of the primary results of the blessing of salvation already bestowed, many of God's children have, when in this condition, considered their case as utterly hopeless, and have thought that God had cast them off for ever; whereas, in very truth, God was just casting them off from self, with its services, experiences, and hopes; that they might take up with Christ alone, and find their full salvation in His atoning death for sinners.

Never become weary of being always a needy soul. The Lord Jesus never becomes weary in having to deal with such. Indeed, the more needy the more welcome to Him. Be assured that when a soul loses its sense of sinnership and need, it is outside the channel of blessing and grace. It is only out of a sense of sinnership and need that the soul can, in this life, be in harmony with the offices and work of our Lord and Saviour Jesus Christ.

It is the same grace that gave all fulness to Christ for the sinner, that also gives the sinner that consciousness of need and sinnership which makes Christ's fulness so suitable to him in every way.

Where there is a soul conscious it cannot do without Christ, and that Christ must be its all for its full salvation; there also is a soul that Christ cannot do without, and one for whom He has already done all for its full deliverance from condemnation, and for whom He will still do all that is needed to bring it safely to the heavenly glory.

Do not judge the love of your Heavenly Father and the love of the Lord Jesus for you according

to your own demerits. Your Heavenly Father
well knew that there would be no good thing in
you by nature, and therefore He never looked
upon you as you are in yourself, but as He made
you to be in Christ. Then take the same view
yourself, ever remembering that it is what you
are in Christ that makes you so much the delight
of the Father. All your failure cannot take you
out of Christ, because it is your Heavenly Father
who put you there Himself, and has so made
Christ and you one, that He loves you as He
loves His Son.

You may, however, say, " How can I be sure
that I am in Christ?" Very easily. The word of
God gives its judgment concerning those who are
in Christ by declaring that "If any man be in
Christ he is a new creature (creation) : old things
are passed away ; behold, all things are become
new." The great distinction here is the new
creature, or new creation. This new creation, or
new life, is distinguished by its manifestations.
The heart that possesses this new life has sorrows
and joys and desires peculiar to itself. It has
sorrow because of spiritual failure and unfaith-
fulness ; sorrow because of cold-heartedness and
lack of deeper interest in Divine things ; sorrow
because of the ease with which the mind slides
away from the consideration of spiritual things

to busy itself with the lesser matters, even the
trifles of the day ; sorrow because of weariness,
and wandering of thought in prayer ; sorrow
because unable to read or meditate on holy things
with more profit ; sorrow in so soon forgetting
what is learned, and sorrow because the things
known have so little influence in the heart and
life.   These are some of the peculiar sorrows of
the heart that possesses the new life—the sorrows
of those who are in Christ.

The heart that possesses this new life has also
its peculiar joys.   The "old things " of the world
are no longer the sources of highest joy, but the
"new things " of the gospel kingdom, the kingdom of grace and love.   It counts it one of its
highest joys to have a realised interest in God's
salvation, and to realise in daily life the presence
and love of the Lord Jesus.

Its ruling desires, too, are not after the " old
things " of a world-pleasing or carnal-pleasing
nature, but after Christ, to live for Him, to be
what He would wish, to do what He would
desire, and thus better to know and love and
serve Him.

This is the judgment of the word of God concerning those who are " in Christ."   The subjects
of this new creation are the objects of God's
everlasting love, and because they are so, He

created them anew by His Holy Spirit, making them the subjects of His grace here, and the objects of eternal glory hereafter.

X.

Concerning receiving Christ and the result thereof.

EVERYTHING here is fleeting and unsubstantial when seen in relation to eternity. Truly, to live well in time is to live wisely in view of the great future, when time shall be no more.

The contemplation of this subject is too often put aside as unpleasant and undesirable. If the putting aside the contemplation could stop the passage of time and hinder the approach of the end, there would be some reason for doing so; but it cannot be : sooner or later every one must learn, by the deeper teaching of experience, that " all flesh is as grass, and all the glory of man as the flower of grass " which soon withereth and falleth away for ever.

Sin has put its stamp upon everything earthly; if, therefore, we would have a sure rest and a satisfying portion for our soul, we must turn from the earthly to the heavenly, and in learning what God has said, and God has done, in the person of His Son, and in the Gospel of His love, find a sure foundation of rest for time and eternity.

In contrast with what is said in relation to the fading nature of "all flesh," it is written, "But the word of the Lord endureth for ever, and this is the word which, by the Gospel, is preached unto you ;" the word of salvation; the word which testifies of Him who is the living and eternal Word, and who is God's salvation to every sinner who trusts in Him.

" In the beginning was the Word, and the Word was with God, and the Word was God. . . . In Him was life, and the life was the light of men. . . . He came unto His own, and His own received Him not ; but to as many as received Him, to them gave He the right (or privilege or power) to become the sons of God, even to them that believe on His name."

" To as many as received Him." Yes, here is the remedy for the woes which sin has wrought. Here is found the true antidote for the curse, and the true treasure which maketh rich indeed. Here is the way of victory over death, and of the removal of all fear of judgment. Here is a full answer to all the law's demands. Here is full salvation and eternal life.

" To as many as received Him." They are the words of the God of all grace and truth ; words of comfort to guilty ones, weary with their endeavours after self-deliverance. It would have been too much for sinners to expect, had it been said that as many as served Him, to the best of their ability, all their days, the blessing should be given ; but it is "not of works lest any man should boast." "That according as it is written, He that glorieth, let him glory in the Lord, who of God was made unto us wisdom and righteousness and sanctification and redemption."

"To as many as received Him." The language is peculiar. It implies need satisfied in Him. Grace does here a twofold work ; it makes man a consciously needy sinner, and then shows him a full supply already provided for his need. To as many lost ones, sinful ones, helpless ones as received Him as God's appointed way of salvation—received Him as their only 'hope, their only Saviour. To such—to such only—to such always—He gives the blessing. They are the saved ones. They are the sons. To them He gives eternal life, and "they shall never perish." To them is the assurance given, "Because I live, ye shall live also." To such there is no need to speak about "preparing for death," for they are always safe in Christ. Having "received Him," all things are theirs—"the world, or life, or death, or things present, or things to come." True, they may sometimes lose the assurance of their salvation and sonship, but they can never lose the salvation and sonship itself; and when they do lose the comfortable assurance, it will be found that it was because they had looked away from Christ, and their minds had been too little occupied with Him.

What anxious souls need for their peace and comfort, is to receive Christ as the Saviour who has fully and completely accomplished salvation on their behalf. What believers need for their continued comfort and peace, is to be daily receiving Christ, not only as their Saviour, but as their ever-living friend and helper.

XI.

Concerning the beginning of the work of grace in the heart as being the sure pledge of its completion.

THE very beginnings of the work of grace in the heart, however feeble those beginnings may seem to be, are a double pledge to the sinner thus favoured. They are a pledge that he belongs to the number of God's elect; and they are a pledge that the whole of salvation is his, whether it be present deliverance from eternal condemnation, or that full and complete salvation yet to be made manifest in the day of glory. "Being confident of this very thing, that He which hath begun a good work in you, will perform (complete) it until the day of Christ."

This is a strong consolation for those who are often doubting about their future, for it gives the assurance that their future will be cared for and wrought out by Him who has cared for and wrought out their past. It is not according to God's way to begin the work of grace, and then leave the receiver of that work to complete it himself. From the foundation to the topstone the work is all of grace—all God's own. "He which hath begun a good work in you, will perform (complete) it."

If the question should arise, "How may I be assured that the beginning of the work of grace has been wrought in my heart? How may I know that God has begun a good work in me?" it can only be satisfactorily answered by referring to those marks or evidences laid down in Scripture, which show the beginning of this good work, and then judging whether we possess such marks or evidences. Amongst such marks are the following: "No man can come to me except the Father which hath sent me draw him." "No man can come" (John vi. 44)—that is, no man has naturally the desire, the willingness, to

come to Jesus, because no man naturally has
the consciousness of his state as a sinner, guilty
before God, and deserving of eternal condemnation.   The drawing of the Father is this willingness, this desire imparted and implanted in the
heart by His gift of the Holy Spirit.   This
willingness, this desire to come to Christ, is
therefore the good work begun.   Again : the
"bread of life" is God the Father's gift.   His
gift also is the hunger for that bread, without
which it is food undesired by man.   Where,
therefore, there is this spiritual hunger after
Christ, the good work of grace has already
begun.

The "good work" is again noticed thus : "In
Christ Jesus neither circumcision availeth anything, nor uncircumcision, but a new creature"
(Gal. vi. 15).   Because of this "new creature,"
or "new creation," in the heart of the awakened
sinner, a new and spiritual eye is given, whereby
he sees, as he never did before, how great is his
individual sinfulness before God, and how richly
he deserves condemnation for his sins.   A new
spiritual ear is also given to him, whereby he
listens with a newly-awakened interest to the
preaching of the Gospel.   New desires are manifested, whereby he longs to be at peace with God,
and to have his sins forgiven.   New trust (or

faith) arises within him, whereby Christ, and Christ only, becomes his refuge for salvation from the wrath to come.

These are a few of the marks which show the beginning of the good work in the sinner's heart; and to those who possess such, is the comforting assurance given : " Being confident of this very thing, that He which hath begun a good work in you, will perform (complete) it until the day of Christ."

XII.

To the Believer—concerning the foundation of an assured hope.

You need to be building upon a firm foundation for better things than the things of earth. You need to have an unwavering assurance of present salvation, and a bright and assured hope of future glory. You need the consciousness of possessing a faithful friend always with you, who can understand and help you, and overrule all things for your good ; one who loves you truly, and whose love nothing can alter. This you need, not only to cheer you amidst the earthly gloom of afflictive providential dispensations, but also to enable you rightly to use and enjoy the

brighter experiences of life, lest they become a
snare and a stumbling-block in your path.

If you look calmly and steadily at facts, you
will not be long before you have the assurance
that these all-needful blessings are really yours.

Have you not an abiding consciousness that
nothing of the mere earthly can fully satisfy you ;
and are you not desiring better and more enduring things than earth can afford ?   Has not your
mind been directed towards God's word, therein
to learn what He says concerning man, and to
man, about the present and the future; and do
you not feel certain that it is only what God says
that can be a sure word of counsel for you ?

Have you not accepted, as an indisputable
truth, what that word teaches you of your sinfulness before God ; and have you not learned from
that word, with some degree of satisfaction, that
there is a salvation provided through the atoning
death of Christ ; a salvation already complete ; a
salvation for sinners, as sinners, in all their sinfulness ; a salvation so sure that God Himself
must cease to be God before that salvation fails ?
Have you not also learned that this salvation
is not for deserving workers, but for sinful
receivers ; and that it is the free gift of sovereign
grace to helpless sinners—not salvation through
Christ for believing, as a kind of reward for

believing, but salvation completed already by the atoning death of Christ for sinners who never would believe, and who never would be in earnest about salvation until the Holy Spirit, by His gracious and quickening influences, teaches them effectually their sinfulness, and makes that salvation to be the desire of their hearts?

Have you not also learned that he who has Christ for his hope already has eternal life, and can never perish; and have you not been led to look to Christ as your only hope? To these questions your reply will doubtless be: "Yes, yes, it is so; it is all true—such have I learned; and though the lesson needs to be taught me over and over again, yet I have learned it all, and find therein the way of hope and consolation." Is this so?' Then you have indeed a sure foundation for eternity — a firm foundation whereon to build an assured hope of future glory. You are among the number of those whom the Father has given to the Lord Jesus to be the objects of His watchful and ceaseless care in this life, and hereafter to be presented by Him, faultless, before His Father's face in heaven.

XIII.

Concerning the course of experimental salvation and its manifestations.

THE Holy Spirit quickens the sinner with new spiritual life. He is thus born again. It is a work complete at once, and one in which the sinner is completely passive. This is regeneration. The sinner knows not that he is born again, but by the results which are manifested in the mind, heart, and life.

His mind is enlightened. He becomes deeply conscious of his personal relationship to God's most holy law, to eternity, and to the judgment to come. These are to him realities such as they had never been before. He sees himself to be guilty before God, and deserving of eternal condemnation. This is repentance.

His heart becomes restless in consequence of his change of mind. He is weary and burdened under a consciousness of guilt. He looks to Jesus dying on the cross as the sinner's substitute. He trusts in Him as his only hope of salvation, and thus with the heart he believes and is saved. This is faith.

His life is now changed. The mind and heart being thus affected, the whole current of his outer life is altered. The man turns from the ways of sin and turns to God. He becomes a true disciple and follower of the Lord Jesus. This is conversion. In other words,—

I. Regeneration is the impartation of a new nature, and is in Scripture termed "being born again." It is an instantaneous work of the Holy Spirit, complete at once, though capable of increase in vigour and manifestation.

II. Repentance is a change of mind about our relationship to God, whereby we become conscious that however moral or religious we may have been, we are really without God, and without hope in the world. Guilty before God and deserving eternal condemnation.

III. Faith is the trust of the heart in Christ crucified, as the way of deliverance from guilt and deserved condemnation.

IV. Conversion is the change of the outward life. Having received Christ as his Saviour, the believer now serves and follows Him as his Lord and Master.

XIV.

Concerning some things to be remembered.

THE Apostle Paul speaks of "putting in mind." The Apostle Peter also says, "I will not be negligent to put you always in remembrance of these things, though ye know them ; " and again, " I think it meet to stir you up, by putting you in remembrance." It is as needful now as in the days of the apostles for believers to stir up one another by putting each other in remembrance of truths already known.   Therefore—

Remember that your salvation is an accomplished fact which nothing can alter.

Remember that it was accomplished when the Lord Jesus died ; for by that death was removed the condemnation which your sins deserved.

Remember that you have nothing whatever to do to make the death of Christ effectual for your salvation ; for it was made effectual for you personally by God your Father, when, in covenant with His beloved Son, He laid all your iniquities upon Him who bore them in His own body on the cross.

Remember it was because that death was effectual for your salvation you were brought by the Holy Spirit's quickening influence (which quickening influence is one of the blessings resulting from salvation already provided) to see your need of this salvation, and your utter hopelessness without it.

Remember that your salvation was not accomplished because of any foreknowledge on God's part that you would, as an awakened sinner, have a desire for reconciliation, and a desire after Christ; because this desire for reconciliation, and this desire after Christ, are also blessings resulting from salvation already provided, and cannot, therefore, be any conditions to procure it. They are God's gracious gift; He foreknowing that you would never have any true desires after Christ, until He awakened those desires by the gift of the Holy Spirit.

Remember that no tears of sorrow for sin, no prayers, no duties of any kind whatever, could have removed you from the position of a criminal before justice, and have left you simply in the position of a child before a loving Father; but that this has been solely the doing of the glorious Three in One—Father, Son, and Holy Spirit, in covenant—whereby Christ Himself took the criminal position as your substitute, that you might take your place as a child, and look up to God as your Father, seeking daily forgiveness for daily sins from Him as your loving and gracious Father.

Remember that your Father readily gives more abundantly the Holy Spirit to His reconciled children, that they may better understand what He has done for them, and what the Lord Jesus has done for them; and to enable them to

look more and more to the Lord Jesus, now at
the right hand of God, so that they may receive
from Him that grace which will enable them
better to love and serve Him.

Remember that the evidence that salvation is
yours, and, consequently, that all the good things
of the covenant of grace are yours, and that
Christ Himself is yours, rests on God's pledged
word.   That word is pledged on behalf of all
sinners who are conscious of their guilt, and of
their need of Christ, and who trust in Him for
all their salvation.   That word declares that they
shall never perish, and that all the blessings of
the covenant of grace are theirs (John iii. 16;
Rom. viii. 32 ; 1 Cor. iii. 21–23 ; Phil. i. 6).

You know that through grace you have been
made conscious of your guilt and of your need
of Christ, and that you rest only in the precious
blood of Christ for salvation.   Therefore to you
is God's word pledged, and that word is unchangeable.

These are a few of the blessings which are
yours; and if you have them in constant remembrance, you cannot fail to have much
comfort thereby, through the gracious influence
of the Holy Spirit; nor fail to render grateful
praise, in heart and life, to the God of all grace,
who has thus loaded you with benefits.

XV.

Concerning heart experiences in a dying hour.

WHEN the believer draws near the end of life, and from his dying bed looks back upon the past, one of his most clear and vivid experiences is not that of saintship, but of sinnership. Then it is that of all the precious truths of God's most holy word in which his soul was wont to delight, none seem so suitable to him as those which declare a full salvation without works—salvation for every needy sinner —through the death of Christ in the sinner's stead. He may have been a disciple of Jesus for fifty years. He may possess much knowledge of the deep things of a covenant God. He may have been favoured throughout his Christian life with much fellowship with the Father, and with His Son Jesus Christ. He may be closing a life of much usefulness in the service of His gracious Master. Nevertheless, it is not from his much knowledge, or his much fellowship, or his much usefulness he derives comfort and peace in that solemn hour, but only from the fact that "the blood of Jesus Christ cleanses from all sin." Thus he first found peace fifty years before. Thus he began his Christian life, and thus he finishes it—a sinner saved by the atoning death of Christ.

That believer is the most likely to have the most vivid realisation, the most full assurance of his complete salvation, living or dying, who makes the atoning death of Christ and his salvation thereby, the foundation of all his thoughts and experiences of spiritual and eternal things in daily life. For a foundation to which the mind so continually refers, is sure never to be far from the consciousness when most needed for comfort.

The Apostle Paul evidently made the atonement, not only the foundation of his labours in his public ministerial life, but the foundation also of all his thoughts and experiences in his private personal life. As to the former, he says: "I determined not to know anything among you save Jesus Christ and Him crucified" (1 Cor. ii. 1). As to the latter, he says: "The life which I now live in the flesh, I live by the faith of the Son of God, who loved me and gave Himself for me" (Gal. ii. 20). These last words reveal the powerful hold which the love of Christ, and the atoning death of Christ, had upon his whole being. His chiefest thoughts were about Christ, and his chiefest thoughts about Christ in relation to himself personally, are seen in those words, "Who loved me and gave Himself for me."

Moreover, after thirty years spent in the service of the Lord Jesus, and not long before the end of his pilgrimage, he writes: "This is a faithful saying, and worthy of all acceptation, that Christ Jesus came into the world to save sinners, of whom I am chief."

Thus to the last taking his place at the feet of Jesus, not as a saint, but as a sinner; and as a sinner who, from thirty years' knowledge of himself, was more than ever conscious how much that name of "sinner" was proper for him beyond all others, notwithstanding his many apostolic gifts and his unexampled labours and sufferings in the service of his Lord.

He ended where he began thirty years before, but with deeper gratitude and fuller joy, because more deeply conscious than ever how much he owed to Him who "came into the world to save sinners."

XVI.

Concerning the written word as a sure foundation for abiding consolation in relation to the present and future world.

"For all flesh is as grass, and all the glory of man as the flower of grass. The grass withereth, and the flower thereof falleth away : but the word of the Lord endureth for ever : and this is the word which by the Gospel is preached unto you " (1 Pet. i. 24, 25). Even a mere worldly man, in the exercise of worldly prudence, would do well to consider these words ; much more so the believer, whose mind has been enlightened by the Holy Spirit correctly to discern and estimate their relationship to the future world—the eternity that is to come.

The utmost consideration that the man of the world may give to this subject, will seldom lead him to include serious thoughts of eternity in his contemplations, and when it does so he will usually look upon that part of the subject as very subordinate, and much more easily and comfortably settled to his own mind than the consideration of what he is to do and what to leave undone of all those plans and pursuits which are in immediate relationship to his present or future position in this world.

The true believer, however, taught by the Holy Spirit, considers his relationship to the world to come as vastly more important than anything pertaining only to his position in this world, and it is therefore his chief desire to have that eternal relationship scripturally and comfortably settled. This is not only of the utmost importance to him

when first awakened from his death in trespasses
and sins, but remains so to the end of his life.

It is therefore well, in view of this relationship
to the eternity to come, that he should always
have something firm and steadfast to lay hold of,
something fixed and stable to refer to, when
everything else seems fading away—when everything else seems passing like a shadow from his
grasp. Something which like a nail will fasten
him in a sure place, or like an anchor keep him
firm to one point, no matter how much he may
be tossed to and fro by the waves of outward
circumstances or inward experiences. Such an
anchor, such a nail is "the word of the Lord"
which "endureth for ever."

Both as regards salvation and true consolation
in the trials of life, it is on "the word of the
Lord" we must alone rely; and it is always
helpful to the believer if he have some special
"word of the Lord" to which he can always
refer, and which he can in a sense call peculiarly
his own, because of the special influence it has
had in past days of soul-struggling and fears, to
fix his mind and hope on the sure foundation of
God's mercy in Christ, and thereby bringing him
some measure of quietness and rest.

Some have found the "word of the Lord" in
the 3d of John, verse 16, to be a special word

for them : " God so loved the world that He gave
His only-begotten Son, that whosoever believeth
in Him should not perish, but have everlasting
life." To this word their minds referred as to a
fixed point, whenever the question of their salvation became prominent in their thoughts. This
they had often found in past days to be a word
of comfort, encouragement, and hope. They had
found it to be as a nail, fixing them afresh in
mind to the sure foundation Jesus Christ, when
from various causes their consciousness of Him,
and of their salvation by Him, had become loose
and dim, often even to doubting their interest in
His atoning death. They therefore prized this
word as a special word for them, and repeatedly
referred to it all their days.

Others have found their special " word of the
Lord" in John vi. 37 : "Him that cometh unto
me I will in no wise cast out." This has often
encouraged their hope in times past. This they
have found to be as an anchor fixing them to
firm ground, when all else seemed beyond their
reach ; and when the question of their salvation
arose in their minds, to this word they continually
referred, and ever found comfort and assurance
therefrom ; therefore they prized it much, and
they did well, for it is "the word of the Lord"
which "abideth for ever."

With many the special word has been that in
John's first epistle : "The blood of Jesus Christ
cleanseth us from all sin." To them no word
ever brought such light of hope and salvation
amid the dark consciousness of sin as this; and
therefore to them it is evermore a word of peace
and consolation ; a beacon in the tempest ; a
safety-buoy amid the troubled waters; and a
precious "word of the Lord" it is, and it
"endureth for ever."

Many and varied are the words of the Lord
which have been specially helpful to believers ;
but whatever may have been "the word" which
the believer has found most influential in the
past for the encouragement and strengthening of
his hope of salvation through the death of Christ
for sinners, even that word should be looked upon
by him as a special word of help in the future,
whenever the question of his salvation may arise
in his mind ; certainly not to the putting aside of
others, but as the one which is to him the special
word of all others.

Believers have often, in their dying hour, referred to the special word which many years
before first gave them a comfortable hope of salvation through Christ ; and they have testified
that it had never lost its special influence for
them all through life, and even at the last it

seemed to have more influence for their comfort than ever.

If a believer has not fixed upon any word as a special word for himself, but has been led to look to Christ as his Saviour rather by the general teaching of the Gospel, such a believer would still find it very helpful, prayerfully and thoughtfully to fix upon some special " word of the Lord " to build upon as a distinct and clear foundation ; for there are times when the most advanced and experienced believers become so enervated or scattered in their minds, either by special temptations or by bodily infirmities, that they cannot take a large general grasp of truth : and it is then that some special word, much thought over, and often mentioned in prayer, becomes as a key, opening the mind anew to Christ ; or as a nail, fixing it in its wanderings to Him ; or as a channel, full of the water of life ; or as the finger of God, pointing directly and always to the sure refuge in Christ ; and as the encouraging word of the Lord, causing the soul to stay itself afresh on Him and His salvation.

It is also very useful for the believer to fix upon some special word in relation to Christian consolation as well as salvation, so that when special trials, afflictions, or sorrows are his portion, he may at once refer to this " word of the Lord " that his mind may be thereby more steadily fixed upon the sure and changeless love of his heavenly Father, and on the constant grace and unfailing sympathy of his Lord and Saviour. How often, in the dark and stormy night of affliction, one such " word of the Lord " has been the channel through which heaven's bright sunshine has filled the soul, by causing it to realise the presence and love of the Lord Jesus.

Many, very many have found such a " word " in the commencing verses of the 14th of John's gospel, " Let not your heart be troubled; ye believe in God, believe also in Me." Some have found their special " word " in the assurance, " I will never leave thee; " and others in " Fear not, thou art Mine." But whatever may have been the special " word " thus useful in the past, it should be treasured up as one to be often referred to in the future. It is the " word of the Lord," and it endureth for ever. This is a firm foundation. All other confidences are as grass, and the flower of grass, which withereth and falleth away.

It is necessary to be cautious that the word of God does not become the instrument for the encouragement of an unhealthy religious emotionalism, by being used in a superstitious or injudicious manner. It is thus used by those who

are continually looking out for some word of
Scripture to be suddenly impressed upon their
minds by what they consider to be the special gift
of God. If many days pass without having such
impressions, they are unhappy, and begin to think
that God is against them, and to doubt His love
and grace. If, on the other hand, some text of
encouragement or promise has suddenly come into
their minds, they consider it to be a special
token of God's favour, and to have come direct
from heaven ; and they again lift up their heads
for a season. The whole experience of their inner
life, and often the doings of their outer life, are
thus influenced and moulded by the sudden impression upon their minds of particular portions
of Scripture. The result is much uncertainty
both in experience and practice. Often injudicious things are done, or wrong views of God are
entertained, or false hopes are encouraged.

This living upon sudden impressions of Scripture texts is very different from fixing upon one or
more as a special word, to be often referred to
by the believer as the foundation truth on which
he relies for salvation and consolation ; truth
which is always for him, and always the same to
him, and which, whenever thought of, always
leads him to contemplate the Lord Jesus as being,
for time and eternity, all his hope and all his help.

XVII.

Concerning the perfect safety of true Believers and the impossibility of their finally falling away.

1. It is impossible that true believers can finally fall away and perish, because of the relationship in which they stand to God the Father (2 Thess. ii. 13).

The Father's purpose concerning them "from the beginning," was that they should be eternally saved. This purpose is accomplished "through sanctification of the Spirit and belief of the truth," that is, through regeneration and faith; both being His own gift and operation. God's purposes cannot be hindered, therefore those chosen by Him to full and complete salvation must certainly be saved.

Again, in Heb. ii. 10, they are spoken of as God's "many sons" whom He is bringing to glory; and that this may be perfectly accomplished, He appointed them a Captain, who is called the "Captain of their salvation." The Lord Jesus is thus made responsible to the Father for their home-bringing.

Furthermore, in Rom. viii. 33 it is taught that the Father Himself has justified them (that is, has freed them from that condemnation which their sins deserved). This He did by providing an all-sufficient Saviour, in the person of his only-begotten Son, by whom the claims of the law against them were satisfied, and their sins taken away, and every hindrance removed that would prevent them reaching their home above. Seeing that this is a finished work, and that all their sins, to the end of their life on earth, of which the Father foresaw they would be guilty, are already legally dealt with and judicially taken away by the atonement made for them through the death of Christ, it is not possible that any true believers can finally fall away.

Moreover, it is stated in 1 Pet. i. 5 that God the Father keeps them by His own power, through faith, unto salvation. They are not kept by their own power, but by the omnipotent power of God Himself. The word also declares (1 Thess. iv. 14) that when the Lord Jesus comes a second time, the Father has determined to bring with Him them also which sleep in Jesus. It is, therefore, evident that true believers, because of their peculiar relationship to God the Father, can never finally fall away and perish eternally.

2. Because of their relationship to God the Son, it is also impossible they can fall away and perish (John x. 27, 28; vi. 37, 39, 40).

True believers are the sheep of Christ. The

Lord Jesus, as their Shepherd and His Father's
servant, has pledged Himself for their safety here
and hereafter. The glory of a shepherd is the
safety and well-being of his sheep. This is a
glory of which nothing can rob the Good Shepherd. Eternal life is not earned by them, but
given to them, with everything else that is needful (John xvii. 2). This is sure.

Moreover, true believers cannot perish, because
they are eternally and vitally one with Christ
(Eph. i. 4; John xiv. 19; Col. iii. 3, 4), and because
of the abiding prevalency of Christ's intercession
for them, and because they are His special reward
for all His sufferings (John xvii. 20, 22).

3. Because of their relationship to God the
Holy Spirit, true believers in Jesus cannot possibly fall away and perish.

The Holy Spirit is within them as a quickening
Spirit; the giver of a life that is eternal and
divine (Rom. viii. 11). This is quite a different
thing from being made partakers of the Holy
Spirit, merely in His bestowment of miraculous
gifts. In Apostolic days, such were sometimes
received by those who, though also much moved
by Gospel influences, were never born again by
the Holy Spirit (Heb. vi. 4, 5; Mark iv. 17).

True believers are also sealed, by the Holy Spirit,
unto the day of redemption (Eph. iv. 30); sealed

as belonging to God in a special manner. His own private property. A seal no power can break or destroy, for God's seal is God Himself in the heart of the believer.

A sinner quickened by the Holy Spirit, and thereby awakened to see his guilty state, and led to seek salvation in the atoning death of Christ, is a sinner sealed by God, and marked as peculiarly His own. He is a true believer, and can never perish.

Thus, because of their relationship to God the Father, God the Son, and God the Holy Spirit—the Three Persons in the one Godhead—true believers can never finally fall away.

XVIII.

Concerning Believers and the curse of the law of God.

A CHILD of God, or, in other words, a sinner who truly trusts in the Lord Jesus for salvation, is not personally under the curse of the law. He never was, and never will be.

In his unawakened and ungodly condition he never was, and why? Because provision had already been made to prevent the curse, which his sins deserved, from alighting upon him personally. He was one of God's eternally loved children; and the love of God the Father for

His children is such, that if they do that which
would bring them under the curse of the Divine
law, He, their Father, will provide a way whereby they shall not be personally responsible for
satisfying that law, or be personally brought
under its direct curse. Therefore, the curse of
the law, which His children's guilt deserved, was
borne by the Lord Jesus, the first begotten of the
family, and its covenant Head and surety, when
upon the cross Jehovah laid the iniquities of His
people upon Him.

Thus the curse of the law, which would have
gone forth against them, was arrested by the
Lord Jesus, as their representative and substitute,
and fully borne by Him on the cross (Gal. iii. 13),
long before multitudes of them were born, or the
sins committed for which He beforehand bore
the curse. Then, indeed, was the curse of the
law manifestly taken from all for whom He died,
as it had been taken away in God the Father's
purpose, and by covenant provision, before the
world was (2 Tim. i. 9 ; Titus i. 2).

Divine justice must, necessarily, be satisfied
for the transgressions of the children, but the
love of the Father provides fully for that. The
heart of God the Father is ever full of love to all
His children. He loves them with an everlasting
love. It is love from all eternity to all eternity.

The changeful scenes of time alter it not.   He loves always, and believers were always His sons. When they first trusted in Jesus they did not then become sons to His eternal consciousness. They were sons before, but they could not per-sonally learn that fact, neither would it be really an object of desire and joy to them until, born again by the Holy Spirit, they became conscious of their lost and guilty state by nature, and came to Jesus, and trusted in Him for their full salva-tion.   Then was manifested the glorious relation-ship which had its existence before the world was.

A child of God may backslide most sadly; but he never comes under a curse in any sense what-ever.   Under a Father's chastening hand he will come, and under multiplied and heavy chastise-ments, if sin be encouraged, but he is still, as ever, a much-loved child, whose sins Jesus took away nearly 2000 years ago, when He satisfied divine justice for them, by His death on the cross.

These truths do not in any way interfere with the free and full proclamation of the Gospel to every creature, for such proclamation of the Gospel is simply the making known everywhere the provision made in Christ for the salvation of sinners ; declaring also that whosoever believeth

in Him shall not perish but have everlasting
life. It is not a proclamation that whosoever
believeth shall there and then, for the first time,
have the curse removed from him, or that divine
justice is then, for the first time, fully satisfied
for his sins, as this would imply that Christ did
not by His death remove such curse, or sufficiently
satisfy divine justice.

The proclamation of the Gospel is God's
appointed way, whereby such Gospel, in being
proclaimed to every creature, reaches those for
whom Christ bore the curse; and they, being
made willing by the Holy Spirit, are brought by
that Gospel to trust in Christ for the salvation of
their souls. Trusting in Christ, however, not to
remove the curse from them then, but trusting
in Christ as one who took that curse fully away
when He died upon the cross.

With every believer rests the responsibility of
faithfully proclaiming the Gospel to his fellow-
creatures as opportunity is afforded in God's providence, either by his own personal labours, if he
be evidently called thereto, or if not so called,
then by assisting those who are; helping them
in every way as far as he is able. Here man's
responsibility ceases as far as regards the proclamation or preaching of the Gospel. For the
covenant and saving results of this proclamation

the Holy Spirit is alone responsible, as this pertains to His office in the covenant of grace.

The Holy Spirit never fails in due time to quicken with new life all those whom Christ redeemed from the curse of the law by being made a curse for them.   The ordinary instrumentality by which He does this is the preaching of the Gospel; but whether by that instrumentality, or some other instrumentality, or no instrumentality at all, He will most assuredly faithfully accomplish His own peculiar work in the covenant of grace, and not leave any sinner to die unquickened for whom Jesus died.

XIX.

Concerning the most prominent truths experimentally taught by the Holy Spirit.

THE most prominent truths, with their effects in experience and practice, which the Holy Spirit usually teaches out of His word to the soul that, notwithstanding every hindrance, really follows on to know the Lord, are as follows :—

1. By the quickening and enlightening influence of the Holy Spirit, the soul is made

conscious of its condition as guilty before God (Rom. iii. 19, 20, 23). This consciousness produces a condition of unrest and anxiety in view of eternity and the judgment to come, accompanied with an earnest desire for salvation and peace with God. At the same time there is a consciousness of utter helplessness and hopelessness in self and self doings, although this latter consciousness is frequently not attained until after many unsuccessful endeavours to procure rest and peace by doing many things of a religious character.

2. The soul becomes conscious of the all-sufficiency of the death of Christ to satisfy the claims of justice, and that in no other way can peace with God be obtained but through the atoning death of Him who died as the substitute for the guilty. The soul is led to acquiesce in this, and to look to the death of Christ as its only hope of salvation from everlasting misery. The soul is now a saved soul—saved simply through resting for salvation on the death of Christ, who in dying bore the curse instead of the guilty (Rom. v. 6–10; Gal. iii. 13; Eph. ii. 13, 17; Rom. iv. 25).

3. After this the soul becomes conscious that Christ is something more to it than a Saviour who redeems from the curse of the law, precious

though that redemption be, for it becomes
conscious of its perfect and changeless standing
in righteousness before God through the perfect
obedience of the Lord Jesus. Resting already on
the atoning death of Christ for salvation, it had
probably thought that fitness for heaven was to
be the result of its own attainments in holiness
and righteousness ; but now it sees that by the
one great work of Christ in its twofold aspect, it
is at one and the same time delivered from the
wrath to come, and for ever made fit for heaven
itself.   Not only redeemed in Christ, but accepted
in Christ (Eph. i. 6). By His obedience made
righteous, as well as by His shed blood fully
justified from all sin and condemnation (Rom. v.
9, 19 ; Rom. x. 4 ; 2 Cor. v. 21).   The desire of
the soul now is not to make itself fit for heaven,
but to live as becometh one already made fit, as
well as already delivered from guilt and condemnation.

4. And now the soul progressing in Divine
knowledge becomes conscious of its position as
one of the family of God : not only a saved
sinner, but a child of God (Gal. iii. 26 ; iv. 6, 7) ;
and it learns that God's purposes and doings in
salvation are the purposes and doings of a wise
and gracious Father on behalf of His much-loved
children for whom He has provided a home of

everlasting blessedness. The soul now takes its place as a child, calling God "Father" with a deeper meaning than it ever did or could before.

5. The soul, still taught by the Holy Spirit, becomes conscious that the work of Christ as the Saviour is a definite work with a certain and assured result ; the effect of a covenant between the Father and the Son for the full perfection of a family in the eternal blessedness provided for them hereafter ; and that such covenant contained every needful arrangement in order that their fall into sin and resulting unfitness for that blessedness, and their consequent liability to eternal punishment, should not hinder His purposes of love : and that the Lord Jesus freely and voluntarily undertook to be the first-born among the many brethren of this family that He might be its Surety—its covenant Head—to fulfil every responsibility necessary for the final home-gathering of the chosen family. Hence the proclamation concerning Him (Isa. xl. 1, 21 ; liii. 11, 12). Hence the charge given Him (John vi. 38, 39). The body provided (Heb. x. 5-7). Judgment work finished (John xvii. 4). Power given to gather in the family (John xvii. 2). The certainty of their standing before the Father in glory (John x. 27, 29; xiv. 1-3 ; xvii. 24; 1 Thess. iv. 16, 17). Hence also the covenant and

sure work of the Holy Spirit (John xvi. 13, 15;
1 Cor. ii. 9-16; Rom. viii. 11; 1 Peter i. 2;
2 Thess. ii. 13).

6. The soul, guided by the Holy Spirit, becomes gradually conscious of its most marvellous
oneness with Christ. Oneness with Him in the
Father's love (John xvii. 23). Oneness with Him
in the election of grace (Eph. i. 4, 5). Oneness
with Him as He stood in the presence of the
Father before the world was (2 Tim. i. 9). Oneness with Him judicially (Rom. vi. 6, 9). Oneness with Him vitally (1 Cor. xii. 27; Rom. viii.
10). Oneness with him experimentally (Gal. ii.
20). Oneness with Him in beauty and glory
(John xvii. 22; Eph. ii. 6; 1 John iii. 1, 2).
This causes the soul greatly to rejoice in the
Lord in the full assurance of knowledge, and of
faith and hope.

7. The Holy Spirit, still leading the soul in
His heavenly teachings, brings it into a happy
consciousness of the constant presence of the
Lord Jesus and of the Father in the daily walk
of life; and causes it to realise more vividly and
more familiarly, and with a more childlike trust
and affection, the presence and love of God in
His relationship as a Father, and the presence
and love of Jesus as a real man at the right hand
of God (one with the Father and the Holy Spirit

as God ; yet as real now as a man, in His glorified humanity, as when upon earth), the friend, the guide, the strength, the joy of the soul every day ; and thus it realises communion more intimate and influential than can possibly result from any earthly friendship or relationship whatever (John xiv. 21, 23).

This is probably the highest experience attainable on earth. The next step being to drop the veil of the mortal body, and see face to face, with a glorified vision, Him whom, having not seen, we love, and in whom, though now we see Him not, yet believing, we rejoice with joy unspeakable and full of glory.

These truths, put into a briefer form, are as follows :—

First.—The soul experiences a state of unrest from a knowledge of its guilt before God, and inability to obey His law, and procure peace and salvation by its own efforts.

Second.—The soul becomes conscious that salvation is through Christ alone, because of His bearing the curse of the law instead of the guilty, and thus looks only to Him, trusts only in Him. This soul is saved though it may not have the full assurance of a higher experience, or a spiritual understanding of the deep things of God.

Third.—The soul learns its full acceptance, as

well as full deliverance in Christ. It learns its standing in perfect and changeless righteousness before God, and rejoices with thankfulness in having been already made meet for the heavenly inheritance (Col. i. 12).

Fourth.—The soul further learns that salvation is not merely the manifestation of God's mercy to undeserving sinners, but the manifestation of a Father's love for His wandering and ruined children, for whom He has made all needful provision, so that they might at last reach the family home above which His Fatherly love had provided for them. The soul now begins to realise sonship as well as salvation, and consciously takes its position as a child of God.

Fifth.—The soul learns that salvation and its attendant blessings are the result of covenant arrangements between the Father and the Son before the world was ; arrangements in which the Holy Spirit also had His part and office : and that nothing can hinder the full accomplishment of the Father's purposes of everlasting love concerning His chosen family.

Sixth.—The soul now begins to realise that it is one with Christ in all that Christ is, or has, as the first-born among many brethren, and their representative before the Father.

Seventh.—The soul becomes more fully conscious of a hidden life before God, which is more its real life than its outward life amongst its fellows, a life of daily heart-communion with the risen and ascended, yet ever-present Jesus, as a loving friend and ever-ready helper in all the incidents, and duties, and trials of the daily path, earnestly desiring in all things to please Him and live to His glory : walking also in daily communion with the Father in a loving yet reverential manner, realising His presence and love as that of a real Father, and earnestly desiring to live always as becometh the child of such a Father.

Such are some of the more prominent truths of the word of God, which the Holy Spirit generally leads the soul into the experimental knowledge of. However different may be the order in which these truths are received as doctrines, the order does not vary much in which they are received experimentally, that is, in which they become the experiences of the heart. Certainly the order of the first two never varies, although, occasionally, they may follow each other without any interval of time between.

It is true that many never attain an experimental knowledge of any but the first two. Indeed, many do not even reach to a mere doctrinal knowledge of the others. Having, however, a heart experience of the first two truths, they are saved sinners ; but having nothing beyond, having no experimental acquaintance with the deep things of the everlasting covenant of love and grace, they cannot enjoy those privileges which are theirs in common with all the redeemed family of God. Alas! how few understand the glorious privileges given them by the God of grace and love!

CONCERNING THE SPIRITUAL CONFLICT IN THE INNER LIFE OF BELIEVERS.

I.

Concerning the inward conflict.

"THE flesh lusteth against the Spirit and the Spirit against the flesh, and these are contrary the one to the other, so that ye cannot do the things that ye would" (Gal. v. 17). "Ye cannot do the things that ye would," is indeed often a true testimony as regards the experience of the believer. He would follow Christ in heart and life, but, alas, he sees how little there is of Christ in either heart or life. He would be spiritually-minded in all things, but often finds that he has been guided by worldly policy and worldly influences, rather than by spiritual principle. He would be meek and lowly in heart, but has cause for sorrow that pride of heart is so often and so quickly manifested. He would

pray, but often finds that he knows not what
to ask, and cannot pray as he ought. He knows
that the reading of God's word should always be
a pleasure to him, but he often finds that the
reading is rather a task than otherwise. He
would be gentle and easily entreated, yet sometimes stands upon his rights with a sternness and
unyieldingness which is not of the Spirit. He
would always please Christ, but, alas, he sees
how often his motive has rather been self-
pleasing, or the pleasing of his fellows. He
would have more firmness in holy desires, but
he sees how faint, even at the best, are those
desires. He would have his mind often engaged
with spiritual things, but finds how much more
readily it runs after things that are trifling and
profitless. He would have a more determined
will against the seducing influences around him,
yet too often his will plays the coward when
most needed to be firm and decided. He would
be thankful to God for the many and great
things He has done for him and given him, but
sometimes he forgets all, in regret for the loss or
refusal of some one thing which his Heavenly
Father has in love denied him.

This is a very sad and very humbling exhibi-
tion of a believer. It is, however, too often a
true one, as many a child of God will sorrowfully

testify, who truly knows the evil of his own heart.

"Ye cannot do the things that ye would." This, however, is not written to make us satisfied with such a state of things, but rather to show us that the life of the believer is one of much conflict amidst many opposing influences, and that we have no sufficient strength of our own to overcome them ; and, also, to teach us to walk with more watchfulness, humility, and self-distrust, and to go more constantly and earnestly to our Heavenly Father, seeking for the increased assistance of the Holy Spirit, that we may thereby live a life of faith on the Lord Jesus, who alone can enable us to war a good warfare, and continually overcome every evil.

It is by thus showing us what we are, in sinfulness and need, that the Holy Spirit brings us more lowly and willingly to the Lord Jesus to find our all in Him.

II.

To the Believer—concerning the way of success in the conflict with indwelling sin.

IT is very necessary for success in the spiritual conflict, that you should ever maintain a consciousness (the more vivid the better) of your position as a child of God, for whose sins judgment has been passed and justice satisfied in the death of Christ, in whom is all your hope.

When conscious of having allowed indwelling sin to get the victory, your thought should never be, "Can I be a child of God and act thus, or feel thus?" for that will discourage you and weaken you for the conflict, and leave the way open for the still further victory of sin. Your thought under such circumstances should rather be, "I know I am a child of God, but how unworthily I act, and how deeply grieved I am at being so soon overcome by the evil within." This will bring you in penitence and sorrow to your Heavenly Father to confess and seek forgiveness for your sin. It will also lead you to look readily, humbly, and thankfully to the Lord Jesus for help, so that while conscious of your inability to overcome in your own strength, you will the more unreservedly cast yourself on the free grace of Christ for help.

Daily grace for strengthening the new life, and for giving victory over sin, is as much an undeserved gift as is the quickening grace which first gave the life. Therefore, let need and unworthiness make you the more thankfully receive the help provided in Christ, and do not allow your thoughts to be so engaged in the contemplation of that need and unworthiness, as to discourage you in seeking the grace which the Lord Jesus gives to all His helpless ones who look to Him.

Of course, if doubt arises at any time as to your position of complete acceptance in Christ, such doubt must be settled without delay. Your very need and helplessness, in regard to salvation, is your solution of such doubt; for this leads your thoughts to Christ's death as the only way of salvation, and to the consciousness that you have no other hope but in that death. This looking to Christ, which in scripture is called faith in Him, is your warrant from the testimony of God Himself to consider yourself a ransomed child of His.

In the life of conflict the believer's experience is ever one of helpless need, therefore he must always have help from another. It is also one of conscious unworthiness, therefore that help must always come in the way of grace as a free gift.

The life of the believer may be much hindered by the evil within; there must, therefore, be active opposition on his part against that evil, and special watchful opposition in relation to each most easily besetting sin. Sometimes our easily besetting sin is not habitually conquered until after years of stern conflict, and even then it is ever at hand to make its power felt.

Whatever your easily besetting sin may be, you will find that the way of victory is to avoid whatever promotes its manifestation ; and when it manifests itself, to deal with it at once, asking your Father's forgiveness for it, and looking to the Lord Jesus for help against it. Do this always. Be not discouraged even though you be overcome by it many times in the day. This active conflict will gradually weaken the habitual nature of the evil, and give you increasing power over it.

III.

Concerning the Believer's relationship to the first and last Adam.

BY reason of our natural relationship to Adam as our first parent, we possess not only a sinful nature, called in Scripture "the flesh," but also a corrupt physical body and a ruined soul. By reason of the relationship of the believer to Christ, he possesses, by the quickening grace of the Holy Spirit, a new spiritual nature which is holy, and a soul eternally saved by Christ's atoning death. He, nevertheless, still retains his sinful nature, " the flesh," as well as his corrupt physical body.

The new spiritual nature in the believer is, in itself, perfect in all holy principles and desires; but, because of being in the midst of hindering and opposing influences, the believer will often have experiences of the most humbling and self-debasing character, through the first Adam fallen nature, so full of sin, and the first Adam death-stricken body, so full of frailties.

He will find that in things of a spiritual kind, with which he would be occupied, he is constantly hindered by the evil within; for the corrupt affections of the sinful nature, or "flesh," never die out in this life, but are ready to show themselves at every opportunity. In addition to this, he finds that the many weaknesses and afflictions to which his corrupt body is subject, are grave hindrances to the full enjoyment of those privileges which are his portion as being one with Christ and a partaker of His life.

All this but shows that our union to Christ, though perfect in God's sight and perfect as regards salvation and vital union, will not be manifestly and experimentally perfect until the perfect spiritual nature, with the ransomed soul, exists in a perfect spiritual body, and the corrupt sinful nature, or "the flesh," with the corrupt physical body, are together put away for ever (1 Cor. xv. 45 to end).

Federally, and in a judicial sense in relation to the divine law, Christ is life to the believer, as Adam was death to him. Through the latter comes the condemnation and the curse. Through Christ comes the deliverance and the blessing.

In relation to the inner experience of the heart before God, Christ is life to the believer, as Adam was death to him. From the latter he receives a nature which is dead to all true godliness. From Christ he receives a spiritual life, perfect in all holy desires and affections.

In relation to the body, Christ is life to the believer, as Adam was death to him. From the latter he receives a weak and perishing body; from Christ he will receive, at His second coming, a spiritual and glorious body like unto His own (Phil. iii. 21).

Moreover, Christ is Himself the believer's life immediately in a direct and positive way. When the first Adam, before his fall, was in the perfection of life and holiness before God, he could not have been a constant and ever-present and ever-flowing source of life to his seed, for he was but a creature. This is the prerogative of the "last Adam"—the Lord Jesus. The believer is not

merely united to Christ by the assimilation of a
spiritual nature wrought in him by the quickening power of the Holy Spirit ; but there is a vital
union between the soul and Christ Himself as He
is now at the right hand of God, so that, henceforth, Christ Himself is the believer's life, and the
more he looks to Christ as such, the more will he
realise this, and the more will the Holy Spirit
work within him and assist him in so doing. For
those who live most upon Christ will have most of
Christ living in them and by them, and will be
most under the influence of the Holy Spirit.

Faith in Christ brings the peace of salvation,
for it looks to Him as the substitute for sinners
who, in His death, bore and removed the condemnation which was their desert. But faith,
rightly directed, does not stop there. It looks to
the ascended Christ living at God's right hand
(Col. iii. 1, 2), and finds a rich treasure in His
fulness (Eph. i. 22, 23) ; and gracious help in
every time of need (John i. 16; Heb. iv. 14–16).
It is this phase of faith the Apostle speaks of in
Gal. ii. 20, where he says, "Christ liveth in me,
and the life I now live in the flesh I live by the
faith of the Son of God." Christ lived in him,
and he lived by Christ.

IV.

*The way of victory under temptation from sinful
thoughts and the power of Satan.*

THE Christian life is one of continual conflict
from its commencement to its close. There is no
hope whatever that it can be otherwise. That
which is born of the flesh is flesh, and never can
be anything else. It continually wars against the
spirit, so that oftentimes, as the Apostle saith,
"When I would do good, evil is present with
me." This was his own experience to the end of
life; and had it not been that he found Christ's
grace all-sufficient, he would to the end of his
days have said, "Oh, wretched man that I am!"
for never did he find any good thing in himself,
that is, in his flesh. The flesh never changes for
the better; our only expectation and our encouragement is, that through the grace of our
Lord Jesus, with watchfulness and prayerfulness,
it will be kept under, and that the spiritual
nature will increase in vigour daily.

The consciousness of all our infirmities, of our
inward lusts, and of our utter helplessness, but
makes the Lord Jesus more precious. The very
lusts we abhor do serve our best interests when
they cause us to look more to Him. Thus they
are among the all things that work for our good

by keeping us in our proper place and exalting
the Lord.

It has been supposed by some that the foe
within us would not be at all troublesome were
it not for Satan. This is a mistake. Satan can
only act outwardly as regards the true believer.
Satan cannot read the heart of man—that is
God's prerogative alone. Neither has he power
to put thoughts, by direct suggestion, into the
heart of any child of God. He can only at the
most do as he did with Peter, make outward circumstances so meet as to draw forth the evil
propensities and lusts of the old nature.

Satan cannot be everywhere, for he is but a
creature, and can only be in one place at a time
tempting and annoying; but a believer's old
nature, the foe within, accompanies him wherever
he goes, and would be as bad in itself if there
were no Satan, only there might be fewer outward manifestations of its evil because fewer
temptations without to draw forth these manifestations; but even then the difference would be
but small, for the influence of the world in its
oppositions and its enticements would still be too
great for the believer without the continued
grace of Christ; besides which there is an inex-
haustible depth of evil in the believer's old fallen
nature which often manifests itself most suddenly

in vain and sinful thoughts, without any outward
instrumentality whatever to draw them forth—
nay, even when the believer is engaged in the
holiest duties—such as prayer, or praise, or hearing the Gospel preached, or reading the word of
God, or endeavouring to do good to others.

It is true that Satan has a multitude of evil
spirits at his command, but as very little is
explained about them in Scripture, their permitted doings are a mystery to us. They are
very inferior, doubtless, both in capacity and
power. The great power is in their prince. But
neither they nor their prince can annoy or hinder
the believer in any other way than by stirring up
the hearts of evil men against them, and thus
making them the objects of his fiery darts of per-
secution ; or by causing circumstances so to meet
in their path as to draw forth into active manifestation the lusts of their old nature ; although,
even in this, he can only succeed when the
believer is in heart first wandering from the
Lord Jesus. The leading thought of evil may be
sometimes aroused, and first brought into active
manifestation, through his or his followers' outward agency ; but even then it is not Satan that
leads the believer. It is the lust within which
really leads him (James i. 14).

When the first thought of evil arises in the

heart through the outward temptations of Satan
or of the world, or without any outward temptation whatever; the way successfully to resist and
overcome is to look to the Lord Jesus at once for
the needful grace to help. Then the temptation
fails. To argue against some temptations only
gives them opportunity to increase in power.
We should immediately go to Jesus with such—
aye, with all.

The believer will do well to bear in mind that
he has within him every vile lust in principle.
This is a very humbling truth, but it is not safe
to ignore it. Habit, education, moral and pious
training, quickening and upholding grace, may
prevent the manifestation of the viler kinds of
lust, even in the heart itself, so that the believer
may think that he does not possess such. It is,
however, no uncommon thing for a believer, after
years of Christian life, to discover a lust within
his heart which had never shown itself before;
not even when in his natural unawakened state.
Yet it was always there, though dormant.
When these things show themselves within, the
way of victory is not to try to hush them or
forget them by thinking of other things; for,
although this may succeed for a time, it will only
give the lust opportunity for firmer, though at
present quieter, hold. Neither is it to try and

remember promises, or try to bring passages of
Scripture against them ; for it is not the evil
power without that we are fighting against, but
the evils within ; therefore the only way of
victory is to bring them to Jesus—not simply
telling Him in a general way, but word for word
expressing the matter before Him ; although the
doing so brings us low in the dust in self-loathing
and abasement.   This is the sure way of victory,
and the way to experience the sympathising
fellowship of our Lord.

Tell Jesus all, and tell Him freely.   Have no
secrets whatever from Him.   To an earthly
physician it is wise to tell every symptom of our
bodily maladies.   Much more so to tell our
heavenly Physician every symptom of our soul's
maladies.   He is already acquainted with every
one of them, but it is for our good to tell them
out to Him, whether they be small or great.

V.

*To the Believer—concerning the importance of
encouraging the habits of the new nature.*

If you have not continual enjoyment of the love
of Jesus, it may be because you are not as yet
sufficiently taken up with Him.   To be fully

taken up with Jesus is the result of increased knowledge, increased experience, and also of habit; for the new nature has its habits, as well as the old.

The chief habit of the new nature is to be taken up entirely with Christ, and as far as this is not the practice of the believer, so far is the habit of the new nature hindered. If this habit of the new nature be repressed by the cultivation of the old habits of the carnal nature, it will grow gradually weaker; but if on the contrary it be encouraged, it will gradually increase in strength until you will be so taken up with Christ every day, and so happy in Him, that it will be quite an exceptional state when you are not.

The new nature is very sensitive, and soon feels and suffers when Christ is not the chief object of the heart and life. When, however, He is so, the graces of the new nature will gradually increase in power and manifestation.

If you would successfully mortify and overcome the evils within, you must not contemplate them, but look away from them to Jesus—to Jesus always. If you would overcome trials from circumstances and persons around you, you must not be absorbed with them, but look ever to Jesus—always to Jesus. Burdens never roll off by looking at them, or thinking about them; but by looking to Him, and thinking of Him. "They looked unto Him and were lightened."

An all-absorbing affection allows no rival in the heart. It rules there continually. It raises a barrier against every opposing influence, and though such opposing influences may at times be very trying, yet the heart is not much moved by them so long as the all-absorbing affection continues to rule within. So when Christ dwells more fully and more consciously in the heart of the believer, that heart is well guarded against every opposing influence.

If you would have Christ dwell more fully in your heart, it can only be by more faith in Him, by looking more to Him, and thinking more of Him. Think more of His goodness, His love, His faithfulness. Think of what He has done for you, and is doing, and has promised to do. So thinking of Him, He will dwell in your heart more fully ; even as the more you think of a very dearly loved earthly friend, the more that friend seems to dwell in your heart. You are more taken up with that friend than before.

Be not discouraged ; your victory is sure, and your joy in the Lord will greatly abound. There is such a conscious nearness to Jesus to be attained here ; such a sense of His presence and His love ; such reality of joy in walking with Him, as most believers have not the slightest idea of. It is an experience that makes the heart so peaceful, so calm, so quiet, so restful, so satisfied, so willing to be anything or nothing for Jesus.

VI.

Concerning the evidence and effect of more grace.

THE deeper the work of grace, the more opposition will it usually encounter in the heart ; and the inward evil will generally become more vividly realised by the believer.

The more we have of each grace, the more clearly shall we discern its opposite within. The more we have of the grace of humility, the more shall we know and mourn over our pride. The more we have of the grace of patience, the more shall we know and mourn over our impatience. The more we have of the grace of faith, the more shall we know and mourn over our unbelief. The more we have of conformity to the image of Christ, the more shall we know and mourn over our want of conformity. The more we have of the grace of self-denial, the more shall we know and mourn over our selfishness. The more we have of the grace of love to Christ, the more shall we know and ·mourn over our want of love to Him: and thus each grace becomes a light to show us how much of the contrary we have by nature. Indeed, by this means we grow in grace, because thus we more fully know our great need of the Lord Jesus, and are led to look more humbly, confidently, and helplessly to Him, to whom we can never look in vain, for nothing draws so abundantly from His fulness as a helpless trusting heart.

The exhortation of the Apostle to Timothy, " Be strong in the grace that is in Christ Jesus," not only means that all grace to help in time of need comes from Christ, but that all of each grace, the manifestation of which our Lord delights to behold in His disciples, is in immeasurable fulness in Himself as the example and source of supply to His people: so that to have more strength in each grace we must have a closer intimacy with our Lord Jesus in all the walk of life.

This intimacy with Him begets in us a corresponding likeness of grace, and more manifestation thereof, so that we become more fully changed into the same image. Nevertheless, this fuller growth will but the more show us how far short we come of reaching unto a full conformity to His image. The nearer the light, the more visible are the imperfections; and it is the characteristic of a growing state of grace, not to see its growth, but to see more clearly its shortcomings. We are predestinated to be fully conformed to the image of Christ. We are righteous now in the sight of God, who sees no sin in us, as He beholds us perfect in Christ; but it will not be until we reach the home above that we shall be consciously and manifestly conformed in full perfection to Him.

It is thus that the Holy Spirit leads believers to a fuller growth in the Divine life; and if the experience that accompanies this growth be often, both in providence and grace, very painful and humbling, yet the end is blessed indeed, for it produces an increased capacity to receive more of Christ's fulness here, and more of His fulness hereafter, with a more exalted position of service in His heavenly kingdom.

Christ's rough-hewn diamonds are precious to Him, but it is His polished ones that shine the brightest, and most reflect His bright image, and have the most conspicuous place amongst His jewels; and though the process of polishing be often painful to the flesh and trying to the spirit, yet the result is worth it all, for that result is "a far more exceeding and eternal weight of glory."

VII.

To the Believer—concerning his dealings with evil self.

LEISURE and solitude do not hinder believers being brought into captivity to sin. There is nothing so distracting as to be alone with self, listening to its suggestions, and influenced by its power; for if self be regarded, or if self takes possession of the mind, more sorrowful distraction results than is ever realised in the midst of the busiest avocations.

Yet how ready we are to regard self, and how ready it is to rule, and how quickly it sometimes gets the upperhand. When this is so, it is a time of sad experiences—experiences which result in deep humbling of soul, and which bring us in much contrition of spirit before the Lord, with a deeper consciousness of our unworthiness than ever before.

When the Lord Jesus would more fully show us what He is, He often begins the lesson by more fully showing us what we are. Blessed lesson, if it more than ever makes Him our all. The way to full victory and the conqueror's crown is often through defeats, but defeats which teach lessons for the future. Care, however, is

needed, lest in the midst of failure we become
so absorbed with evil self, and so occupied with
its changeful, but always saddening manifestations, as to forget that Christ is still and always
our strength for combat and for victory.

That is a most unhealthy religious experience
which is continually occupied with self—evil self
—the old self. True, it may be hated intensely,
but we may, to our great discomfort, be too
much occupied with what we hate, as well as
with what we love. You may say that you are
compelled to be much occupied with that which
so continually shows itself. If this be so, you
need prayerfully to seek wisdom and grace, so
to deal with the evil within, that it may not be
any hindrance to your spiritual life.

The old nature may be very strong in you,
as it is and has been in many of God's children ;
but this should only be the better opportunity
for you more fully to show forth the riches of
God's grace than others can, whose old nature
is not so strong, by manifesting how very powerful, how very efficacious is that grace to oppose
and give the victory.

This old self—evil self—must be mortified
continually. The path of spiritual wisdom and
profit is to do, or bear with alacrity and quietness, whatever the evil self dislikes in the clear

path of duty. If evil self dislikes certain engagements or associations to which duty may call in
the service of the Lord, be sure you do not
shrink from them, but readily and steadfastly go
on, walking therein with the Lord Jesus as your
friend and helper.

Do not think that the Lord will remove or
hinder or alter certain circumstances or associations, simply because evil self rises against them.
If He were to do so He would encourage evil in
encouraging this self to have its own way. Your
old evil self cannot be permitted to conquer and
direct the Lord; and it would come to that, if He
were to order all things to please it.

If self rises because of certain very trying
circumstances, and there is murmuring, unbelief,
dissatisfaction, and discontent, these very trying
circumstances are much more likely to be continued, or their intensity increased, until the old
self is completely brought down and mortified,
and grace completely reigns. When such a result
is arrived at, the time of blessing and it may be
the time of deliverance is at hand.

Do not therefore suppose that God will so pity
the evil within as to forbear His providences,
lest that evil should be stirred up. No, if self be
not subdued and humbled by present providences,
present providences may speedily be removed to

make way for others, compared to which the present would be as a bed of roses. Love, infinite love would prompt it, if that love sees that the evil of old self still rises and frets and opposes.

If ordinary remedies fail, and cutting off the child's limb is the only way to save the child's life, the mother will not only accede to this, but even request that it may be done.

VIII.

Concerning dissatisfying experiences.

To take counsel of our own heart is to trust to a deceitful foe. Very often the evil and the good are so mingled in the heart experience that an earnest and ingenuous soul, afraid of judging too favourably, judges according to the evil rather than the good. Indeed, it often believes the good is all evil too.

When the Apostle Paul said that in him (that is in his flesh) dwelt no good thing, he doubtless implied that in him dwelt the principle of every evil thing, and this made him continually conscious that he had no strength of his own in which to stand in successful opposition to that evil ; but the grace that taught him this, also taught him that all-sufficient strength was in another for him, and that his way of joy and victory was in leaning upon, and looking to, and rejoicing in that other—even the Lord Jesus Christ.

When dissatisfying experience leads us to look more to Jesus for help and rest, it ends in blessing. Hunger makes food sweeter. Weariness makes rest more welcome. So this experience makes Christ more desirable, and is part of His wise dealing with us, that we may the more look to Him, welcome Him, rejoice in Him. Yet many believers are continually being influenced by their dissatisfying experience in quite a contrary way. It hides Christ from them because they are ever looking to it, and not to Him. They are wretched because they are not what they want to be. They doubt their sincerity because they see so many evils within, some of which, to their great grief, occasionally find an outlet in the daily life. They are often confounded at seeing themselves content to appear to others better than they really are, and therefore question the reality of all their religious profession.

Often they sorrow for a sin, and confessing, seek forgiveness for it from their Heavenly Father, yet find that they easily fall into the same sin again, and therefore they think they

cannot be true believers. Again, they do not feel
that love, and do not realise that ardour and joy
in holy things which others speak of, and they
think they must have been deceiving themselves
and can never really have been in the right way.
Again, they see so often that their prayers and
reading of God's word are gone through as mere
matters of duty, with but little thought, and still
less reality, nay, that at times the inclination
would be to leave them undone, but lest conscience should reprove for duty neglected, they
are gone through as mere matters of form. They
know these things and they are unhappy, thinking that the Holy Spirit cannot have given them
new life. Then again, they remember how little
gratitude they have towards the Lord Jesus, and
how seldom they seek to exalt His name, and
how much they think of themselves and their
own comfort and ease, and they are thereby
greatly dismayed, and believe they never had any
real faith in Him or real love for Him.

Thus it is that many children of God, by looking only to their experience, become downcast and
often despairing, whereas, if all their consciousness of failure and unworthiness did but lead
them to see more than ever how much they need
the Lord Jesus as their strength for conflict and
service (the very lesson He would teach them),

they would—while deeply humbled and truly
sorrowing because of their frequent failures, and
their little likeness to their Lord—seek His grace
the more earnestly, that thereby they may be
enabled to overcome all the evil over which they.
mourn.   Then would they rejoice in having such
a sure refuge, such an unfailing helper.

Yet how few do this—how many remain dis-
consolate all their days, having only the faintest
shadow of a hope that, at last, God will appear
for their deliverance. This ought not to be.
This is not the spiritual experience of the New
Testament, though too often the experience of
real believers.

IX.

*Concerning the trials arising from a keenly
sensitive nature.*

THERE are sometimes seasons in the life of the
believer when, after days of quietness, there comes
a combination of perplexing, annoying, and peculiarly trying circumstances, as if the ordinary
perplexities of a whole week or month were put
into a few hours, and this, too, just when the
spirit feels less able to bear them.   We think if
they had come but the day before we could have

better borne up against them, but now the spirit
is depressed and overwhelmed. Then follows a
tumultuous rush of contending feelings, with a
disturbed mind. Now is the opportunity for the
old nature to show its evil propensities, and it is
never slow to embrace such opportunities. Now
is the soul overcome and tossed in a tempest it
cannot allay ; struggling in bonds which it cannot
sever; until at last it comes weary and downcast
to that gracious and compassionate Jesus who
calms the storm and looseth the prisoner, and by
whose gracious intercession the downcast and
erring one is assured of forgiveness from his
Heavenly Father.

There are some believers who possess three
strongly marked peculiarities, which require them
to be more constantly on the watch than others,
whose natural characteristics are not of so decided
a character. These peculiarities are—keen sensitiveness, deep feeling, and much firmness of purpose. These may either cause the possessors
unusual and unutterable agony of soul, or, through
grace, unusual and unutterable peace and joy in
the Lord, and make them, in a marked manner,
faithful in His service beyond many.

Firmness of purpose is usually the servant of
the feelings ; we need therefore to be on our guard
continually as to the nature of the feelings rising

within, for if they are not under the control of
faith, if they are not such as will exalt the Lord
Jesus, if they lead us not nearer to Him, they
will lead astray and be most certainly to His
dishonour and to our harm.   Firmness of purpose
will then but make the heart-wandering more
decided ; and what agony of soul eventually
ensues, until deliverance and peace is found in
returning to Jesus once more !

When anything very trying occurs (suddenly
or otherwise) it wounds keen sensitiveness, and
this soon arouses deep feeling ; and as these are
blind guides if permitted to rule, they are sure to
result in evil ; and when firmness of purpose is
brought into their service, it makes matters still
worse.   Now, when anything trying occurs, the
way of wisdom and victory is to prevent feeling
leading us, by *at once* seeking a guide more wise
and mighty than feeling.   To accomplish this,
the soul, at once recollecting its own weakness
and need, and the willingness and power of Jesus,
should immediately bring the matter to Him.
This should be done *immediately ;* delay is
dangerous; delay brings tumult ; delay brings
defeat.   If, before deep feeling be powerfully
aroused, the matter be put into the hands of
Jesus, then He rules.   The sensitive nature is
indeed wounded, but it looks to Jesus.   Deep

feeling is now awakened, but it leads to Jesus. Firmness of purpose, being subordinate, makes us still more decided for Jesus, and stays the heart more firmly on Him.

X.

To the Believer—concerning a divided heart.

You ought to be rejoicing in the Lord and quietly waiting upon, and walking with Him.

Perhaps, however, this is not your experience; but there is in your heart turmoil, darkness, and distress, instead. This condition is often caused by self-will. Should this be so, the remedy is in your own hands. The word of God shows you that self-will and all that is of the flesh should be mortified, crucified, subdued, by putting away everything that comes between your soul and Jesus Christ and that hinders your joy and peace in Him.

Perhaps you have never yet made a decided stand for the Lord in this matter. You may have made a decided stand for Him as regards the things of the outward life; but you have not yet done so as regards the things of the inner life, the desires of the flesh—of self-will.

The cause of all your turmoil and distress of

soul is, because the will is divided between self and Christ. It is a divided house, and cannot stand. Until your will ceases altogether to be the slave of self, and seeks only to bow to the Lord Jesus, you will never know true peace or quietness of soul. When, however, that is done, your inner life will be completely changed, and you will be wholly on the Lord's side both as regards the inner life and the outward life. You will also be wholly on the Lord's side as regards His providential arrangements, with which self is sometimes so dissatisfied, and against which the will, self's active slave, rebels so strongly.

It is impossible to serve two opposing masters, and the endeavour to do so will only result in darkest conflict, certain defeat, and deepest sadness. Were you not a child of God you would not have such conflict, for self would be sole master. Now, however, that is impossible, nevertheless it will always try to divide the house, and hinder the rightful master having dutiful and loving obedience, if you do not watch against it, and continually seek grace from Christ for victory over it. " Be strong in the grace which is in Christ Jesus," and you will then be able to say, "I can do all things through Christ which strengtheneth me."

. Where self reigns, and the will is crossed, there is terrible turmoil within. But when Jesus reigns, and the will is crossed, there is peace within; because the will, as His servant, readily and lovingly acquiesces.

Consider well these things. All your reading and study of Scripture will be in vain, if self rules, and the will is not brought into complete subjection to Christ; for the measure of your subjection of will to Christ in all things will greatly influence the measure of your true progress in spiritual knowledge, and in the power of the new life.

You will ever find that the land of self is the land of darkness—even darkness that may be felt; but that the land of Christ is the land of light, and peace, and joy. The former is the land of Egypt, the latter the land of Goshen. The cruellest of Pharaohs is self, but what liberty, what joyous liberty does the Lord Jesus give!

XI.

Concerning the influence of little things.

LIFE is usually made up of so-called trifles. These, however, are God's disciplining servants; and have more or less influence upon our comfort or joy.

Trifles are relative things ; and what are trifles
to some, and easily put aside, are to others of
great weight and influence, and cannot be put
away at will.   Much depends on peculiar temperament and circumstances.   Moreover, nothing
is a trifle to the Lord Jesus that has an influence
on the comfort and peace of a disciple of His.
He intends that His disciples should be influenced
by these things, and, therefore, the better way is
not to endeavour to ignore them, by trying to
cast them aside, or, Stoic-like, to be above them ;
but to acknowledge them to the Lord Jesus—to
take these so-called trifles to Him, and make
them subjects of prayer and communion, and
reasons for His help.   These trifles are disci-
plinary, and will profit us much, if made the
cause of increased communication between the
helpless and the Helper.

Some believers can calmly bear great disasters,
looking to the Lord.   Great things do not move
them much ; yet the very same believers may be
deeply influenced by a headache or by a gram-
matical slip in conversation, or by an article of
furniture being in the wrong place, or by a book
being mislaid, or by a dinner being half an hour
too late, or by a favourite dish being ill-cooked,
or by a rainy day, or by not receiving an expected visit, or by having an unwelcome one, or

by a servant misunderstanding a request, or any other things of a like nature. Great things, because of their very greatness, do not always reach the lower depths of our being—just as too great a rush of water fails readily to fill the narrow-necked vessel ; whereas the little things, like continuous driblets, reach deeper down, and bring to the surface hidden things to our great humbling of soul before God.

If these things do thus influence us, the Lord means us to acknowledge the fact, and bring them all to Him ; that by His grace these little things may work abundantly for our good.

The finest Christian characters are moulded by a proper use of those things called trifles.

XII.

Concerning self-love.

SENSITIVE watchfulness over, and godly jealousy of self, within due bounds, are a positive Christian duty ; but if carried beyond a certain limit, they produce darkness of mind and unrest of heart, and greatly hinder the realisation of those blessings which, through grace, are the privilege of all believers.

The best way to live is to live out of 'self,' and on Christ. This is to live a life of faith ; and the more faith we have in Christ, the more of Christ shall we have in the heart. "That Christ may dwell in your hearts by faith." Great faith is the peculiar portion of those who look much, and always, to Christ. This prevents the believer from looking too much within, or from being perplexed or distressed when the old nature interposes ; for the soul knowing that its strength is always in Christ, at once refers to Him, and obtains the needed help.

It is necessary always to distinguish between that self-love which is proper, and the encouragement of that evil self which has its principle and power in the old nature. Self-love is really a duty. It is self-love that prompts to self-preservation, and it has its highest manifestation in that heart inquiry, "What must I do to be saved?" which results in trust in Christ, and in safety and salvation through Him. No sinner ever seeks to be saved because of love to God, or a desire to please God, but really from self-love and a desire for self-preservation ; and the gospel meets this desire and fully satisfies it. Then follows in due course the desire to love and serve God in Christ.

Another legitimate manifestation of self-love is a due care for our health and comfort as we pass

on day by day through life, and as providential
circumstances permit. To neglect this is to neglect a Christian duty. True, it is a duty to
"mortify our members which are upon the earth,"
"to crucify the flesh," "to mortify the deeds of
the body," because these phrases allude to the
evil principle of the old fallen nature, and its
manifestations as mentioned in Col. iii. 5–8 ; but
to mortify that self, which is the true object of
our love, is altogether a mistake ; and the doing
so has had the most mournful results in the by-
gone days of asceticism.

Indeed, self-love is the standard of the moral
law in relation to our love for others ; "Thou
shalt love thy neighbour as thyself ;" although
the new commandment of spiritual love goes
beyond this, and will lead a believer to love the
brethren more than himself, and, if need be, to
lay down his life for them.

"Crucifying the flesh" and "mortifying the
deeds of the body" do not mean starving ourselves and denying ourselves the proper amount
of bodily rest, or repressing the true natural
feelings of the heart, or engaging in certain work,
or in placing ourselves in certain circumstances
and associations, not because of the evident and
unmistakable call of the Lord, who has shut up
every other way and given peculiar fitness for

this, but because such work and such associations and such circumstances are the most trying and objectionable and painful to us personally. This is not what is meant by crucifying the flesh or mortifying our old evil self. This is rather to mortify that self which should not be mortified, and frequently results in not only leaving unmortified that very self or " flesh " (the evil principle and its passions) which is the true and only object of mortification, but in the further encouragement and strengthening of it, besides placing an effectual hindrance to the judicious exercise of those gifts which have been bestowed upon us for useful service.

It is right in all things to avoid being a self-worshipper, but it is no less right to avoid being in this sense a self-hater.

To deny self is a duty to which all believers are called when self is in any way a hindrance to the faithful following of Christ. But this consists in refusing to listen to the solicitations of any one however beloved, or be guided by any influences however attractive, or remain in any position however honourable amongst our fellows, or cultivate any associations however pleasant, which would hinder faithfulness to Christ in following and serving Him according to the teachings of His own word. Yea, in being ready and willing to give up all things, and even life itself, rather than be unfaithful to Him.

XIII.

Concerning spiritual growth.

HOWEVER firm, apparently, our decision for the Lord Jesus may be before men, and however sincere our aim after full conformity to His image, all will be in vain unless He Himself be our strength. Moreover, true decision for the Lord is not to be carried out by mere impulsive actions or special plans, but must, if success is to be attained, be the constant aim in the daily life; and although we may sometimes fall far short of this because of the hindrances arising from peculiar temperament, yet we must not be discouraged, nor desire to lower the standard to suit our peculiar temperament, but rather seek that our peculiar temperament may be modified by His grace, so that we may daily reach nearer the standard and become increasingly conformed to our Lord's image in all things.

Peculiar temperaments are sometimes like wild creatures that must be either tamed or chained; and constant watchfulness and prayerfulness, with firm decision through the grace of the Lord

Jesus, can alone accomplish either. He gives grace, not to help our peculiar temperament nor to excuse it, but to overcome it if such temperament be a hindrance to consistent and loving service, or to fellowship with, and joy in Him.

The believer carries within him a foe as artful and deceitful as any outside, but more annoying and more untiring than those outside, because ever at hand and always ready to seize every opportunity to manifest its evil propensities. No believer fully knows what spirit he is of in any of his actions, even in his best, so much is there a mixture of the flesh in all he does. This shows the great necessity for, and the great benefit of, the Saviour's intercession. He pleads for the acceptance of the good for His own sake; and for the forgiveness for His own sake of the bad; and thus our imperfect services, our mingled doings, find favour. Were it not for this, not one of our religious doings or duties would be, in the least degree, acceptable to God.

Moreover, the Christian life, while one of warfare, is one of progress; we should go on from strength to strength, and why? because it is the nature of this life to grow, to expand. We must grow spiritually if we would maintain a successful warfare. Either the old nature grows or the new; and while the new life can never die because of its union to the Lord Jesus, and because of the covenant faithfulness of the Holy Spirit, yet very much depends upon the faithfulness, the watchfulness, and the prayerfulness of the believer whether that life be one of healthy growth, so that all in beholding its manifestations shall see that the believer adorns the doctrines of God his Saviour in all things; or a poor, half-dead, stunted thing, such as few can see to be in existence at all, and none can see to be in beauteous, healthy activity. Oh, for more growth in divine life. Oh, for deeper rooting into Christ. Oh, for stronger growth up into Him. The one depends upon the other. The rooting and the growing correspond, and the fruiting too—all in Christ.

Our hearts are ever a sowing and a growing ground; and we may be assured that if the wheat is not growing luxuriantly within, the tares are springing up a prolific crop.

Furthermore, believers are, in one sense, God's granaries, from whence goeth forth the good corn of the gospel; even as from the Egyptian cities went forth to the starving nations around the good corn which, under the wise hand of Joseph, had been stored up against the day of need. Let us see to it that we send out the good corn unmingled with deleterious seeds, lest men refuse it and rather starve than eat, or eating, die.

XIV.

On the proper order of faith and experience.

In relation to the conflict within, and also in relation to unavoidable circumstances, we should always remember that the Lord Jesus is on our side, and therefore all must end well if, in all things, we walk by faith in Him. Whatever the soul truly needs for its good, faith will find in Christ. It is not, however, the realising experience that is to be the chief thought, but the trusting in Jesus.

To believe when all is dark and trying is more divine and more honouring to Christ, than to believe when all is light and joyous. To trust with the eyes shut shows more true trust than trusting with the eyes open.

To rest without hesitation and questioning on the word of God is the truest faith, and such faith is built upon a sure and unchanging foundation.

Faith believes all that the word of God says of the Lord Jesus in His wonderful and loving relationships to His people, and rests in Him in such relationships, and is content with Him, and runs not after frames or feelings. It takes God at His word, notwithstanding that everything else may give no comfort, or may even seem to contradict the word of the Lord.

Pleasant experiences, and comfortable feelings, and powerful realisations, desirable though they be, are never obtained by being made the chief object of pursuit and desire, but result from a living faith on the Lord Jesus, as He is made known in His word as the salvation and strength and joy of His people. If we would rejoice in the love of any one, we do not make the joy the chief object of thought, but the person himself and his love. The joy will then follow without being thought about or sought after. So is it between the soul and the Lord Jesus.

It is a great mistake to seek comfort and assurance from " feeling " instead of " faith," and to walk in the daily path under the power of " feeling " instead of " faith," and to endeavour to overcome indwelling sin by the influence of " feeling " instead of by " faith." These are very serious errors, and they are sure to prevent peace and joy, and to result not only in doubt and darkness, but in greatly hindering the believer in his endeavours to overcome indwelling sin.

Some of the children of God have been in the greatest distress of mind through this mistaken and unhealthy longing after feeling. Indeed, it has laid such hold on the minds of some by

long encouragement, that sadness and melancholy,
instead of a bright joy, is all the testimony they
could bear to the power of the Gospel.   Oh, this
sad, this soul-depressing struggle after strong
feeling, instead of quiet faith — a faith which,
though it cannot see, yet quietly waits and
trusts.

Feeling in religious life is necessary.   Heart
experiences of divine truth are an essential part
of the divine life within.   Realisations of the
blessings and privileges of the Gospel are the
believer's portion in a large measure, even in
this life, and are comforting and sustaining ; but
such feeling, such heart experiences and realisations must be under the direct and continued
influence of a living faith, guided by the word
of God.   The true spiritual order is, first knowledge, then faith, and, afterwards, a realising
experience.   First, rightly to know and understand truth ; then to believe in it for ourselves ;
then to realise it, or have the experience in the
heart, followed by such feeling or emotion as our
personal experience of its blessedness is calculated
to arouse.   But when this order is reversed, and
men want to realise truth before they believe it
for themselves, or want to have joy, peace, or
some other feeling before they exercise faith in
Gospel promises, the result is sure to be con-

fusion, darkness, and doubt, and a stumbling-block to all true progress in spiritual life.

We are not to make feeling or experience the foundation for our faith, but God's word only. We are not to realise, and experience, and feel, as an encouragement to believing, or as the way to faith, but we are to exercise faith in God's word, even if we have no deep realisations, pleasant experiences, or joyful feelings whatever.

Much of the joy of believers may be the joy of circumstances. The result, therefore, is that, when circumstances are changed, the joy of the believer ceases, whereas, if his joy were in the Lord, no circumstances would alter it, yea, even adverse circumstances would, through His grace, cause the soul more than ever to look for consolation and joy in Him.

XV.

To the Believer—concerning the way of consciously receiving power from the Lord Jesus in heart conflict with the evil within.

IT is the general experience of believers to find that self—old evil self—is an active enemy to spiritual life. As they advance in spiritual life they know more of self than they ever did before, and know it to be often a sore trouble to them, and a great hindrance to fellowship. It is too mighty for them, therefore they know their safety is in bringing it to their Lord, that He, being on their side, may put self in its proper place: yet, when quieted, they find it is only for a little time; soon it again rises, often suddenly and without notice, and sometimes, to their great grief, with renewed vigour.

There are these three with the believer:—his old self—"the flesh," "that which is born of the flesh is flesh;" his new self—"the spirit," "that which is born of the Spirit is spirit;" and the Lord Jesus Himself. So long as the believer walks with Jesus in the power and principle of the new self—"the spirit," the old self—"the flesh" cannot triumph; but when the believer ceases to do this, the latter is sure soon to have the victory. Our wisdom is to set the Lord Jesus always before us—looking to Him as He is now at the right hand of God in Heaven —walking in intimate fellowship with Him, and keeping watch against that old enemy—our old evil self.

There is nothing more difficult in all Christian experience than this keeping down of self. More sorrowful humbling, more deep abasement before our Heavenly Father, believers have had from the inward manifestations of self, than they could tell to any living being. Indeed, it is this old evil self that causes us to feel our need of Jesus more than the daily trials we meet with in our providential path.

When you have any cross to bear, when anything more than usually trying meets you in your path, if you would walk safely and cheerfully, you must bring it at once to the Lord Jesus, to receive from Him all needed power and grace ; but if, through want of watchfulness, old evil self takes hold of it, an opportunity is afforded to the flesh, by which it is not slow to profit, and the result may be murmuring, impatience, irritability, uncharitableness, and, of course, a complete hindrance to spiritual progress. The old self thus gains power every moment, and the soul has received from this enemy a blow which has already wounded its spirituality. What is to be done? shall the cross be taken to Jesus ? That should have been done before, and because it was not, there is a double burden upon the spirit, the cross and also old evil self, now becoming mighty and struggling for full victory. The cross—the special trouble—is now a secondary thing ; the great danger is from old self, and against this you have first to seek aid. What, then, is to be done ? The soul is, as it were, bound in the fetters of old self, and cannot exercise itself in spiritual things as it was wont to do. It seems utterly powerless, but there is no time to lose; something must be done, or what is yet within the heart will speedily make itself manifest outwardly. What, then, is to be done? simply this; immediately remember that *the eye of the Lord Jesus, as a friend, is upon you, and that the presence of the Lord Jesus, as a friend, is with you.* These two thoughts alone often make the soul more steady. Then, earnestly crying, "Lord Jesus, save! Lord Jesus, help!"—rest helplessly upon Him, believing He is your sure helper; lean upon Him, cast yourself upon Him, keep Him before your mind, and thus you are sure to receive power from Him, and to receive it consciously, so that—although a short time before you were downcast, overcome, filled with fear and dismay—you are now calm, restful, steady, and undismayed, through looking to Him, in whom you know you have now found strength for your day, grace for your time of need.

The evil thus subdued, confess to your Father the evil itself and the shortcomings which allowed the evil to gain such power, knowing that "He is faithful and just to forgive us our sins, and to cleanse us from all unrighteousness."

This forgiveness and cleansing of the conscience puts you right again; and the lesson you have deeply learned is the necessity of walking close with the Lord Jesus, looking always to Him. This experience of consciously receiving power from the Lord Jesus does not relate merely to the victory of the believer in that particular position of inward struggling just alluded to, but bears a very intimate relationship to the holy and joyful walk of the believer throughout the whole of his earthly pilgrimage.

Bear in mind, then, that in all temptation and difficulty the way of victory or deliverance is to remember that the eye of the Lord Jesus, as a friend, is upon you, and the presence of the Lord Jesus, as a friend, is with you, and He Himself waiting to be your strength against the foe ; and that to ask with confidence and to expect with certainty will surely result in consciously receiving power from Him. The power of the Lord Jesus thus working in you, you will find that greater is He that is in you, and for you, than the mightiest that can be against you. This conscious receiving from Christ should, however, in a measure, be our constant experience, whether under special temptation or not, so as not merely to recover ourselves when from want of watchfulness we have been brought under the power of old evil self, but to prevent old evil self from in any way gaining the upper hand.

You will observe that the experience here alluded to is not merely receiving power and grace from the Lord Jesus, but receiving it consciously. Many believers know they have received grace and strength only from the result; such an one would say—"I must have received grace, or I could not have overcome; I did overcome at last, therefore the Lord must have assisted me;" this is true, and this is the only experience many have of receiving power from above. This, however, is not consciously receiving power from the Lord Jesus. True, the victory may frequently be ours, for He does more for us oftentimes than we can ask or think; but we do not realise the presence and power of our Lord during the conflict. Consciously receiving power from Him gives the full assurance of victory whilst engaged in combat, and gives also calmness and firmness of soul, not doubt and dismay, as is too frequently the experience of believers when in temptation and affliction.

A believer might say—"Can I receive power from the Lord Jesus, and be conscious of it as a special experience continually? I do receive power, or I could not go on at all in the narrow way; He does give grace, but does He not do it in a mysterious way unknown to me, and of which I have no distinct consciousness, except as I see the result in being able to resist and overcome evil?" That question may be answered in asking another. Does not the Lord Jesus give rest to the weary, and do not the weary consciously receive this rest from and enjoy it in Him? But rest is only one of the blessings we require and find in Jesus; we need strength, we need nourishment, as well as rest. If the Lord Jesus be our rest, He is also our strength, and our bread from heaven; and this we ought to know and enjoy as much as the former.

The infant knows when it is resting in its mother's arms, and it no less knows when it is receiving food from its mother's hand; so should believers, looking to the Lord Jesus, consciously receive spiritual rest, nourishment, and power from Him.

To put it in another way; the Lord Jesus is always with each individual believer — each individual believer is always with the Lord Jesus. These facts are not always realised, but the want of realisation does not alter them; they are true notwithstanding.

Now the soul living by faith says:—"The Lord Jesus is with me alway—I am with the Lord Jesus continually." This is realised in the conscious experience of the soul, and joy and peace are the result.

Again; the Lord Jesus is continually giving to His people; His people are continually receiving from Him; and although they seldom realise this with full consciousness at the time, the fact is not altered thereby; He ever gives—they ever receive. Now, the soul living by faith says : — " The Lord Jesus is my strength; my eyes are upon Him by faith, now at the right hand of God, as my present helper, and as all my trust. He is now helping me, as I am looking to Him ; and I am now receiving power from Him to sustain me in the path of life, and to uphold me lest I fall."

This experience of continually receiving is realised more fully the closer we walk with the Lord Jesus. It is an experience which keeps the soul very low in itself, and is ever accompanied with conscious self-helplessness. We must stoop to rise. The highest experience of a soul in Jesus is not from climbing or striving mightily, but from sitting down very low. Jacob's ladder was not from heaven to the top of a high mountain, but to where Jacob lay low, with a stone for his pillow. Lying very low in ourselves, then heaven opens, Jesus is seen nearer, the soul is strengthened because strong in Him, the soul is happy because happy in the Lord.

A maiden carrying an empty pitcher desires to fill it at a streamlet flowing down the rocky sides of a mountain. Being conscious of strength and buoyant in spirit, she lifts the pitcher high that the water may run into it; soon, however, she finds the pitcher too heavy, and takes it away when only half full. Another comes on the same errand, but conscious of weakness she does not lift her pitcher high, but places it on the ground, under the waterfall, where it is soon filled without wearying effort. So is it with believers. They have often found their most hallowed and most precious seasons of holy communion, and of received help and joy, when, unable to reach forth with vigorous effort unto the Lord Jesus, they have come as empty vessels, and have laid low before Him in their helplessness; then the refreshing streams flowing from that Fountain of living waters, have filled them with fresh delight and renewed vigour. This, after all, is our safest position, for often in lifting high, old evil self is also lifted up.

To seek salvation in Jesus is wise; yet, at the best, it is but a selfish view of the Lord, if we are thus content. Let us not be so, but let us seek continued power from the Lord; power for conflict, so that "strong in the Lord and in the power of His might," "strong in the grace which is in Christ Jesus," we may ever go forth to victory. Blessed indeed is the salvation, and the rest we have in Him; blessed, too, the position of victory we gain through Him.

In this way we honour the Father, for He has made the Lord Jesus the channel of every blessing to His people. In Him, by the Father's appointment, is the fulness of every grace for our need; and only out of that fulness can we receive any grace whatever.

In this way we also honour the Holy Spirit, for His glorious office is to take of the things of Christ and show them to believers; graciously testifying of Christ in their hearts by teaching them of His riches which are unsearchable, and of His love which passeth knowledge.

Third Part.

CONCERNING A LIFE OF FAITH ON THE LORD
JESUS, AND WALKING IN FELLOWSHIP
WITH HIM IN THE DAILY PATH.

I.

*To the Believer—concerning personal dealing with the
Lord Jesus in the providential path.*

SALVATION you already possess, through faith in
the Lord Jesus who died to save sinners. Full
deliverance from condemnation you now enjoy,
through faith in the Lord Jesus, whose death
is your deliverance. Complete acceptance with
God the Father is now your happy portion,
through faith in the Lord Jesus, by whose precious blood and perfect obedience you stand
completely cleansed from guilt, and completely
righteous in His sight.

Your aim now is to enjoy more fully these
blessings which are yours, and to go on from
strength to strength, growing in grace and in

the knowledge of our Lord and Saviour Jesus
Christ.

What great things are now yours! not a
spiritual promise in the whole Bible but is
yours; and all are given for you to rest upon
and enjoy. You are an heir of God, and a joint
heir with Jesus Christ; a living member of that
family which God delights to call His own.
You are the special object of the love and care
of the Father and of the Lord Jesus, and also of
the Holy Spirit. Your heavenly Father and
His beloved Son Jesus Christ, do both hold you
in their hand (John x. 28, 29); and the Holy
Spirit dwells within you (1 Cor. iii. 16). The
Three have all agreed in covenant to bring you
safely home to glory. Your eternal happiness is
therefore assured beyond the reach of sin and
Satan to hinder.

All things are yours, and are directed and
overruled by the Lord Jesus specially for your
good. All grace is yours here, and all glory is
yours hereafter; and all because Christ is yours,
and you are His. Your trust in Him for that
salvation you deeply feel your need of, is the
evidence that not only the salvation, but that
all else is yours. Yes, the first link in the chain
of eternal joys and treasures is, when the soul,
conscious of its need of salvation, finds that

need fully met in a crucified Jesus. This links you in experience with all of eternal glory. Such, then, is your happy position now. For this you strive not. For this you work not. It was a portion prepared for you before all worlds. It is a free gift and never recalled. Live, then, in the enjoyment of what is so freely given you of God ; and seek increased grace for victory over your evil heart, and for a quiet but decided testimony for Jesus, wherever in providence He has placed you. The power, or strength of grace, which you need for this is given you in Christ Jesus. He is to you not only the salvation of God, but the power of God, and the power of God to be made use of daily, in all daily need. Therefore " be strong in the grace which is in Christ Jesus." Bring, in conscious helplessness, all your need to Christ ; not merely in a general way, but bring each need distinctly and individually to Him, as each need arises ; asking Him to be your help and strength therein. This He has promised to be, and He keeps His promises. Whatever need, or trial, or affliction you take to Christ, He at once accepts as His.

If you would have full joy in Him, and constant strength for all from Him, you must make much use of Him, as your living and ever-watchful, ever-present friend. You cannot give Him anything of your own, worthy His acceptance. Nevertheless, by bringing your need to Him, you not only obtain help, but you give Him glory by acknowledging Him thus, as your only hope and helper. Be intimate and constant in your dealings with Him, as the special friend and helper given you by your Father to be your guide, and strength, and joy all through life. Seek not to climb to any fancied height of excellency, as your qualification to walk with Him. The path of lowly need and of self-nothingness is the path in which He meets with His beloved ones. Look to Him in that path, and walk therein by faith in Him. So will you rejoice in the Lord always, and continually realise His presence and love.

Pray to your heavenly Father, that the Holy Spirit may work in you with increasing power; but ever remember that this power of the Holy Spirit is given to believers to enable them to look more to Christ, to live more upon Christ, and to realise more fully the presence and love of Christ, and to receive more grace out of the fulness of Christ; for the power by which to live to God, and walk in faithfulness and victory, is the power and grace of Christ (John i. 12, 16; 2 Cor. xii. 9; Eph. vi. 10; Phil. iv. 13; Col. ii. 10; 2 Tim. ii. 1., iv. 17).

II.

About looking to the Lord Jesus.

A BELIEVER should look to the Lord Jesus and walk in fellowship with Him, as One who, though invisible, is yet personally watching over him as his almighty, ever-gracious, wise, and loving friend.

The believer is not to think of the Lord Jesus as invisibly with him on earth, in His presence and form as man ; because in that presence and form He is now in heaven, and will abide there until His second coming.

The Lord Jesus is the true and eternal God, as well as man ; and therefore He knows all things both in heaven and on earth. The believer should not, however, think of the Lord Jesus as God apart from His presence and form as man ; for though the human nature and the Divine are ever distinct, yet He who possesses them is ONE PERSON. We cannot say that the man Christ Jesus is in heaven, and that the God Christ Jesus is everywhere ; but that the ONE PERSON, the Lord Jesus Christ, who is God and man, is everywhere; though, as regards His human form and presence, He is at present always and only in heaven.

A believer in looking to Him, should fix his thoughts upon His human presence in heaven, and walk in fellowship with Him as He is there; conscious that the Lord Jesus knows him, and sees him as fully and intimately as though there were no space between the believer on earth, and His own presence in heaven.

It is thus the believer is said to have his conversation in heaven, from whence he looks for the Saviour the Lord Jesus Christ. While in the body he is absent from the Lord, as regards His human presence; but he is exhorted to seek those things which are above, where Christ, in the real likeness of man, sitteth on the right hand of God.

It is from the Lord Jesus in heaven, that all grace comes to help believers in time of need; and it is through looking with faith to Him in heaven, that we are encouraged, and strengthened, and made joyful in our pilgrimage on earth. The Holy Spirit is especially sent to aid us in thus looking to the Lord Jesus, and in living by faith on Him.

The martyr, Stephen, just before he was put to death, looked up steadfastly into heaven and saw the glory of God, and Jesus standing on the right hand of God; but what he thus saw with his bodily eye, was only the clearer vision of what his faith had realised in every-day life.

The Lord Jesus never hides His face from a
believer, but there are many earthborn clouds
which may blind the eyes of a believer, and
prevent him looking to the Lord Jesus. Indeed,
a believer may be said to be blinded by whatever
he allows to come between his soul and the Lord
Jesus, so as to prevent him realising the presence
of his Lord, and walking in fellowship with Him.

His eyes may be blinded by encouraged evil;
so that he looks not to the Lord Jesus as his
daily Saviour and ever-present deliverer.

His eyes may be blinded by his sorrows; so
that he looks not to the Lord Jesus as the comfort of his soul.

His eyes may be blinded by his earthly joys;
so that he looks not to the Lord Jesus as his
chief delight.

His eyes may be blinded by his activities of
service; so that he looks not to the Lord Jesus
as the rest of his soul.

His eyes may be blinded by his weaknesses;
so that he looks not to the Lord Jesus as the
strength of his life.

His eyes may be blinded by his afflictions;
so that he looks not to the Lord Jesus as his
sympathising friend.

His eyes may be blinded by his disappointments; so that he looks not to the Lord Jesus as

the head over all things, and as one who is engaged to make all things work together for his good.

His eyes may be blinded by his feelings, or want of feelings; so that, through contemplation of self, he looks not to the Lord Jesus as the only true object of contemplation and faith, from whom all joyful experiences flow.

His eyes may be blinded by the contemplation of the evil within ; so that he looks not to the Lord Jesus, as one, by whose obedience he is made righteous, and in whom he stands unchangeably perfect and accepted before God ; and in whom is all his strength for victory over indwelling sin.

His eyes may be blinded by religious rites and ceremonies, so that he looks not to the Lord Jesus as his all—his all for salvation, so that no religious helps are needed to make his salvation through the precious blood of Christ more secure —his all for friendly help and sustaining grace in daily life, and, as such, more ready of access than is any earthly friend.

These are some of the clouds which may blind the eyes of a believer, to the great loss of that daily peace and joy which is the privilege of all who look to Jesus, and walk in the light in fellowship with Him.

III.

On need met in Christ.

IN every path of life there is the experience of need ; for if need be not felt in one way, it is sure to be in another. This need is ordained by the Lord for each of His children, with a view to the peculiar spiritual training of each. Wisely and graciously He works, and with untiring discernment as to what is best suited for each, for He well knows that what is suitable for one will not be suitable for another. No two of His dearly loved ones have been led in exactly the same path of experience, although all are led by the hand of the same Father, and by the hand of the same Friend and Saviour, the Lord Jesus (John x. 28, 29).

Need is the chief characteristic of our pilgrim path ; and it is so, that we may the more regard that fulness which is for us in Christ Jesus, or, rather, that we may the more regard the Lord Jesus Himself, who delights, out of His own fulness, to give grace for grace and sure help in time of need.

Often His best and most blessed help is not in the exercise of His power to deliver, but in the gift of His grace to bear—not in the removal of tribulation, but in giving joy in the midst thereof.

In the prayer of the Apostle for the Ephesian converts, he asks that Christ may dwell in their hearts by faith. Now, need is one of the chief means through which this indwelling of Christ in the heart is realised; for when the believer opens his heart's need to Jesus, it is faith opening the door of the heart to Him, and He then comes in and dwells there as its friend and helper.

There are two ways in which Christ dwells in the heart of the believer—vitally and experimentally. He dwells there vitally through the quickening power of the Holy Spirit, by which the soul becomes one with Him in spiritual life. This dwelling is never altered by any failure or unworthiness of ours. He dwells there also experimentally, and this is through faith; faith in action; faith prompted to action by a conscious need that nothing but Christ can satisfy. The heart of the believer is opened to admit Christ, when, in conscious need, that heart brings before Him, in faith, its griefs, and fears, and difficulties, and wants. He then comes, oh, so readily, so joyfully, to be the all of that heart, and to make it happy with His gracious and helpful presence. Christ in glory has not ceased His earthly fellowships, but, as when on earth, His fellowship is still with the needy and the helpless who look only to Him (Isa. lvii. 15).

Heart-trembling is not always a sign of unbelief. It may sometimes be a sign of conscious weakness and unworthiness. Such an experience is one for which the Lord has a peculiar regard, and is one that, looking to Him for help, ever brings in His own time peculiar manifestations of His presence and favour (Isa. lxvi. 1, 2).

Contrasts show forth more fully the Lord's glory. It is when His perfect power meets our perfect weakness, and His greater grace our deeper ill-desert, that both His power and grace obtain their highest glory in us. As long as Christ lives (and He liveth for evermore), so long shall a consciously helpless soul never lack an arm to lean upon, or a consciously guilty soul a full deliverance from condemnation and guilt. " I am He that liveth and was dead ;" these are precious words. " He that was dead,"—there is our deliverance from endless death. " He that liveth,"—there is our assurance of earthly help and endless life. " Because I live ye shall live also "

IV.

*Concerning sincerity of heart in walking before God
and before men.*

IT is necessary to be very sincere in all we say
concerning our personal spiritual life, and to be
careful never to make use of phraseology that
would seem to indicate an experience beyond
that which we really possess.   A free and un-
thinking use of such phraseology cannot but be
injurious to the spiritual life, for it has a tendency
not only to promote a merely superficial and
sentimental knowledge of spiritual things, but to
encourage an artificial experience, a mere coun-
terfeit, by which the conscience becomes eventually so deluded, and the spiritual sensibilities
of the soul so deadened, that there is but little
relish for a deeper and truly spiritual heart
work.

There should be more of watchful heart-living
before the Lord, and sometimes less of lip-living
before men.   Religious phrases and sentiments,
which seem to indicate a deep religious experience, may come from a source no deeper than
the intellect, or from a mere natural emotion,
easily excited under the influence of religious
associations.

There is something unhealthy in the spiritual
life when there is more of religious fervour and
more of Christian ardour in our converse and in
our more public or social doings than there is in
our hearts, for the heart should be as a fountain,
and the outward life as overflowing waters therefrom. It is well then to have more heart culture
before the Lord, and in the Lord, by quiet
dealings in heart-walking with Him in daily
life.

How seldom is the soul walking with the Lord
in the consciousness that it is overcoming through
Him! How often in the presence of seeming
obstacles there is lacking a prayerful determination to do or suffer all things through Christ,
and for Christ.

Seeming obstacles in the path of duty should
but cause a believer to buckle on his armour
more firmly. The removal of a seeming obstacle
would perhaps be more pleasant to the flesh, but
it might not be so profitable to the spirit. It is
not therefore well to seek pressingly its removal,
except in complete subjection to the Lord's will,
but rather grace and wisdom to overcome it, and
that it may be so sanctified as to bring us in
heart and life closer to Him than ever. What
may seem now to our weak and blinded vision
to be an obstacle, may be seen eventually—when

we know things better than we can do here—
to have been just the very thing that kept us
from making fearful shipwreck on some hidden
rock to which the great enemy of souls was
trying to draw us.

The great thing is to be as little children before
the Lord. We should be strong men and women
spiritually before others, and the only and sure
way to be so is to be always as little children
before the Lord, looking to Him at every step as
needy and helpless ones, and resting with believing hearts on His assurance of help and grace.
We should never go to the Lord as strong ones,
but as weak ones, as very children. It is not
strong ones to whom He gives grace, nor rich
ones to whom He gives treasure, nor wise ones
to whom He increases knowledge, but the weak,
the poor, the ignorant, are those whom He blesses.
Happy is that soul which learns to profit by
learning that it has nothing in itself, but everything in Christ.

We should make heart work of all our dealings
with Christ and doings for Christ. So many say
and do without the heart being engaged. As
the heart is, so are we before the Lord. We
may be very religious, very active, very faithful
amongst our fellows and be much loved by them,
and yet be very, very far from pleasing the Lord.

There may be a correct walk, according to man's judgment, without a correct heart; but the trees of the Lord's planting bear fruit as the result of a good root—a heart rooted in Christ.

The Apostle Paul could say, "For me to live is Christ," because he could say, "Christ liveth in me." The fruit of his life was Christ, because the root of his life was Christ. This is ever the secret of a happy, useful, and consistent life in the Lord's service.

V.

On the excellency of a resigned will.

IF we use all earthly things in subordination to the Lord Jesus, no earthly things will draw us away from Him; but if earthly things, however excellent in themselves, have a greater influence with us than Christ has, He will soon plant a thorn where we expected only pleasant flowers. It is thus we are taught more effectually that Christ must be our all in everything here below.

The great cause of the want of spirituality of mind in believers is that they do not live in daily life as before the Lord, walking as in His presence with a sincere heart, being perfectly sincere before Him, perfectly open with Him in all things, and sincerely desirous of growing in the knowledge of Him.

When there is lacking a resigned will and a contented mind, great spiritual tempests arise, and much sorrow and turmoil follows. It is quite possible to live a conqueror's life henceforth, but the very idea of a conqueror's life implies foes to combat and defeat. The Lord will not be more on our side ten years hence than He is now. He is always on our side, and always with us; but it is a resigned will that embraces Him; it is a contented mind that sits down with Him.

When a child of God places any matter in the Lord's hands, waiting upon Him whilst using such means as the Lord, in His providence, puts within his reach, relying, however, not on the means, but on the Lord, the result is sure to be one of blessing from Him, although we may be unable to see His meaning, or understand His work. Faith here rests satisfied, knowing that the Lord is always good, and that He makes all things work together for the good of His people.

Continual risings of doubt and fear, or discontent concerning any matter, show that it has not been unreservedly and completely put into the Lord's hands. Until this be truly done, the experience concerning it will not be such as becomes a disciple of Jesus Christ. The flesh in the believer is always ready to influence the heart to murmur and rebel, but it is unable to do this concerning any matter that has been unreservedly and completely placed in the Lord's hands.

It is well to remember that the best help, in every season of need, is the realised presence and love of Jesus, through faith in His promises. To have Jesus Himself more consciously near, and His love more fully realised in the path of peculiar trial, affliction, and conflict, is more supporting and more blessed than the ordinary experiences of the believer in the ordinary and less trying path of life. It is always well to look above second causes for the secret of things and to the believer such secret reason is ever found in that eternal love which chose him in Christ Jesus before the world was. That love, in union with infinite wisdom, plans all the path of grace, and all the path of providence to the end of the journey here.

VI.

*To the Believer—concerning intercourse with unbelievers,
and fellowship with fellow-believers.*

You will, necessarily, meet with much in your
social and private life that will, for the time
being, prevent your mind being specially occupied with thoughts of Christ and spiritual
things.

It is necessary always to make a distinction
between that judicious occupation of the mind
which is necessary for the proper consideration
and carrying out of needful things, and that
wilful occupation of the mind with those things
which are not necessary, and the known tendency
of which is, not only to prevent the mind
thinking of Christ, but to give the mind a
distaste for thoughts of Him. The former are
not sinful, although it is well, in them, to refer
everything to Christ as a friend and helper, so
that they may be the pathway of daily communion with Him. The latter are, however,
decidedly sinful, and should, therefore, be firmly
resisted and discouraged.

Communion with Christ does not necessarily
imply that the believer should be always thinking about Him or always talking about Him,

but it does imply a mind that will not readily engage itself with what it knows to be injurious to the spiritual life, and a mind glad to embrace every opportunity which will help the soul to realise more fully its interest in Christ, and to promote heart fellowship with Him.

In intercourse with near relatives who are unbelievers, much caution is needed, lest we increase their sin by giving increased opportunity for opposition to the word of God. Between a desire to bear testimony for the Lord, and a desire not to give offence to those we love in the flesh, the believer is often in a perplexity. He is also often tempted to speak about religious truths rather from a desire to satisfy his own conscience, than from any higher motive.

Where your religious principles are already well known, it is often better not to speak on religious subjects in a direct manner, unless in answer to questions, but rather to let your light shine by quietness of manner and gentleness of speech, and by acts of special kindness and forbearance.

In all things prayerfully and thoughtfully take counsel of Christ in His word. Try to exercise in all things a calm spiritual judgment, for lawful things are not always expedient for the soul's good, or for the real good of others, and we are to consider wisely what is for the good of others, as well as for our own.

Believers often experience that earthly fellowship even with fellow-believers is unsatisfying.

Perfect joy in fellowship can only exist where the fellowship is between perfect beings, and for that we must wait until we reach heaven. So long as we are imperfect ourselves, we must not expect perfect joy and uninterrupted harmony in even true Christian intercourse ; yet, to a considerable extent, much of the pain and disappointment experienced might be avoided if fellowships were founded upon, and moulded by, mutual fellowship with the Lord Jesus. Then the closer the mutual fellowship with Him, the sweeter and more complete and more profitable will be the fellowship between the disciples. Discords to spiritual harmony exist in every heart, and these may soon have opportunity to manifest themselves, unless the Lord Jesus be the bond of union always.

Our most earnest desire in fellowship with each other should be increased fellowship with Him, knowledge of Him, likeness to, and love for Him, and a fuller consecration to His service. Christ should be the Alpha and Omega—the beginning and the ending of all we engage in here. Without Him the sweetest of earth's

harmonies may end in sad discord. With Him
we may have, even in earthly fellowships, much
of hallowed union and heavenly enjoyment. To
a soul that makes Jesus all in everything, there
will be the most joyful communion where He
is the most manifested.

Too often, however, the fellowship of believers
is founded merely upon oneness in Church relationship, or oneness of doctrinal views, or oneness
in religious activities, and not upon oneness in
Christ. No wonder, then, that they tend not to
spiritual progress and growth in grace. Where,
however, Jesus is first, always first, there the
cup of fellowship will be both pleasant and
profitable to the true-hearted believer.

VII.

*To the Believer—concerning rest and help in Jesus
amidst seemingly adverse providences.*

REST only and wholly in the Lord Jesus. Simply
rest, and quietly wait as one who knows not into
what path the hand of the Lord may next guide
your steps, yet as one well assured that all must
be well, because it is His hand that guides and
His presence that cheers. You may have still
increasing evidence in your pilgrim path that

this is not your rest, nevertheless walk trustingly onward and leave all with Him.

When darkness overtakes a traveller in a difficult and dangerous road, and one to which he is quite a stranger, it is a great relief to his fears to hear the voice of a friend who well knows the path and who has trodden every step. So, though the future of your journey to your heavenly home be all unknown to you, it is fully known to the Lord Jesus, and He who is the light and joy of that home to which you are journeying, will be your light and joy in the journey there. He will, as it were, turn the home light upon your path, so that, in your measure, you will walk in the light of heaven ; for to walk in the light of His countenance and the brightness of His presence while here upon earth, is indeed to walk in the light of heaven.

He well knows the path you tread to-day, and will tread to-morrow. Therefore look not at the storm, for it cannot harm you, it would sooner harm Him. Tremble not at the dark waters, for they cannot overflow you; if they did they would overwhelm Him also, for He says, "I am with thee." Fear not the darkness, He is your guide. Look only to your guide. Look always to your guide.

Consider well the lesson taught by the experience of the Apostle Peter. When this apostle walked on the sea, he did not begin to sink until he looked away from Jesus. It was then that the boisterous wind caused him to fear, but it was his fear that caused him to sink, and not the boisterous wind. In his fear, however, he cried, "Lord, save me!" and quick was the response of love, for "immediately Jesus stretched forth His hand and caught him, and said unto him, O thou of little faith, wherefore didst thou doubt?" Thus showing that however stormy the path, though it be sufficient to cause the stoutest natural heart to tremble, the disciple of Jesus, walking therein at His call, has no cause for doubt or fear.

"And when they were come into the ship the wind ceased." The wind did not cease when the Lord stretched out His hand to Peter, but they walked together hand-in-hand all through the storm. They walked along the waters, rough as they were, and with the wind as boisterous as when Peter saw and was afraid; but Peter walked unharmed, and now without fear.

Blessed companionship did Peter have. Never would he have had such a special manifestation of the love and watchful care of his gracious Lord but for that storm—and thus they walked along together. How the disciples in the ship must have wondered when they saw Peter walking safely and firmly on the rolling waves, even as many now wonder when they see believers happy in the midst of the sorest calamities, not knowing that the secret power that sustains them is Jesus Himself, not knowing that He is with them there, and in a spiritual manner holds their hand.

The wind blew hard and rough until Peter and his compassionate Guide and Protector entered the ship together; then, and not till then, did it cease. The Lord Jesus, to quiet Peter's fears, might have spoken to the winds and waves, as He did upon another occasion, and at once have produced a calm on the troubled ocean, but no; He would still further teach Peter, and teach all, that those who walk with Him are as safe on the deepest waters, when the most violent tempest blows, as when there is a great calm.

It may please our gracious Lord Jesus not to quiet the troublous waters around you, but to let the storm continue at its height for a season, that you may the more learn what a precious guide, and preserver, and comforter He is; and that you may, as it were, go hand-in-hand together with Him over the stormy waters. Blessed fellowship indeed! Some of the sweet-

est, happiest lessons have the Lord's loved ones
learned in the path of deep trial; for there they
have learned how, in the night, He can give
songs; how, in the midst of tribulation, He can
cause the heart to rejoice; how He can make
the rough winds, as they fiercely blow, and the
mighty waves, as they onward roll, the means of
more intimate fellowship between the disciple and
Himself, and the opportunity for showing more
fully His watchful care and changeless love.

VIII.

On living upon Christ.

IT is quite right to grow in the knowledge of our
Lord Jesus, but it is not right to be impatient
about it; nor is it right to neglect to walk in the
power of what we do know, simply because we
do not learn as fast as we should like. Those
generally who hold truth firmest, are those who
learn it slowest. Sometimes what is quickly got
is as quickly lost. Patient waiting and patient
learning is the best every way. The result is
sure to be more enduring.

Some need more and sterner discipline than
others. Some are the easy trophies of grace,

others need to be hedged up on every side, and to be dragged from their idols with force more effective than pleasant. As self is the great god of fallen humanity, so the fallen humanity in the children of God still longs after its old idol. Some of the children need to be chastised into obedience because self-will is rebellious. Others will obey, but like to do it after their own mind, and so they need to be taught by many falls. Others, however, having been brought, through grace, to have no will but the Lord's, having now done with self-choosing and self-pleasing, are readily drawn after the Lord by His gentle and gracious hand. Happy are these, for no anxious care is theirs. They find in the Lord all their salvation and all their strength.

The most real part of a believer's life is that inner life before the Lord, which, with all its struggles and hindrances, its defeats, sorrows, and victories, is only known in its fulness to Him, who knoweth all the thoughts of His tried ones. Such a life is too deep for utterance in all its realities ; and the soul often feels that it would rather draw a veil over it which no eye can pierce but the eye of Jesus, than risk being misunderstood by others.

It is a cause for thankfulness if the Lord Jesus does not permit us to lean on any creature whatever. When we keep quite close to Him and do not even expect rest in anything or anybody else, nothing will move us. Let us then ever remember that Jesus is always with us. We have not to make His presence a fact, but to live conscious of that which is already and always a fact. We rest on that, and what our lips cannot even whisper forth of the struggling within, let our heart speak in silent communings with that loving One, who well knows all we are, and all we feel.

We want a deeper heart-life from the Lord Jesus; a conscious, a felt power within, a subduing, mellowing, directing, absorbing influence which no words can better describe than these— "Christ liveth in me;" not a shadowy, sentimental, mystical Christ, but the life of the real Christ who is at God's right hand, incorporated as it were into our innermost being, so that Christ may be more the life of the soul, than the soul is the life of the body. This is a high experience, and the attainment of it is through making Christ everything in our daily life.

The fulness which is in Christ is not for Himself, but for others. His fulness seeks rest, and finds it nowhere but in empty and needy souls. These empty, needy souls seek rest, too, and find it nowhere but in Him and His fulness. There thus exists a mutual suitability for each other.

IX.

On prevailing faith.

"MANY are the afflictions of the righteous," is as true now in the experience of God's children as it ever was.   It is also true now, as ever, that "the Lord delivereth him out of them all."   There is no chance work either in the affliction or the deliverance.   Both are appointed by the Lord, and appointed in love, as far as regards those called "righteous"—that is, those who, knowing no good in themselves, seek only for acceptance before God in "Jesus Christ the righteous," always desiring to walk before Him in newness of life.

All things work together for the good of those who trust in Christ, therefore, although some things are as bitter medicine, yet good is the promised issue ; and the promises of God have never yet failed.

It is not so easy to believe when everything is painful and unpleasant.   There is hard work for faith, as well as easy work ; but the hardest work faith ever has, is most successfully accomplished by greatest weakness—by greatest weakness looking trustingly to Him whose strength is all-sufficient.   "Most gladly therefore will I

rather glory in my infirmities (weaknesses) that
the power of Christ may rest upon me" (2 Cor.
xii. 9). The almighty power of Christ finds its
most suitable opportunity in the greater weakness of His needy ones. It is thus that weak
ones so often do greater feats of faith than those
who are strong to labour.

The Lord Jesus delights in a childlike trust.
Too often His people want to come to Him with
a trust that is man-like—that is, with a trust
that has some self-reliance, some self-reasoning,
or self - ability, or some self - wise plans and
arrangements, or a trust that commends itself
by the many things the hand has accomplished.
Whereas a childlike trust—that trust which is
the result of becoming like a little child—has no
self-reliance, or reasoning, or ability, or plans, or
great works to encourage it, but has only a consciousness of need, and ignorance and helplessness; and looks hopefully to Him who has never
yet been known to fail His trusting ones.

The childlike trust which grows out of weakness, pain, and affliction, is more honouring to
the Lord Jesus than the trust which grows out
of health, and ease, and the impulse of many
activities.

In weakness and affliction how precious it is to
know that we have a Person to look to; a Person

to lean upon ; and that Person such a gracious and faithful friend as the Lord Jesus, who loved us so much as to die to save us.   However much the mind may be interested in doctrines, nothing satisfies the heart but the consciousness of the sympathy and love of a real living friend, such as the Lord Jesus is.   Doctrine is for our instruction and belief—Jesus Himself is for our heart-trust, and love.

Jesus is not a friend for sunny hours only, but also when the storm comes, and the thick black cloud, for He is in both storm and cloud with His ever-ready hand and His ever-loving heart.   No changing providences imply any change in Him. All glory be to His name for evermore !

X.

On being led by the Spirit.

To be led by the Spirit of God is that which distinguishes believers from unbelievers.   The latter, however religious they may be, are always led by the flesh.   The former, on the contrary, though often annoyed and perplexed and defeated by the flesh, are not led by it, but by the Spirit of God.   "For as many as are led by the Spirit of God, they are the sons of God " (Rom. viii. 14).

The Holy Spirit in His leading the children of God, first gives them a new nature whereby they desire to know, and trust, and love, and follow the Lord Jesus Christ. He then encourages, assists, and leads the believer more and more to hunger and thirst after Christ. To learn of Christ. To trust in Christ. To love Christ. To follow Christ, and to look to God as a Father unto whom he is reconciled by Christ. This is what is meant by being led by the Spirit of God; so that it is a very easy matter for a soul to know whether it be led by the Spirit of God or not.

The Holy Spirit never leads to Himself, but always to Christ. He leads outwardly by His written word; but He does not there teach us that His office is to lead us into the knowledge of Himself, but into the knowledge of our Lord and Saviour Jesus Christ. He does not in His word lead to Himself as the source of life and strength, but to the Lord Jesus, who alone is our strength and life, that we may be strong in the grace which is in Him, and live a life of faith on Him, who is "our life," now at the right hand of God. The Holy Spirit leads us not to Himself as our master, but to the Lord Jesus : "Ye serve the Lord Christ." Even in the exercise of His office as the Comforter, He speaks not of Himself;

for the Lord Jesus is the comfort of His people, and the Holy Spirit acts as the Comforter by showing more of Jesus to the soul.

It is only by the Lord Jesus becoming more a reality to the soul, and more its desire, that a believer can be conscious the Holy Spirit is working in his heart with increasing power— even as our Lord Himself said, " He shall testify of Me."

It is the glory and joy of the Holy Spirit to lead believers in the path of spiritual life and spiritual progress; but the sum of all spiritual progress and spiritual life is—more of Christ in the mind, better to know Him—more of Christ in the heart, better to love Him and be more influenced by Him—more of Christ in the life, better to serve Him.   Therefore, when the Holy Spirit more powerfully leads the believer, the sure result is, that Jesus is better known, loved, and served than before.

XI.

To the Believer—about realising Christ's presence.

LET the fact of the love and presence of Jesus influence your other thoughts about Him, and your converse and communion with Him.   You do not make His presence and love a fact, by believing it. The fact exists already, and you have His word for it.

Many children of God think, that before they can have the realised joy of Christ's presence, there must be a consciousness of His presence imparted to them by some spiritual impression upon their minds. But it is not so. It is simply by believing. In this matter the saying is true, "According to your faith so be it unto you." The restful joy results from the resting faith. The faith rests on the fact, as guaranteed by the Lord's own word ; and this is the most sure foundation for your faith.

Do not seek the joy directly, for it comes indirectly, and not by specially seeking for it. Simply rest in the fact that Jesus is with you ; and contemplate Him in His assured presence and love. Let your mind habitually refer to His presence as with you always, and His love for you as unchanged ; then rest, and peace will follow.

Furthermore, rest in the fact that you are a child of your heavenly Father, and that He will make all things work for your good ; and as you thus contemplate these facts, and your mind increasingly and habitually reverts to them as facts, unquestioned facts, for which you have

God's own word, the resulting peace and joy will soon follow. So many believers look more for the experience of peace and joy, than they look to Jesus and His word, by which means alone that peace and joy comes. By making the desired experience most prominent, and making that their aim, many lose a joy that would otherwise be theirs.

"The just shall live by faith;" that is, shall live by trusting, simply trusting; trusting Jesus and His word; and the more this trusting becomes the habit of the soul, the more will peace and joy be the result. Do not then allow your thoughts to be fixed upon the desired joyful experiences; but upon the Lord Jesus Himself, and that relationship to Him which is yours, and for which you have His own faithful word.

The Lord's way of helping His people in trial is most frequently not by removing the trial, but by Himself becoming their companion, and friend, and helper in it. Therefore the more sure way of blessing is to look to the Lord Jesus in the trial, to take it from His hand, and walk with Him in it.

The Lord did not still the waves and tempest at Peter's cry, "Lord, save, or I perish!" but He took him by the hand, and walked with him in

the midst of the terrible uproar around; and
Peter, doubtless, found those tempestuous waves
a pathway of much blessing, because a pathway
of fuller intimacy with his Lord, and more complete reliance upon Him. In trial and affliction
especially, the soul's thought should be, *He holds
me.*

XII.

*To the Believer—concerning growth in grace and the
fuller experience of life in Christ.*

WHATEVER leads the soul to contemplate itself
and its circumstances, is sure to be injurious
unless always viewed in the light of Christ.
The eyes of many of God's children too readily
look within and around, instead of upward; and
the result is, their hearts are more often filled
with doubt and darkness, than with light and
confidence. To a heart whose trust is full trust,
there is enough light in Christ to illumine the
darkest path on earth that ever man trod.

We want to be more settled in Christ. The
experience of believers is frequently of too inter-
mittent a character. He is always a shining sun
to them. Alas! that they should so often get
into the cold and cheerless shade of self. The

reason why so many walk in spiritual darkness, is either, because they know so little of His love and faithfulness, or because they are so little looking to Him, and walking with Him.

Love for Christ, or joy in Christ, is not always according to the amount of doctrinal knowledge. There may be very much knowledge of revealed truth concerning Him, and yet but little true joy in Him, or desire after Him. There may be, on the other hand, but little knowledge—doctrinal knowledge—yet much joy in Him as a personal Saviour, and Friend, and Helper. The possession of much scriptural knowledge about Christ, without living more fully upon Him by faith, is like being in the possession of much food, and understanding well its nature and excellency, but not partaking of it. The failure of spiritual strength, like the failure of physical strength, is caused either by hidden disease, open irregularities, improper food, or insufficiency of that which is good.

Cleave to Jesus ; abide in Him ; abide, trusting in Him ; abide, looking to Him for strength ; abide, following Him—abide thus, whether it be darkness or light, joy or sorrow. Abide in the consciousness of His love to you : that love never changes—then never let your sense of that love change ; abide in it, and abide in love to

Him, by always preferring Him to the world. Never doubt His love for you, and never let the world hinder your manifestation of love for Him.

Unless you have the same mind as Christ in all things you will find that those things will be often a sore trouble to you, in which you are not of the same mind as He is. Living by faith in Him includes the wish to have everything as He sees best, and to walk contentedly with Him in every incident in the path of life He appoints ; so that you would not have anything altered until He sees fit.

Sometimes it is needful to look to Jesus as a shield, who defends us from our enemies while we remain still and passive. The soul is consciously helpless, and its victory is only in looking to Jesus wholly to undertake for it. At other times the soul looks to Jesus more as the giver of strength to resist, to fight, to conquer. Then is the time for the soul's activity, and foes must be met face to face. In such instances it is not so much that the Lord is our shield, behind which we, utterly helpless, abide in safety ; but that He is the power which nerves our arm, and encourages our hearts to go forth and fight the good fight of faith. It is our wisdom to know how rightly to use Christ in our ever-varying circumstances ; whether to run behind Him, or stand by His side and press on against every foe.

The great hindrance to growth in grace is not so much a sudden fall before strong temptation, as a general faint-heartedness in every duty. A sort of spiritual paralysis that benumbs the faculties of the soul, and pervades its spiritual actions. Under such circumstances there is increasing need for prayer, for confession, for humbling, for patient waiting on the Lord, and decided separation from everything that would encourage this spiritual torpidity.

Where there is growth in grace, such growth is sure to manifest itself by a closer walk with the Lord Jesus, and by an increased and increasing experimental knowledge of Him, and an increasing power over evil within and around. This will, of course, be first the consciousness of the believer himself, but afterwards of all those with whom he has to do in daily life, for Christ is always seen without, when Christ is actively living within.

If evil be consciously encouraged in the heart of the believer, or if evil rises within which he does not at once oppose, by bringing it to the Lord, seeking help against it,—such evil will surely increase in power (though it may be for a time secretly and quietly) until it be eventually not only a complete hindrance to the soul's walk in fellowship with the Lord, but the cause of growing inconsistency in life.

The way of safe walking is to look at the evil as an enemy to be overcome at once, by bringing it to the light before the Lord Jesus, and looking to Him for grace to overcome it. Evil thus treated will result in increased fellowship with the Lord, by bringing the believer to Him on an errand of need which is sure to meet with success.

We often have the brightest and most assuring experiences of the grace and compassion of Christ through our inward evil, when thus brought out into the light before Him in lowly and contrite acknowledgment. "I dwell in the high and holy place, with Him also that is of a contrite and humble spirit, to revive the spirit of the humble, and to revive the heart of the contrite ones" (Isa. lvii. 15).

How frequently believers complain that they are not clear and steady in looking to Christ. This is simply because something in the mind hinders the clear and steady view of Him. It is impossible to think fully of two things at a time, especially if those two things have an absorbing influence. He should ever be chiefest in the mind. Experience comes from habit of thought; and whatever be the character of the thought, that also will be the character of the experience, whether of Christ, of self, or of the world, whether good or evil, hope or fear, joy or sorrow, faith or unbelief, earthly or heavenly.

Christ should be always first. Everything and everybody else should be subordinate to Him, and held and loved, and used in the light of His countenance.

XIII.

To the Believer—concerning a rightly directed faith.

WE cannot walk in fellowship with God abstractedly, as He is the infinite God, but we can walk in fellowship with each of the three Persons who are the one God. Abstractedly considered, God is an infinite Being beyond our comprehension. Relatively to us He is revealed in personality. This is so encouraging and so well suited to us ; for we are so constituted, that we can only have fellowship with persons. The Father is one Person with whom we, as persons, can individually walk and have fellowship, as children with a father. The Lord Jesus is another Person with whom we as persons can have individual fellowship. The peculiarity of the Lord Jesus is that He is a Person with two natures, one of which (the human) makes Him one with us in our humanity, which is not the case either with the Father or the Holy Spirit. The Holy Spirit is another Person with whom we can have personal fellowship distinct from the other two; although His special office is to assist us to walk in fellowship with the Father and with the Lord Jesus. Thus we can talk to each of the Persons distinctly and separately, knowing at the same time that the three Persons are the one God.

Remember that amongst your chiefest thoughts of the Lord Jesus one must ever have a prominent place, and that is the thought that He is ever looking down upon you and watching you with tenderest love, and ordering all things for your good; sometimes it is spiritual medicine, at other times it is spiritual food, but at all times it is spiritual good, and just what is best for you; for He sees and knows beyond any one else just what is best for each day and hour; so, always when you think of Him, think of Him as thus looking down upon you and ever caring for you.

Be careful to avoid mysticism and the exercise of a fanciful imagination in your thoughts of the Lord Jesus. Of course your eye cannot see Him until you leave this world. In thinking of Him looking down upon you from heaven, you are thinking what is true; but if you try to realise that you see Him with you, about you, or above you, you are wrong. This it is that has made so many enthusiastic and misguided devotees, glorying in their visions, or in sights of the Saviour and His wounds.

True heart-experience is ever the result of true knowledge. Whenever the experience of the heart is not guided by a right understanding of God's word, it becomes dangerous and delusive both as regards the inner life and the daily walk ; and if not ending in superstitious enthusiasm as it often does, it nevertheless not unfrequently ends in an imaginative and emotional experience of a most unhealthy kind, either encouraging religious passion to an alarming extent of excitement both physical and mental, or promoting a shrinking and gloomy pensiveness or asceticism ; both greatly opposed to a calm and gradual growth in grace, and in the knowledge of our Lord and Saviour Jesus Christ.

Such persons are guided more by the promptings of their inward feelings than by the simple word of God. They too often mistake the impressions of a fervid imagination, and the feelings of an easily excited emotional nature, for the influences of the Holy Spirit within them.

An unduly imaginative temperament, if not a diseased, is at least an unhealthy one, having a constant tendency to disease. If not curbed by grace and kept in check, a too-active imagination is like a high-spirited runaway horse with the bit between his teeth. Woe be to the rider thereon. Yet grace can gradually overcome even that. "I can do all things through Christ." "Is anything too hard for the Lord?"

The religion of the Gospel is the religion of sanctified common sense that can give a reason for things, because guided by the plain teachings of God's word. The exhortation of the Apostle to "grow in grace and in the knowledge of our Lord and Saviour Jesus Christ," directs to a double growth—growth in grace, which is heart-growth, and growth in knowledge, which is mind-growth. The healthiness and correctness of the heart-growth depend greatly upon the healthiness and correctness of the mind-growth. This should lead us to great watchfulness and prayerfulness concerning what we hear and read and how we hear and read ; for errors clothed in the garb of truth have been a great hindrance and stumbling-block to multitudes.

XIV.

To the Believer—on living to the glory of Christ.

ALL things are for the glory of Jesus and were
created for Him.   When we look at all things in
this relationship all is well, for self and self-
pleasing have no place in the presence of such a
glorious issue as the honour and glory of the
name of Jesus.   This is ever the Father's purpose
in all He does.   He makes everything else but
secondary and subservient unto the exaltation
and glory of Jesus' name.   So should we.   Thus
we have fellowship with the Father.   The Holy
Spirit, too, works ever in all His works of grace
and power with the same end in view—the glory
of the Lord Jesus.   So again should we.   Thus
we know the fellowship of the Spirit and are
co-workers with Him.

The Holy Spirit is always assisting us in our
calm, judicious, prayerful thinking about Jesus
and His word, and also in looking to Jesus for
grace to help in all we do, so that in all things
He is the servant of Christ to us, leading us in all
to think of Christ and to act for Christ and continually to look to Christ.   In fewer words—the
Holy Spirit helps us to look to Christ for everything, and to serve Christ in everything.

The natural mind makes self the centre, and self the end. The spiritual mind makes Christ the centre, and Christ the end. The more we seek Christ, and the less we seek self, the more we please Father, Son, and Holy Spirit.

Christ is the source and end both of grace on earth and glory in heaven. Growing in grace is living more upon Christ, and living more for Christ, and growing more like Christ here on earth. Grace in the heart is glory in its beginnings. Glory in heaven is grace in its full consummation. Perfect fulness of eternal glory is the portion of all true believers, but some will have a capacity for a more exceeding weight of glory than will others. Our starting-point in glory will depend upon our attained capacity here. Our peculiar position in the family above will be after the measure of our growth in this life. The higher the spiritual attainments, and the larger the spiritual growth here, the higher the position and the larger the capacity in heaven.

If the Lord Jesus becomes truly and habitually the personal object of an individualising and growing faith and knowledge, the result will be increasing spiritual power, increasing peace, joy, and light in heart and life; for Christ dwells in the heart by a faith in Christ who dwells in heaven, and whose history and record are in the Bible.

Look not into your heart to find Christ there, but look to Christ where He is now in heaven; and looking to Him and trusting in Him, you will realise a power not only from Him, but a power which is Christ Himself in you. Look not however to the experience within, for as soon as the attention is turned to that, the realisation of Christ in His presence, and love, and power, is gradually weakened until the consciousness is lost, only to be restored by again looking out and away to Christ in heaven.

The Christ of the Gospel history; that is—the Jesus Christ of "yesterday." The watchful, loving, gracious, and present working Christ at God's right hand; that is—the Jesus Christ of "to-day." The unchanged and unchanging Christ who lives for evermore; that is—the Jesus Christ of the "for ever;" is the "all" of God to man; and to learn of such a Christ and live upon such a Christ, is the highest experience of the soul here or hereafter.

XV.

To the Believer—concerning the discipline of love.

LONG and trying discipline is for some special purpose not yet seen, but it will be by and by.

Be patient, still wait, wait on. The Lord may seem to work slowly, but there is wisdom as well as love in the worker.

There must be patient receiving as well as patient waiting. Often the Lord, in His discipline of love, not only withholds what the heart longs for, but gives what the heart shrinks from naturally. If this be not patiently received at His hands, the discipline is of no avail, and the Lord has to begin the discipline again, and sometimes again and again, but all in love, and that the believer may at last leave it to Him to give, or take away, or withhold, even as He pleases. He wants the believer to look to Him as his all, both in providence and grace, in temporal things and in spiritual.

To enjoy rest in the Lord Jesus in every providence however trying, each trying providence should be interpreted in strict accordance with His covenant love and faithfulness. To the believer He is all love. His providences contradict not this, however unpleasing, undesirable, or disappointing they may be.

Trying providences and pleasing providences are alike often permitted by the Lord's people to become veils which hinder them from looking to and rejoicing in Jesus, instead of opportunities more fully to learn His love and prove His grace and truth. To use trying and even pleasing providences as such opportunities, is not always easy; but our sufficiency is in Him in whom dwelleth all fulness for us, and who never suffers a disciple of His to seek for more grace in vain. The Lord Jesus by affliction calls His people to draw still nearer to Himself in daily fellowship, in secret and personal intercourse, so that, having become the still deeper necessity of their souls, He may still more become their fulness of life, and peace, and joy. With believers who are often in much affliction, the question should not be, "Why am I thus afflicted by Him more than many are who appear to be always well?" but rather, "Why am I so loved by Him more than many are; I who deserve this love no more than they?"

One of the sure results of living by faith, is to bring everything in the daily life, and every thought of the heart, in subjection to the Lord Jesus, to have no will but His. An unmortified member of the flesh is a usurping tyrant lording it over the will, and completely hindering a life of faith. If only partly mortified, its power may be hidden for a time, but will not be lessened, and when opportunity serves it will quickly show that power most painfully, sometimes like a torrent that would carry all before it, or like a whirlpool in the heart, wrecking every good feeling and desire.

Walking with Christ you are sure to walk in the path of safety and blessing. What if the way be sometimes marked with rough and thorny places! What if the difficulties and perplexities be many and unexpected! Looking unto Jesus, they will be but His opportunity to prove to you more vividly, more fully, what a ready helper, and what a faithful and ever-present friend you have in Him. All that the Lord does in relation to you is prompted by special individual love for you.

You would realise more of His love if you were to individualise it to yourself, even as you do His death for your individual personal salvation. Concerning the latter, nothing will satisfy you fully but your ability consciously to adopt the language of the Apostle, " He gave Himself for me." So, in relation to His love, nothing can fully satisfy you but to be able consciously to say, " He loved me "—loved you as if He had singled you out that He might fix His special personal love upon you—upon you individually and personally. This He really has done. It is no vain supposition, but a fact, a wonderful fact for which you will praise Him hereafter, world without end.

The most prominent object of the soul's regard, at all times, should be the glorified man, the Lord Jesus, ever living, and loving, and sympathising, and succouring; who is ever present with us, and to whom, though He is God, we can speak in holy, loving, childlike confidence, and with whom, because He is man, we can realise a nearness and relationship we could not do if He were only God. He it is who so often assures and comforts us by His presence and love. In walking with Him in holy fellowship, rocks give forth honey, stormy waves are a peaceful path, dark valleys become filled with light, and the heart is untroubled, though perplexities may arise so great that it may appear as if the earth were removed and the mountains were cast into the midst of the sea.

In your spiritual warfare increasing victories will make future ones of more easy attainment, and will cause you to realise the power, and love, and sympathy of our Lord Jesus more fully, than if the conflict were less sharp and severe. This is the way to a more perfect knowledge of Him, and a more perfect fellowship with Him. This, too, is the way in which the soul's rooting in Him is deepened and strengthened, for as tempests overhead do often but make the trees strike deeper their roots into the earth, so the tempest-tossed disciple, finding no safety but in Jesus, strikes, by faith, firmer roots into Him as the tempest increases ; then, by and by, the result is seen in more vigorous manifestations of growth and fruit before men.

There is so often such an alternation of sorrow and gladness in the experience of believers. Sometimes, however, the experience may not reach quite so far as real heart sorrow, but is more of a heart-heaviness or depression from mental or physical causes ; but whether it be heart-sorrow or heart-heaviness, our best position is still to wait on the Lord. Although from these causes we have not that joy in the Lord which we desire, yet we can be content with His will. Affliction, pain, trial, are not evil things ; nothing is evil but sin. We should be dissatisfied with nothing but sin. The heart can have rest in Jesus, even in the most trying circumstances, if the mind be free to think of Him, unhindered by weakness or disease, or by too great encouragement of other thoughts. If unable to think much of Him there should be quiet contentedness about it, if the cause of that inability be weakness or disease, and so beyond our own control, else we fight against the Lord.

XVI.

On pilgrim trials and pilgrim fellowships.

HE who well knows what it is to pass through
stormy waters and fierce fires—He—even Jesus,
is always with His people in similar experience,
according to His word (Isa. xliii. 12), "Fear not
. . . thou art Mine ; when thou passest through
the waters I will be with thee, and through the
rivers, they shall not overflow thee : when thou
walkest through the fire thou shalt not be
burned, neither shall the flame kindle upon
thee."

He does not say there will be no waters to
pass through, nor fires to walk through, but He
does say that they shall not harm us.   Mark
the blessedness ; it is not that He sends help
by His angels, that would not be sufficient for
His loving heart; it is, " I will be with you."
How comforting and assuring is this !   Had
omnipotence been joined to an angel, while the
help would have been sure, the loving sympathy
and precious fellowship could not have been the
same, but, for our help and joy, omnipotence is
for us in a man—a man true and tried in every
respect—true God and real man.   So the weary
one finding his weak and trembling hand held

by a man, and one who is not ashamed to call him brother, he finds also that it is held by omnipotence, for He is the Son of man with fellow-feeling to sympathise, the Son of God with omnipotence to help.

Because of this it is that some of the children's furnace-songs are the sweetest that ever heart and tongue united could pour forth, and some of their deep-water experiences the most precious and most blessed of all met with on the journey home, even because He, who is always near, seemed nearer still.

It is true that sometimes, when the flames are fiercer than usual, the believer may, for a time, be unfit for anything; but by waiting upon Him, and looking to Him, the heart-pangs are gradually lessened, and the mind regains its calm, and He with His help and comfort seems more real than ever. These times, however, often make the soul long for home.

There are some voids which the believing heart experiences that are never filled up on earth, and never meant to be, even by the Lord Himself. These more than ever disassociate us from earthly things, and make us the more conscious that this is not our rest. Still, though the void is never filled on earth, the Lord gives grace to wait until—in heaven's light and heaven's joyous associations—earth's voids are completely removed. Happy, happy time yet to come! Then will the hidden things of His providence be revealed to our wondering gaze, and then will the marvels of His wisdom and love become the more manifest through the very things which on earth sometimes made hearts very sad.

That time is yet before us; we are journeying to our home. Ours is a changeful journey; oftentimes pilgrim fellowships cheer the spirit and seem to shorten the way; but a little while and the fellow-pilgrim is at home, while we are still journeying on. All this makes the present rest in the ever-present One more necessary, and more welcome, and the future rest with Him, if possible, the more desirable. So we pass on; soon to see Him and see loved ones in the better land, the home of love on high.

When the spiritual and the natural heart (distinct from the carnal) have the objects of their affection in heaven, no wonder that heaven itself becomes the more desirable. We hasten on to it daily; and though we may have now and again to walk through the fires, yet He is ever with us; and though the waters be sometimes stormy through which we have to pass, He holds us with His hand, that once pierced hand of His, whose loving grasp no storm can unloose, and soon will He bring us to our desired haven. Then let us quietly and patiently wait the "little while;" joyous times are coming for weary pilgrims in the calmer and smoother paths above. Amongst our pleasant remembrances in those heavenly paths will be some of the rough sea walks we have had here, with Him as our companion.

Do not these things teach us that nothing on earth is truly pleasant apart from Jesus? Yes, indeed, with Him life's sternest realities wear a smile, though tearful eyes cannot sometimes see it; without Him the brightest things are darkness. Fair flowers may seem to bloom around us; but outside that paradise they are but painted vanity and death.

XVII.

Concerning personal relationship between God and man.

IT is important for the believer to consider the individuality of the love of the Father, and of the Son, and of the Holy Spirit, for each member of the chosen and ransomed family; and the peculiar, personal dealings, in grace and love with each, as distinct from the love and grace manifested towards every other member of that family.

If this fact were more a matter of heart realisation with each child of God, it would have unspeakable influence for power, for joy, and consolation, in the providential path appointed for each. The way in which God has revealed Himself to man, shows that He is not satisfied with being the God of creation and providence, known and worshipped in a general manner, merely as a God great in wisdom, goodness, and power.

The very fact that Scripture reveals God to us in a threefold personality, is sufficient to show that personal intercourse with man was His object. The very fact also, that fallen man in his groping after the unseen, apart from revelation, has fashioned to himself gods who were supposed to have personal dealings with him, and that of the most intimate character, even to the lesser and more ordinary affairs of life, shows that man, even though fallen, naturally longs for this direct intercourse with the Unseen, in order that a power beyond his own may work with him, and for him, and around him, for his personal good, however mistaken his views of that good may be.

The fall of man from his creation state of per-

fection has so completely darkened his mind, that
he can never find out the right way of personal
intercourse with God, nor even the true knowledge of that God in whom alone he can find all
that his soul needs. God, however, rests not at
a distance from sinful man, but overrules the Fall
to the opening out fuller and more wonderful
personal dealings than Adam realised before he
fell; for instead of manifesting destroying wrath
at the sin of Adam, a Seed was promised such as
man could never have looked for naturally—one
so wonderful in His work that He must be
Divine—and one so human that he must be the
seed of the woman.

Man was cast out of Eden, but not cast away
by Jehovah. All Old Testament history shows
that Jehovah was personally and intimately dealing with man. Personally dealing in judgment
with some. Personally dealing in love and grace
with others. Indeed the one great subject of
that history is a personal God dealing personally
and in intimate nearness with man. Jehovah in
His great condescension showed Himself frequently in the form of a man to men; dealing
with men, not merely as a God of holiness, wisdom, and power, but as a God possessing affections; as a God who could pity, and grieve, and
rejoice, and love—manifesting Himself as one

who sought His happiness amongst men, and who delighted to walk with men.

The Lord's yearnings over Israel; His pleadings with them ; His chastisements ; His startling language of mournful kindness when He reproaches them because of the way they treated Him, and His heart's joy in prospect of the glory and honour which in a future day awaits the Zion He loved so well—all testify of One whose delights are with the sons of men, and whose joy is in loving and intimate intercourse with them.

The New Testament record reveals the fuller outflow of this by the Father, Son, and Holy Spirit—the three glorious Persons in the one eternal Godhead.   True, it had been seen all along man's history, yet it was not until God had become man in Jesus of Nazareth that it was fully revealed how much it was in God's heart to have personal intercourse with man.   In that record we learn of reconciliation effected at Calvary ; even the personal and individual reconciliation of each of those sinners whom the Father, in His everlasting love for each, gave individually and personally unto Christ in the eternal covenant of grace.   In that record we learn that a most intimate and eternal experimental intercourse begins personally and individually with each sinner when the Holy Spirit enters his heart, and

quickens him to new life. Then indeed has God
in love and grace come so near to that individual
as not only to be with him but to be in him.
Intercourse thus begun will never end. This is,
however, at first unrealised by the newly
quickened one. His thoughts are not of personal
intercourse with God in love and confidence, but
of his own personal sin and guilt, and of the
personal punishment he merits hereafter, and of
the way by which he can escape that punishment.
Then the Gospel becomes indeed good news to
him, for therein he learns that a personal substitute is provided for the sinner by God Himself
in the gift of His only-begotten Son.

He finds in the death of Christ not only a way
of deliverance from his fears, but a way to more
personal thoughts of God, and to closer relationship and more intimacy with Him than he had
ever thought possible. Reconciliation, deliverance,
peace, forgiveness, redemption, acceptance, are all
intensely personal, and he begins to understand
them as such. He comprehends as he never could
before that God is to him a personal God, and a
personal Father; not one who merely takes upon
Himself the character of a Father, but the real,
loving, gracious Father of His sinful children.

He is now also brought into personal intercourse with the Lord Jesus as a personal Saviour

and friend and helper, and as one who is
the first-born among many brethren ; not one
who condescends to speak of Himself as merely
having the feelings of such, but really, tangibly,
personally, unchangeably so.   Heaven now is to
him no longer a dim and perplexing uncertainty
of the future, but a bright and sure prospect of
endless fellowship with a real Father and a real
Christ.

Thus far many believing ones rejoice in the
personal and individual realisation of God's inter-
posing love in personal action on their behalf for
salvation.   Where many however fail, is in not
realising that God's dealings in providence are
quite as direct, and personal, and real for each
one as they are in salvation.   Yet nothing can
be more clearly revealed in Scripture than the
reality of God's dealings with men as individuals
in all that pertains to their providential path
through life.   The Lord always desired His people
Israel to understand that He was not only the
true God, but in a special manner their God ;
working amongst them day after day in everything small or great.

This personal relationship is, however, much
more intimate and gracious and loving in His
providential dealings with His spiritual Israel
now, even with those whom He has led to seek

for refuge in His once crucified Son. Every step
in the providential path is watched over by each
of the glorious Three with the tenderest love.
No rough places in the way but have been fore-
seen and arranged for. No lessons to be learned
but had long been prepared by the most wise and
loving of teachers. No trials, but were planned
to work out great and exceeding good by Him
who hath all power in heaven and earth. No
difficulties, no sorrows or joys are matters of
chance. All flow from the same source from
whence salvation flows ; and Jesus is head over
all things to His Church, that Church composed
of individual believers who each stand in full
individual and personal acceptance and changeless perfection before God the Father, as one with
His beloved Son.

XVIII.

*To the Believer—on the way of fellowship with the
Lord Jesus.*

IT is a happy experience ; a very path of pleasantness to walk the daily path looking unto Jesus.
There is such a deep reality in the soul's intercourse with Him. Those only who watch His
providences, and who walk with Him by faith,

can have any clear consciousness how close and
intimate is His watchful care, and how personal
He is in His manifestations to the soul.   Such
feel a reality and a nearness in the Lord's presence
with them, and the Lord's doings for them, far
beyond that which the most intimate earthly
association can possibly afford.   This fellowship
with the Lord Jesus is usually one of gradual
attainment.   The difficulties in relation to the
evil within should neither hinder nor discourage
you.   Much difficulty is sure to be encountered
in attaining a habit so foreign to our fallen human
nature as this of fellowship with Him.

Let the Lord Jesus be much in your thoughts.
Seek to know Him better every day.   We only
know what He is now by what He was when on
earth as related of Him in His word.   As God
He has no " yesterday," for He is eternal ; but
as " the man Christ Jesus," He had a " yesterday,"
and that is contained in the Gospels.   What He
was there, what He was then, He is " to-day,"
and will be " for ever."   It is therefore well to
read the Gospels frequently.   Endeavour to realise the incidents in the life of Christ, especially
those in which His power and grace were manifested, not only towards His disciples, but towards
all who sought His help and instruction.   Picture
them to yourself quietly and calmly and as

vividly as you can. Make them living realities
to your consciousness; but look at them chiefly
as the index of His heart. Think of His gentleness, meekness, and patience, His forbearance,
and compassion, and considerate affection in His
dealings with His weak, wayward, and often
selfish and unbelieving disciples. Thus read His
heart life in His life of earthly ministry. It is
His "yesterday," and as He was then, so is He
"to-day," and will be "for ever."

In walking with Him in the consciousness of
His living presence with His people now, let your
thoughts not be so much from earth upwards, as
from heaven downwards. In other words, try
to accustom yourself to think of the Lord Jesus
at the right hand of God in all His fulness of
love and grace and power, ever supplying your
need; rather than to think first of your need and
then to think upwards to Him for supplies. The
former keeps you ever thinking of, and ever near
to the Lord Jesus. The latter may have a
tendency sometimes to make you think too much
of your necessities and infirmities, and in such a
way as almost to be overwhelmed by them.

Fellowship, or personal intercourse with Christ
is grounded on one or more of the following experiences. First, a consciousness of our need of
Him. Second, a consciousness of our obligation

to Him. Third, a consciousness of our covenant relationship to Him. Fourth, a consciousness of His love. Our communion with Him may at one time be founded on the first, at another time on the second, or third, or fourth, or on several together.

In each of these ways of communion there is personal intercourse with a personal friend, because of a personal and particular consciousness in our souls in regard to Him.

The most prominent way of communion in the experience of believers is that of need, because that is generally their most prominent consciousness. In this way every want, every care, every weakness is made the means of communion with the Lord Jesus, when from conscious helplessness we are brought by these things nearer to Him that we may obtain help in all.

Communion through the consciousness of obligation ought to be as constant as the communion through need ; but it seldom is so, because the consciousness of what we want is generally deeper than the consciousness of what we have received ; therefore the soul oftener comes to the Lord with its need than with its thanksgiving. This communion through consciousness of obligation, is, however, sweeter far than that through need, for it leads the soul to think more of the giver than of the gift, and whatever leads us to do that, leads

us to a higher communion. In this way of communion, the believer remembers what the Lord
has done for him through grace, in the way of
salvation, light, life, and forgiveness, and what
He has done in the way of providential blessings,
by watchful care, by delivering mercies, by help
in time of need. As each act of favour rises in
remembrance, the soul is lifted up with heartfelt
gratitude for good given. This has a very great
influence to bind the grateful soul in closer
affinity to the giver. It is well to remember
how much we need, because of our weakness,
and ignorance, and sinfulness. It is still better
to remember how much we have received, because
of His free grace and infinite love.

The communion through consciousness of
covenant relationships is, however, higher than
either, for it leads the soul to the more particular
contemplation of Christ in those special relationships which the Father has caused Him to bear
towards us in choosing us in Him before the
foundation of the world, and as being given to
us by our Father, as our Covenant Head, our
ever-living Friend, the first-born among the many
brethren of that family, of which sovereign grace
has made us members.

The communion by way of consciousness of
His love is the highest of all, for it is the con-

sciousness of heart to heart. The believer's heart is filled with a deep sense of the individual personal love of Christ for him. The believer thinks not of his love for Christ, but of Christ's love for him, and is happy, very happy, in the consciousness thereof. The highest experience of this communion is inexpressible, and the soul is therefore silent in calm blessedness and restful joy before Him. A joy unspeakable, and full of glory (1 Peter i. 8).

XIX.

Further thoughts and counsels to the Believer concerning the way of fellowship with the Lord Jesus.

IN your endeavours to walk in higher, closer, and more constant fellowship with the Lord Jesus, you may expect to meet with many difficulties and hindrances; especially from that innate evil which remains in all believers to the end of life.

The increased activity of the inward evil, although cause for deep humbling of soul before God, is yet no cause for discouragement. It gives you a fuller experience of your utter inability to do anything good of yourself, and this experience is necessary that you may have just views of yourself, and that you may not hinder

the work of grace in your soul. When our Lord
Jesus was on earth, it is said in one part of His
history, that the unbelief of the people prevented
Him doing many mighty works. So is it always
even with His own people; self and unbelief
ever prevent His work of higher grace in their
hearts. He can only be perfect strength to those
who fully realise their own perfect weakness, and
who trust unreservedly in Him. He can only be
the perfection of beauty and the object of the
soul's highest joy to those, who, conscious of
their own vileness, have altogether ceased from
self-satisfaction and undue self-esteem.

Like all believers you, doubtless, have your
special and peculiar hindrances in seeking to walk
in the path of higher fellowship with the Lord
Jesus ; you will, however, find it exceedingly helpful, in successfully combating such hindrances, to
observe the following words of counsel :—

FIRST.—Try continually to think of the Lord
Jesus as a glorified man, who is ever watching
over you,—ever loving you,—ever caring for you
—and listening to you.

Avoid all unnecessary things that have a tendency to lead you astray from Jesus. If you are
of necessity called to encounter such things in
the strict path of duty, they will, if you are
watchful and prayerful, tend more, through grace,

to your spiritual good than otherwise. In such a case a victory over circumstances will bring more glory to the Lord Jesus, and more spiritual profit to your soul, than an alteration of circumstances ; but if not in the path of strict duty before the Lord, do not read those books or papers, do not converse on those subjects, do not spend your time in those engagements, do not encourage those associations or habits, which, however apparently innocent in the sight of others, you know have a direct tendency to injure the spirituality of your mind, and to prevent you thinking of Jesus, and to hinder that quiet trustful look to Him in all the necessities and in all the joys of the day, which is such a true channel of blessing to the soul.

Many say that when they are in good health and free from perplexing cares, they are happy, and can think of the Lord Jesus and His love ; but when they are weak, and ill, and surrounded by providential difficulties, darkness and coldness seem to fill the heart, and they cannot rejoice in Him, and feel Him near. But a religion that, when most needed to cheer, most fails to do so, is not the religion of the Gospel,—*that* cheers the downcast, strengthens the feeble, encourages the timid, heals the broken-hearted, gives light in darkness, rest to the weary, and stable joy to the

sorrowful. The reason why professing Christians
do not realise these things so frequently as they
ought, is because they err in the way they seek
after them. If you would realise them, it can
only be by having the chief and most prominent feature in your soul's experience the
constant assurance of the presence of an unseen
but real man—a glorified man, a man who,
though in His human form and presence always
abiding in heaven until the time of His second
coming, is yet ever watching over you and
caring for you with an unceasing love, however
little you may have been conscious of it. A true
man, who is also the true God, and yet, because
He is man, "made in all things like unto His
brethren," He is one to whom you can tell with
confidence and comfort all your need, all your
evil, all your sorrows, and with whom you can
walk in holy intercourse, as an unseen but true-
hearted friend, and as the first-born among many
brethren and an almighty and ever-loving helper.

In "this man"—God as well as man (His
name is Jesus), all the lines of Jehovah's thoughts,
and works, and ways do centre, whether we
regard the counsels of eternity, the doings of
time, or the consummations of the future.

All God's manifestations of Himself to man are
through "this man." Our heart-experience of

God, if true, must correspond with His manifestation of Himself, and as this is solely in and
through a man, so our experience of Him must
be in and through a man also; the same man, one
with the Father as God, one with us as man.

All God's fulness for all man's need, is in "this
man." Those have most of God's fulness in
their souls, who have their hearts most filled with
"this man." Happy indeed are those in whose
hearts Christ doth more vividly dwell; realised
there by a faith which ever thinks of Him, looks
to Him, rests in Him, talks with Him in daily
life.

SECOND.—Endeavour to attain the constant
habit of speaking to Jesus as a true-hearted man
and a loving friend, telling Him the circumstances
of your daily life according as they arise—one by
one—and as you remember them ; many things
you will forget, but do not be discouraged ; the
habit of referring everything, small or great, to
that unseen friend, will grow upon you as you
practise it daily; for that which is difficult to
practise at first, becomes easy, comparatively,
from long habit.   It will be so in this—try—still
try—ever try—go on and on—no matter if you
have been to your own mind going back—begin
again—do your best, imperfect as it may be,
seeking His help to do better; and be assured of

this, the loving Lord Jesus will never cast your failures in your face. He is too pleased to see His loved ones pressing nearer to Him, to do that.

THIRD.—Let your duties be done for Jesus.

Let your sufferings be borne for Jesus.

Let your study be to learn more of Jesus.

Let your aim be to grow more like Jesus.

Let your one purpose ever be to please Jesus.

Jesus—the man—the friend—the first-born amongst many brethren.

Live, looking into His face.

Live, sitting at His feet.

Live, walking by His side.

Live, leaning on His arm.

Seek not your joy and satisfaction in successful labour for Him, but only in Him for whom you labour—evermore in Him. Oh! this is a happy life indeed, this makes even the path of suffering a way of sunshine and peace, for "Thou art with me," and there is no sunshine like the light of His countenance.

FOURTH.—Guard against the natural temper and disposition of your mind, so that when evil within first manifests itself, it may at once be brought to Jesus.

You will find your chief foes more frequently within you than elsewhere. You will more often have need to ask Jesus to save you from, and help you against, yourself, than to save you from or help you against anything or anyone else.

The evils arising from the varieties of natural temper and disposition of mind, are many. Some have a keen sense of the ridiculous—others have a fretful disposition—others again are sharp and hasty in temper—some are hilarious—others gloomy, prone to brood over ills, fancied or real—some are argumentative—many selfish ; and thus the fountains being dissimilar, the many streams flowing therefrom are dissimilar too; but whatever be the evil arising from these sources, when it first shows itself it must at once be taken to Jesus. The least evil is too strong for us successfully to overcome. We must at once tell Jesus about it. Delay is dangerous. Delay gives strength to the evil. To seek to overcome in any other way, than by bringing it to Him, is simply to prepare the way to be overcome by the evil.

If your easily besetting sin be a hasty temper, as it is with very many believers, be on your guard against it, or it will be the cause of great hurt to the soul, and great hindrance in the walk of fellowship. When anything occurs calculated to irritate and vex you, do not speak to anyone until you have first spoken to Jesus in your heart, asking Him for help and grace—then speak to others as circumstances require; but do it very slowly; quick utterances at such times are dangerous. Speak as little as possible so long as the annoyance lasts; and be silent before the Lord, in heart communing with Him, until through His grace you get above it all and obtain the victory. Be very decided in the practice of this silence and slow speaking; for one hasty word in a moment of annoyance causes a wound to a spiritual mind, and is a greater hindrance to the soul's higher joys in fellowship with Jesus than strangers to that fellowship would think possible. Be assured that none can maintain a happy walk of fellowship with the Lord Jesus who will not, when they meet with so-called vexations and annoyances, at once thus recollect themselves (keeping silence for a few moments, the better to enable them to do this), and then speak very slowly, while at the same time the heart continues looking to Jesus for help; thus bringing Him between the soul and the annoyance. This makes the soul steady, the temper does not easily give way, hasty words are not uttered, because Jesus is there, very near, very gracious, very helpful.

FIFTH.—In seeking after and maintaining a walk of constant fellowship with the Lord Jesus, it is essentially necessary that you do not in any matter or in any relationship, whether personal or social, secular or religious, walk contrary to the light you may possess, and that as more light is given, you conscientiously walk according there unto at any cost.

The sum of all is—" As ye have therefore received Christ Jesus the Lord, so walk ye in Him." You received Him, the dying One, as your all for salvation from eternal misery ; so walk in Him, the living One, as your all for the needs and joys of the way home.

Fourth Part.

THOUGHTS AND COUNSELS CONCERNING JUSTIFICATION, SANCTIFICATION, &a.

I.

Concerning Justification.

To be justified is to be acknowledged by the authority of the law as being free from guilt and condemnation, or, as being perfectly righteous.

Justification is therefore a legal act, and consists in the judicial expression of the satisfaction of the law with the person whose acts are called in question; either pronouncing its satisfaction because his acts are found perfectly to agree with its righteous precepts, or if his acts be found to transgress those precepts, pronouncing its satisfaction if it be found that its penal claims, because of such transgressions, have been fully met.

Thus, one who has perfectly obeyed the law will have the authority of the law upholding and justifying him, in pronouncing him righteous; and one who has transgressed the law will have the authority of the law upholding and justifying him, in pronouncing him free from guilt and condemnation if its claims against him, on account of his transgressions, have been perfectly satisfied.

All mankind are declared by the word of God to be transgressors of His law, and guilty before Him (Rom. iii. 19). If therefore any amongst men are justified before Him, it can only be because the claims of the law against them, on account of their transgressions, have been fully met. The law thus satisfied upholds and justifies them in pronouncing them cleared or freed from guilt and from judicial condemnation.

Of this justification of sinners, we learn in Scripture—1. The author. 2. The source. 3. The means. 4. The completeness. 5. The realisation. 6. The manifestation. 7. The result.

1. The author of this justification is God Himself, as it is written :—"It is God that justifieth" (Rom. viii. 33). He whose laws have been transgressed becomes Himself the justifier of the transgressors. Their justification, being the work of God, is necessarily a perfect work and a firm foundation for awakened sinners to build upon for the assurance of their full deliverance from condemnation.

2. The source of this justification is the grace or favour of God, as it is written:—"Being justified by His grace" (Titus iii. 7). Justified without any worthiness whatever on the part of sinners to influence Him to accomplish their justification, but with a full knowledge on His part of all their great and aggravated unworthiness. "Being justified freely by His grace" (Rom. iii. 24). Justified freely without any consideration of their after repentance or good works, but with a full knowledge that no repentance or good works would ever be manifested by them until He constrained them thereto by the power of the Holy Spirit.

3. The means of this justification is the precious blood of Christ, as it is written:—"Being now justified by His blood" (Rom. v. 9). God provided a way of fully satisfying the claims of His own law against those guilty ones He would justify, so that while their justification should exalt His love, it should also honour His justice. To this end He appointed His co-equal Son to undertake the great work (Gal. iv. 4, 5), a work which the Son readily undertook and faithfully performed, according to His own word—"Lo, I come to do Thy will, O God" (Heb. x. 9); and again, "I have finished the work which Thou gavest Me to do" (John xvii. 4). By His death

the claims of the law, against those for whom He died, have been perfectly and for ever satisfied.

4. The completeness of this justification is seen in the resurrection of Christ from the dead, as the representative of those for whom He died, as it is written—" Who was delivered (delivered up) for (because of) our offences, and was raised again for (because of) our justification " (Rom. iv. 25). He was delivered up, and willingly delivered up Himself into the hands of the law, that by His death the claims of the law against them, because of their offences, might be satisfied. His death was their deliverance according to law. His resurrection testified to the completeness of the law's satisfaction, and to the completeness of the removal of the guilt and condemnation, and therefore to the completeness of the justification of those for whom He died.

Moreover Christ was so completely the sin-bearer of His people, that the law beheld all their sins upon Him when on the cross, and not upon the sinners for whom He died, as it is written— " Who His own self bare our sins in His own body on the tree " (1 Peter ii. 24). And again, " The Lord hath laid upon Him the iniquity of us all. . . . He shall bear their iniquities " (Isa. liii. 6, 11); " He hath made Him to be sin for us " (2 Cor. v. 21).

Though in Himself the spotless Lamb of God; evermore holy, harmless, and undefiled; yet, as thus bearing the sins of many as their representative before the law, those sins became judicially His own, and He Himself therefore needed to be justified from them. This He perfectly accomplished by His atoning death; according as it is written—"He that is dead is freed (justified) from sin" (Rom. vi 7). "Who shall lay anything to the charge of God's elect? It is God that justifieth, who is he that condemneth? It is Christ that died, yea rather that is risen again, who is even at the right hand of God; who also maketh intercession for us" (Rom. viii. 33, 34). Similar language the Lord Jesus uses concerning Himself, "I gave My back to the smiters, and My cheeks to them that plucked off the hair. . . . He is near that justifieth Me; who will contend with Me? Let us stand together; who is Mine adversary? let him come near to Me. Behold the Lord God will help Me; who is he that shall condemn Me" (Isa. l. 5–9). So by the death of the substitute, both the substitute and the sinners are free.

The completeness of this justification is further seen in the ascension of Christ to the right hand of God in heaven, as the representative of those whose sins were laid upon Him on the cross, and for whom He died. No one with sins upon him could enter that holy place, whether those sins be his own personally, or the sins of others as their representative; but the Lord Jesus has entered there—even He on whom were laid the sins of many. He entered not there, however, until He had judicially put them all away, as it is written —" When He had by Himself purged our sins, sat down on the right hand of the Majesty on high;" and again, "But this man, after He had offered one sacrifice for sins for ever, sat down on the right hand of God " (Heb. i. 3, x. 12).

His presence there is another sure evidence that the justification of those for whom He died is now and for ever complete.

5. The realisation of this justification is by faith, as it is written :—"Therefore we conclude that a man is justified by faith without the deeds of the law" (Rom. iii. 28, v. 1).   That justification which has been completed for the sinner by God Himself through the Lord Jesus entirely apart from, and independent of anything the sinner himself could do, is in due time known and trusted in by the sinner, when, through the quickening work of the Holy Spirit in his heart, he is awakened to see his need of it.   In consequence of this work of the Holy Spirit, the sinner's conscience becomes so burdened under a

sense of his sinfulness and guilt, and his deserved condemnation, that nothing but this free grace and completed justification through the blood of Jesus will suit his sinful and helpless condition. He now trusts in the Lord Jesus, and is content to rely for deliverance from condemnation and guilt solely in the atoning death of Christ. This is faith in Christ for salvation. Through this faith peace is brought to his troubled conscience, and he takes his place amongst the justified ones. He is thus justified in his own experience by faith.

His faith has nothing whatever to do with his justification in relation to Divine law and justice, inasmuch as nothing could procure that but the precious blood of Christ. This has been already shed, and he is thereby justified, or cleared freely and completely, in relation to Divine law and justice ; but he needs to be justified or cleared in his own experience in relation to his own troubled conscience, and this is only accomplished by faith in the completed work of Christ for sinners.

His faith has nothing whatever to do in making the atoning sacrifice of Christ more efficacious for his personal and individual justification, for this would imply that the death of Christ was not sufficient to satisfy the claims of the law, but that the faith of the sinner was needed to perfect the work of Christ. This cannot be, for the faith of the awakened sinner needs itself to be accepted through the merits of Christ, and it cannot, therefore, prevail to make those merits more efficacious, or assist them to justify or clear him before the Divine law. That justification or clearance from guilt and condemnation is already completed by the shed blood of Christ, and is ready for the awakened sinner's faith to lay hold of when he becomes conscious of his need of it. His faith, even at the strongest, is but the eye that beholds this and is satisfied, the hand that lays hold of this and is conscious of safety, the heart that rests in this and is content, the opened ear that listens to the glad tidings and rejoices, relying fully on the sure word of God.

Thus an accusing law is satisfied by the atoning death of Christ, and an accusing conscience is satisfied by faith in that atoning death.

6. The manifestation of this justification is in the changed life of the believer. As it is written—"Ye see, then, how that by works a man is justified, and not by faith only" (Jas. ii. 24). The good works of the believer, as well as his faith, have nothing to do with his justification in relation to the law. They are but the legitimate result and manifestation of

that already completed justification. His good works are the justification before men of his profession of faith in Christ, and of salvation by Christ. If his works contradict his profession, he deserves the condemnation of his fellows. If his works correspond with his profession, they justify him before men in making that profession ; and although he may not always receive their approval for his good works, they will at least clear him from their just condemnation.

Thus the threefold relationship of justification, as regards clearing from condemnation, consists in—justification or freedom from the condemnation of the holy law of God, which is by the precious blood of Christ—justification or freedom from the condemnation of an accusing conscience awakened by the Holy Spirit, which is by faith in that precious blood—justification or freedom from the just condemnation of our fellow-men, which is by our good works, the result of a new spiritual life and a living faith.

7. The result of this justification is the certainty of eternal glory, as it is written— " Whom He justified, them He also glorified " (Rom. viii. 30). Divine justice having no further claim against those justified by the death of Christ, the assured result is their full and final salvation. He who ordained and completed the

one, will as certainly accomplish the other in
His own time.   The justified will be the glorified,
to the praise of the glory of His grace, world
without end.

The clearing of sinners from judicial condemnation is not, however, all that the word
of God teaches concerning the justification of
those whom God justifies. A legal standing in
perfect righteousness is also provided for them, as
well as a legal deliverance from guilt and condemnation.   The former is provided in the
perfect obedience of the Lord Jesus to the holy
precepts of the Divine law as their legal representative and covenant Head, as it is written—
"By the obedience of one shall many be made
righteous" (Rom. v. 19).   The latter is provided
in the shed blood of the Lord Jesus as their
legal representative and covenant Head, as it is
written—"The blood of Jesus Christ cleanseth
us from all sin" (1 John i. 7).

In consequence of this twofold legal work of
Christ on their behalf, His people possess a twofold legal justification ; inasmuch as, because of
His penal death on their behalf, the law justifies
them in pronouncing them cleared from guilt
and condemnation, and because of His life of
obedience on their behalf, the law justifies them

in pronouncing them perfectly righteous. In Him they are thus complete—completely delivered, completely righteous, and therefore completely justified.

His righteous life was obedience to law. His atoning death was also obedience to law. It is by this one obedience in life and death His people are free, His people are blessed. By the obedience of His righteous life His people are made righteous, but no blessing would have resulted to them on this account, so long as the just claims of the law against them, because of their transgressions, were unsatisfied. By the obedience of His atoning death, however, those claims were fully satisfied, and thus every legal hindrance was removed which would have prevented them receiving the full blessing which the perfect obedience of His righteous life, on their behalf, had procured for them.

Thus is brought about the wonderful arrangement spoken of in 2 Cor. v. 21—"He hath made Him, who knew no sin, to be sin for us, that we might be made the righteousness of God in Him." Thus, also, is brought about the twofold result spoken of in Eph. i. 7, 11—"In whom we have redemption through His blood;" "In whom, also, we have obtained an inheritance." By His precious blood believers are

redeemed from the claims of a condemning law.
By His perfect obedience and their acceptance in
Him as perfectly righteous, they have obtained
an inheritance.   By His precious blood the gates
of hell are closed against all sinners who trust in
Him, so that they enter not that dread prison-
house.   By His perfect obedience, on their
behalf, the gates of heaven are opened to them,
and they freely enter in, joint-heirs with Him in
the heavenly inheritance.   Blessed is the redemption ; blessed is the inheritance ; but blessed,
infinitely blessed is the name of Father, Son,
and Holy Spirit—one God—by whose infinite
love and covenant grace and mercy the whole
work of justification has been so fully completed.

Thus the Gospel more than restores in Christ
what was lost in Adam.   Before his fall, Adam's
righteousness was but a perfect human righteousness, and the only revealed result of that, an
earthly paradise.   Whereas, in Christ all believers
are provided with a Divine-human righteousness
through the obedience of Him who is God and
man, in which, notwithstanding their continued
consciousness of unworthiness, they evermore
stand complete and accepted before God, and the
revealed and assured result of that is a heavenly
and eternal paradise.

But one thought more on this subject.   Christ

and His people are one in eternal union by electing love, as it is written—" According as He
hath chosen us in Him before the foundation of
the world" (Eph. i. 4). He was thus the ever-
living and mystical Head of His people, and
they His members. When He came forth from
the Father, and was made under the law, partaking of flesh and blood like unto His people, even
the children whom God had given Him, He was
their legal and responsible Head, as well as their
ever-living and mystical Head; and the law
looked upon Him and them as one body in law
relationship.

Christ, the legal Head of this one body, wrought
out by His obedience a spotless legal righteousness. His people, the members, wrought out by
their disobedience the blackness of sin and guilt.
He the Head takes upon Himself the whole of the
sin and guilt, and removes it out of the way
altogether, by His atoning death on the cross.
There remains now for the one body, comprising
Himself and His members, His own spotless, legal
righteousness which no sins of His members could
ever defile. In this they stand together, evermore one in perfect righteousness.

He needed not this legal righteousness for
Himself, for He is the everlasting God, whose
eternal attribute is perfect righteousness. His

righteousness as the eternal God, is not, however, the righteousness in which the one body, Head and members, stand complete. That must be a righteousness under the law ; and under the same law which had been dishonoured by the unrighteousness of His members ; and must be wrought out by one possessing the same nature as the transgressors. Therefore He voluntarily came forth from the Father, and "as the children are partakers of flesh and blood, He also Himself took part of the same. . . . For verily He took not on Him the nature of angels, but He took on Him the seed of Abraham" (Heb. ii. 14, 16.), and was "made under the law" (Gal. iv. 5). It is in this legal position, as the Head of His people, He utters the words, "It becometh us to fulfil all righteousness" (Matt. iii. 15) ; and His fulfilment was perfect.

In that spotless legal righteousness, the Head and members, as one body, now and evermore stand together complete and accepted before God the Father, according as it is written,—"I in them and Thou in Me, that they may be made perfect in one" (John xvii. 23). "Who—is made unto us righteousness" (1 Cor. i. 30). "He hath made Him who knew no sin, to be sin for us, that we might be made the righteousness of God in Him" (2 Cor. v. 21). "He hath made us accepted in the Beloved" (Eph. i. 6). "Ye are complete in Him" (Col. ii. 10).

Wonderful indeed are the doings of everlasting love and sovereign grace. "He that glorieth, let him glory in the Lord."

II.

Concerning Sanctification.

"To be sanctified," in the general signification of the term, means, "to be set apart or separated;" with the idea of separation from impurity or profaneness ; or of being set apart for some special use or purpose ; or as possessing some distinguishing moral or spiritual characteristic or relationship.

From what separated, and for what object set apart, and by whom, and in what manner, can only be learned by the special relationship in which the term is used. Sometimes it is God who sanctifies man, and sometimes man who sanctifies God, and sometimes man who sanctifies himself, or is sanctified by his fellow-man. Rightly to understand the special use of the term "to sanctify," its general signification, "to set apart, or separate," must not be lost sight of. As for instance, in the special use of the term in relation to God, as in 1 Peter iii. 15, "Sanctify the Lord God in your hearts"—the meaning is— set Him apart in your hearts as the only true and holy God, and as the chief object of your love, reverence, gratitude, and praise, and the sole object of worship.

The term sanctification and its cognate terms are used in the New Testament, in relation to men, to denote six different kinds of sanctification, or sanctification in six different relationships. These may be distinguished as, 1. Judicial. 2. Spiritual. 3. Experimental. 4. Practical. 5. Official. 6. Social.

1. Judicial sanctification is that standing in perfect holiness before God, which is the portion of all true believers in Jesus.

In Him they are sanctified, or separated, or cleansed from sin, as it is written : "When He had by Himself purged (or made a cleansing of) our sins, sat down on the right hand of the Majesty on high" (Heb. i. 3). "The blood of Jesus Christ His Son cleanseth us from all sin" (1 John i. 7). "Unto Him that loved us, and washed us from our sins in His own blood" (Rev. i. 5). "We are sanctified through the offering of the body of Jesus Christ, once for all" (Heb. x. 10) ; and not only so, but those sanctified by that offering, are by that offering for ever perfected ; as it is written—"For by one offering He hath perfected for ever them that are sanctified" (Heb. x. 14). Thus judicially they are perfectly sanctified, in being perfectly and for ever cleansed from their sins, as well as perfectly justified, in being delivered from the condemnation those sins deserved.

In Him they are also sanctified or set apart as holy ones, as it is written—"Sanctified in Christ Jesus." "Who of God is made unto us sanctification" (1 Cor. i. 2, 30). Their judicial sanctification in Christ is their radical or root sanctification, and is always perfect and complete both as regards their judicial cleansing, and as regards their being set apart as God's holy ones in Christ, their root and representative. This sanctification or standing in perfect holiness can never be altered, even by the sins which the sanctified ones mourn over, and confess before their Father. In relation to those who are thus sanctified, it may indeed be said : "If the first fruit be holy, the lump also is holy ; and if the root be holy, so are the branches" (Rom. xi. 16). They are thus "accepted in the Beloved" (Eph. i. 6) ; "complete in Him" (Col. ii. 10) ; and God "remembers their sins and iniquities no more" (Heb. x. 17).

2. Spiritual sanctification is the work of the

Holy Spirit, in the impartation of a new principle of spiritual life; in consequence of which the sinner is regenerated or born again. " God hath from the beginning chosen you to salvation through sanctification of the Spirit and belief of the truth " (2 Thess. ii. 13 ; 1 Pet. i. 2). This sanctification of the Spirit always precedes, and always results in the exercise of, saving faith. Like judicial or radical sanctification, it is always perfect and complete in itself ; being a new creation pure and perfect from the hand of God, by the direct operation of the Holy Spirit. " That which is born of the flesh is flesh, and that which is born of the Spirit is spirit " (John iii. 6). The " flesh " or the old corrupt carnal nature which is " born of the flesh " remains corrupt to the end of life. The " spirit," or the new and perfect spiritual nature which is " born of the Spirit," remains perfect to the end of life. The " flesh " will lust against the " spirit " and often powerfully and successfully to the grief of the believer; but it can never destroy or alter it. In the new nature there is nothing of sin, though it abides continually in immediate contact with the sinful nature of the believer. It is born from above ; born of God. It had its origin from heaven. There is its chiefest attraction ; and there is its true and eternal home.

3. Experimental sanctification, or the sanctification of the inner life, consists in cultivating the vigorous growth of "the spirit," or new spiritual nature of the believer, and in subduing and conquering the opposing influences of "the flesh." By this the believer becomes more consciously and distinctly separated from the evil within him; and his mind, will, and affections are made more effectually the servants of "the spirit," or new nature, and the ready channels of its outward manifestations. The law or constraining principle of sin in "the flesh" is overcome and kept under when the law or constraining principle of holiness in "the spirit" is in healthy and vigorous action; and the believer is able to live in "the spirit"—to live in the consciousness and power of his new nature—the law of holiness in "the spirit" triumphing continually over the law of sin in "the flesh."

The Apostle's words in Rom. vii. 25 evidently show that he felt the necessity of constantly identifying himself with "the spirit" or new nature within him, if he would succeed in this experimental sanctification. He there says— "So then with the mind I myself serve the law of God; but with the flesh the law of sin." "With the mind," influenced by the spiritual principles of the new nature, he delighted in and

served the law of God " (ver. 22). " With the
flesh," influenced by its corrupt principles, " he
served the law of sin " (ver. 23). To the end of
his life he carried within him these opposing
principles. According as he identified himself
with, and lived under the influence of the one or
the other, so did he succeed or fail in experimental
sanctification ; whether it was " I myself with
the mind," or " I myself with the flesh." If the
former, he was spiritual, and served the law of
God. If the latter, he became carnal, and served
the law of sin.

The increased vigour of the new life within,
and consequent success in experimental sanctification, results from the prayerful cultivation of
faith in the Lord Jesus. A faith that not only
regards Him as the Saviour, by His atoning death,
from condemnation and the wrath to come, but
a faith that also regards Him as He is now living
in heaven at the right hand of God, the source of
life, and strength, and light to His people—a
faith that is continually looking to Him, and
living upon Him—a faith that brings everything
to Him ; every need, every care, every duty,
every sorrow, and every joy—a faith that seeks
in all things to honour Him and exalt His name
—a faith that brings the soul into closer and
more continuous intimacy with Him, than with

any earthly friend, however near or dear—a faith
that knows and trusts in His changeless love and
gracious care, when everything is dark and trying in the providential path, or in the heart's
experience—a faith that rests content in Him
when everywhere else there is turmoil, disappointment, and unrest. It is by the cultivation of such a faith as this, that the new, the
spiritual nature within the believer, becomes
increasingly vigorous, and experimental sanctification more complete.

The Apostle Paul asks concerning himself :—
" Who shall deliver me from the body of this
death ? " and immediately gives the answer out
of his own experience in the words following—
" I thank God, through Jesus Christ our Lord "
(Rom. vii. 24, 25). In Jesus Christ he found the
source of that strength which gave vigour to the
new nature within him, and which alone could
enable him to maintain successful warfare against,
and obtain constant deliverance from, the ruling
power of the " flesh," which he here calls the
" body of this death." Though always weak in
himself, he said—" Most gladly therefore will I
rather glory in my infirmities (weaknesses) that
the power of Christ may rest upon me " (2 Cor.
xii. 9).

The word of God also teaches that success

in the sanctification of the inner life is always accompanied by love to the brethren, for the Lord's sake—that is, love to all who love the Lord Jesus; as it is written, "The Lord make you to increase and abound in love one toward another, and toward all . . . to the end He may establish your hearts unblamable in holiness (or "sanctification") before God" (1 Thess. iii. 12, 13). "Seeing ye have purified your souls in obeying the truth unto unfeigned love of the brethren ; see that ye love one another with a pure heart fervently" (1 Pet. i. 22).

When the mind of the believer is influenced by the word of God, and his will and affections are influenced by "the spirit," or new nature within —all under the gracious influence of the Holy Spirit—the whole inner and outer life of the believer is sanctified and subject to Christ and His word, notwithstanding the opposing influences of the old nature—the body of sin. This is in accord with the prayer of the Apostle for the Thessalonians. "The very God of peace sanctify you wholly, and I pray God your whole spirit (mind) and soul and body be preserved blameless unto the coming of our Lord Jesus Christ" (1 Thess. v. 23).

Judicial sanctification is God's work by Christ for man. Spiritual sanctification is God's work by the Holy Spirit in man. Both are perfect, and changelessly complete, because entirely the work of God Himself. Experimental sanctification is however man's own work, although graciously assisted therein by the Holy Spirit; and like all the works of man, it soon shows the marks of imperfection. The consciousness of this often brings the believer before his heavenly Father in penitence and shame, to seek forgiveness, and increasingly to receive, out of the fulness of Christ, grace to help in time of need.

4. Practical sanctification, or the sanctification of the outer life, is the result of experimental sanctification, or the sanctification of the inner life; and consists in the manifestation of the graces of the new nature in daily life, by the sanctification or the setting apart by the believer of all his mental, physical, and other providential gifts for the service of the Lord Jesus; and in, their separation from all worldly, unholy, or self-glorying purposes, as it is written—"Be ye holy (or "sanctified") in all manner of conversation" (or "living") (1 Pet. i. 15). "As ye have yielded your members servants to uncleanness, and to iniquity unto iniquity; even so now yield your members servants to righteousness unto holiness" (or "sanctification") (Rom. vi. 19). "I beseech you therefore, brethren, by the mercies

of God, that ye present your bodies a living sacrifice, holy (sanctified), acceptable unto God, which is your reasonable service" (Rom. xii. 1). "Let us cleanse ourselves from all filthiness of the flesh and spirit (or "mind"); perfecting holiness (or "sanctification") in the fear of God" (2 Cor. vii. 1). "Whatsoever ye do, in word or deed, do all in the name of the Lord Jesus, giving thanks unto God and the Father by Him" (Col. iii. 17).

The believer's practical sanctification being his own work as well as his experimental sanctification, its imperfection is but too soon manifest. Those who best know themselves, and who seek to walk in the light with the Lord Jesus, know too well how imperfect the sanctification of the inner and outer life is, even at the best: for however blameless the life may be before men, the enlightened spiritual mind is conscious that, before God, there is nothing perfect in purity and holiness which comes from a heart where the old evil nature still abides; making his best and holiest thoughts and actions such as God cannot look upon or accept, but through the perfect merits of the Lord Jesus Christ.

The believer's judicial and spiritual sanctification is perfect in spotless holiness now and evermore; but perfect experimental and practical sanctification, in the sense of spotless holiness, cannot be attained here on earth. That is the perfection of the experimental and practical life in heaven only, where the believer shall have no body of sin, no corrupt principle of evil within to hinder and pollute.

Nevertheless, though perfect experimental and practical sanctification in the sense of spotless holiness, can never be attained here; perfect experimental and practical sanctification in the sense of completeness or unreserve, is not only possible here, but is the duty of every believer; yea, it is his high privilege, and his heavenly calling while still in this life. For this, a full capacity has been given him by the quickening grace of the Holy Spirit. For this, a full provision of grace to help has been made for him in the fulness of the Lord Jesus, his ever-living and ever-gracious Head.

Imperfect sanctification in the sense of reserve and incompleteness, too often means, only half a heart for Christ and the other half for self and the world. It too often means, not loving the brethren for the Lord's sake, and because they love the Lord; but only having a certain regard for those of them who are in a good social position, or whom it is useful or respectable to know. It too often means, living a little for

Christ, but a great deal for self - gratification and self-glorying. Such a double mind, such a divided heart, and such an attempt at divided service, is completely opposed to God's word, and is sure to produce instability and failure.

One with such an experience may not be a true believer, but if he be, the power of the new life within him is sure to be increasingly weakened and its growth completely hindered, while "the flesh" is increasingly encouraged and strengthened in its evil.

It is a hopeful sign when such a condition of soul causes continual self-dissatisfaction, self-humbling, and self - loathing and fear as before God, with an earnest longing for deliverance. But even then, if this state be continued in, it will end either in a state of spiritual lethargy and indifference, or of spiritual darkness and despair.

When however such a condition of soul causes no fear, and there is a contentedness with it, and no desire that it should be different, while still there is the desire to be considered a true believer, such an one is called upon by God seriously to judge himself by His word. To that end he is there confronted with such words as these by which to weigh himself as in a balance—"To be carnally minded is death, but to be spiritually minded is life and peace. So then they that are

in the flesh cannot please God. But ye are not
in the flesh but in the spirit, if so be the Spirit of
God dwell in you. Now if any man have not the
Spirit of Christ, he is none of His " (Rom. viii.
6, 8, 9). "Examine yourselves whether ye be in
the faith : prove your own selves. Know ye not
that Jesus Christ is in you except ye be repro-
bates?" (2 Cor. xiii. 5). "If any man be in Christ
he is a new creature ; old things are passed away;
behold, all things are become new" (2 Cor. v.
17). "For in Christ Jesus neither circumcision
availeth anything nor uncircumcision, but faith
which worketh by love" (Gal. v. 6). "They that
are Christ's have crucified the flesh with the
affections and lusts" (Gal. v. 24).

Perfect sanctification in the sense of complete
and unreserved separation of the outer and inner
life for Christ and to Christ, never implies the ex-
tinction of indwelling sin—nay, it creates a more
delicate sensitiveness to that sin, and a more
humble and subdued walk with God the Father
and with the Lord Jesus in consequence thereof,
and a greater readiness to confess at once when
there is the least motion of sin within, or consciousness of failure in the daily walk, accompanied with greater gratitude and love to God the
Father, Son, and Holy Spirit, for the rich provision which sovereign grace and infinite love have

made for the free forgiveness of sin, and for the free gift of life everlasting. This increased sensitiveness to sin and greater readiness to confess, does not alter the completeness of the sanctification, but is rather an evidence of it. Even as a less sense of sin is an evidence of an imperfect sanctification both of the inner and outer life.

"Christ liveth in me." This was the expression of the Apostle's experimental sanctification. Christ had full possession of all his inner life— mind, will, and affections.

"For me to live is Christ." This was the expression of his practical sanctification. Everywhere and always Christ was everything to him. In his Lord's service, neither bonds nor afflictions moved him; neither did he count his life dear to him. His one desire was that Christ might be magnified in his body, whether it were by life or by death.

"The life I now live in the flesh I live by the faith of the Son of God, who loved me and gave Himself for me." This was the secret of his success in both. Christ never failed him. Over every difficulty he was more than conqueror through Christ his Lord.

Jesus Christ is the same yesterday, and to-day, and for ever. He is evermore worthy of our best affections; evermore worthy of our life service; and evermore the ever-present helper of his people.

5. Official sanctification, though included in the believer's general practical sanctification, is nevertheless special and distinct in itself, for it consists in being set apart for special official service. The Lord Jesus was thus sanctified both by Himself and by His Father, as it is written— "Say ye of Him whom the Father hath sanctified and sent into the world" (John x. 36). "And for their sakes I sanctify Myself" (John xvii. 19). He was in all respects the perfect servant, always doing the will of His Father who sent Him, glorifying Him in all He did (John viii. 29, xvii. 4).

Believers, too, have this official sanctification in a general sense, for wherever in providence the Lord places them, there have they official service to render for Him who hath sent them to be His witnesses, and to bring glory to His name (2 Tim. ii. 20, 21). When a believer is called by his Lord to any particular office for special service, it is still that he may be a faithful witness for Christ. When the response to this call is without reserve, and the whole man, body, soul, and mind, is given up to Christ for this object, the sanctification is complete ; though there be daily a consciousness of the need of a Father's forgiveness for not being more like unto Christ, the Father's perfect servant.

6. Social sanctification relates to a man's moral position amongst his fellows, and consists in his

being set apart or separated from the loose and immoral social practices by which he may be surrounded. This may relate to those who are not true believers in the Lord Jesus, or indeed to those who unhesitatingly profess to be unbelievers, but who are relatively brought under the moral influence of the Gospel, as in 1 Cor. vii. 14, where the question relates to the moral sanctification of the unbeliever by marriage union, and to the moral sanctification of the children as regards their social position, although both children and husband, or both children and wife, might still remain unbelievers.

III.

Concerning the responsibility of the natural and the spiritual man in relation to the Law and the Gospel.

MAN naturally has power to avoid moral evil and to reach a very high standard of moral and social excellency before his fellows (Matt. xix. 20) ; but he has naturally no power to perform one spiritual act or understand one spiritual truth. " The natural man receiveth not the things of the Spirit of God, for they are foolishness unto him : neither can he know them, because they are spiritually discerned" (1 Cor. ii. 14). To perform spiritual

acts and understand spiritual truths, he must
first have spiritual life; and this is the gift of
God through the operation of the Holy Spirit
(John i. 13, iii. 3-6; 1 Cor. ii. 9).

The Holy Spirit never assists a "natural man"
to understand spiritual truths or perform spiritual
acts. He first makes the man spiritual by giving
him spiritual life, and therewith the capability to
perform spiritual acts and the capacity to understand spiritual truths—truths which a "natural
man" cannot possibly understand, "neither can
he know them, because they are spiritually discerned." After giving the new spiritual life, the
Holy Spirit graciously assists the actings of the
new life.

God never requires the spiritual acts of the
spiritual life from those to whom He has not
given that life. He requires from such a perfect
obedience in heart and life to His moral law,
such as He required from Adam before his fall.

Adam, before his fall, possessed a perfect
nature, with a natural power, fully enabling Him
to obey the Divine law. In his fall he lost that
perfect nature and that natural power to obey
perfectly, and brought all his descendants into
the same helpless position as himself. The Divine
law, however, remained in force notwithstanding
the loss of Adam's natural power to obey it

perfectly, and it remains in force for all his descendants, and must condemn them.

Natural acts, at their highest and best, can never bring salvation, for, at their best, they are but the acts of a fallen and sinful man ; therefore a natural man, at the best, is but a sinner under condemnation.

Until a sinner be spiritually quickened, he will not and cannot believe in Jesus unto salvation, because this believing unto salvation is the spiritual act of a spiritual life already given.

All men, naturally, can be better than they are, and have power naturally so to be ; and because they are not, and according as they are not, in relation to light given, will be their measure of condemnation.

All men, who have heard the truths of the Gospel, will have increased condemnation if they reject them, and do not regard Christ as the Son of God and the true Messiah—as the true God and only Saviour, and as true God and true man, and refuse to order their lives according to the light of Christ's teaching (Matt. x. 14, 15, xi. 20--24 ; John iii. 19, xv. 22--24). But no one will have increased condemnation and punishment hereafter, because he does not possess the faith of God's elect, that is, does not exercise saving faith in the Lord Jesus, because such faith is the special gift of God to whomsoever He pleases, and is, as already stated, a spiritual act, the result of being born again by the Spirit of God (Eph. ii. 1-8).

God makes no man responsible for being born again. The quickening of a sinner with new life is His own sovereign act. When, however, a sinner is born again by the power of the Holy Spirit, he becomes responsible for the putting forth of those spiritual acts which are proper to the new spiritual life thus imparted.

A sinner born again by the Holy Spirit possesses a higher kind of life than Adam did before his fall. The latter possessed only a perfect natural life, a life which was not in direct union with God Himself, as is the new spiritual life which a sinner born again by the Holy Spirit possesses, and by the impartation of which he becomes in a measure a partaker of the divine nature. The possessor of this new spiritual life can never lose it, even though, while he is in this world, it remains in immediate and constant contact with, and is continually opposed by the body of sin which is within him. Had Adam possessed this spiritual life before his fall, he could never have lost it any more than a believer now can, because of its direct union with God Himself.

The perfect natural life was Adam's only

power of obedience, and the Divine will of his Creator as made known to him was the standard of his obedience, and was not beyond the natural power given him.   He lost that perfect natural life, and therewith his ability to obey in natural perfection the standard which still remained, and which was still the measure of his natural responsibility.

This standard, and the natural responsibility to it, still remains the same for all his natural descendants.   But the responsibility is the responsibility of the perfect natural life such as Adam had before his fall, and not the responsibility of a spiritual life such as Adam did not then possess, and such as his descendants do not possess until born again by the Holy Spirit.

This new spiritual life takes a man out of the natural Adam family with its natural responsibilities, and places him in the new spiritual family with its new spiritual responsibilities and relationships.

Unless these things are kept distinct, much perplexity will arise, by making the natural man responsible for the spiritual acts of the new spiritual life, instead of the natural acts of the perfect natural life, which, in other words, is making a man responsible for not being born again.

Concerning natural responsibility — that has been greatly increased in relation to those to whom the light of revelation in the New Testament Scriptures has come; and a natural man will have increased condemnation if he does not believe the written record which God has there given of His Son, for this is part of his natural responsibility. But such a man will not have increased condemnation for not believing on the Son of God as his own personal Saviour, because that is outside his natural responsibility altogether, and is part of the responsibility of the possessor of the new spiritual life, of which life the first manifestation and evidence is a newly-awakened consciousness of sinnership, and guilt, and of deserved condemnation, and of needed salvation.

When a sinner is born again by the Holy Spirit, he is by that act apprehended by the hand of grace to be a partaker of the salvation already provided for him in Christ Jesus. When born again he then possesses, and not until then, the new spiritual life by which alone he can apprehend those new covenant blessings, for the full enjoyment of which he has been thus apprehended by the grace of Christ.

The heathen who never had an opportunity of hearing the truths of the Gospel, will not be judged according to what they had not, but

according to that natural light they possessed
—their own consciences bearing witness (Rom. i.
18, ii. 14).

However much the natural life may be in
accordance with the moral teachings of God's
word, such accordance has no relation to salvation, but to less condemnation and punishment
hereafter.

Salvation, or deliverance from the wrath to
come, is altogether a different matter; and is the
free gift of God without any works whatever on
the part of sinners. It has been provided by
God Himself in sending a deliverer or Saviour
in the Person of His Son Jesus Christ, who, by
His death on the cross as substitute for the
guilty, did legally procure full deliverance and
salvation from the condemnation and the curse
of the Divine law, for all sinners who, personally
conscious of their guilt, look only to Him and
His death as their hope of salvation, relying upon
His word that whosoever believeth in Him should
never perish, but should have everlasting life.
(John iii. 16, 36, vi. 47 ; Acts xvi. 30, 31 ; Rom.
iii. 24, v. 8, 9, vi. 23 ; Gal. iii. 13 ; Heb. ix. 28,
x. 12).

After this believing unto salvation, which is
the result and evidence of the new spiritual life
already given by God, there follows the new life

of obedience—a life of gratitude—the outflow of a salvation already accomplished and of a spiritual life already given (Rom. vii. 6 ; 1 Peter ii. 24).

IV.

Concerning the distinction between the relationship of God to the national Israel of the past and the spiritual Israel of the present dispensation.

JEHOVAH stood in a twofold relationship to the children of Israel. Religiously, He was their God. Politically, He was their invisible earthly King and Ruler, dealing with them according to an earthly political system of His own devising. The rulers and judges amongst them were His servants to carry out the laws which He as the king of the nation gave them. He thus stood in a special relationship to the Jews, such as He did not to any other nation. He was their God whom they were to worship, and their political king whom they were to obey.

As their God He gave laws relating to their mode of worshipping Him. As their king He gave laws relating to the temporal government and well-being of the nation. These laws of worship and of civil government were interwoven the one

with the other, and according to their obedience
to them they prospered in earthly things. If
they disobeyed them, they were punished as
kings of other nations punished their rebellious
subjects—by fine, by banishment, or death.
Jehovah sometimes inflicted the latter directly,
by means of pestilence, famine, or the sword.
The punishment inflicted was the death of the
body—death temporal and physical, as distinct
from the punishment inflicted upon body and soul
hereafter, which is eternal. The former is the
earthly judicial act of the king of the nation.
The latter is the eternal judicial act of God as
Judge of all the earth.

When an Israelite was put to death by
Jehovah for transgressing the laws of the kingdom, it did not necessarily imply that his body
and soul would be lost in hell. Good political
government may require the death of a criminal ;
but before the sentence of the law takes effect, he
may, through grace, become a saved soul. He
dies as a criminal notwithstanding, in obedience
to the laws of the kingdom.

This is the kind of death alluded to in Ezekiel
xviii. ; where Jehovah speaks as the king of the
Jews to His rebellious subjects ; dealing with
them as responsible subjects of the kingdom, and
subject to political laws and penalties. Those

who were true to those laws should receive at
His hands temporal good and constant protec-
tion, even though they might not be the Israel
within the Israel ; that is, though they might
not be quickened with new and spiritual life,
and thus made members of the spiritual Israel.
If they rebelled against their king, and continued
in their rebellion, they would be punished ; but
if they turned from their rebellion they would
be pardoned, and thus escape the death penalty
which, as rebellious subjects, they deserved. The
repentance, and the consequent escape from death
alluded to, was not the repentance of spiritually
quickened sinners, who thereby escaped from the
second death, death eternal ; but the repentance
of rebellious subjects, who thereby escaped the
death penalty of the law of the land. Concerning the latter, Jehovah's language was "Make you
a new heart, and a new spirit, for why will ye
die, O house of Israel ?" (Ezek. xviii. 31) ; that is,
He exhorted them to give up their rebellious
spirit, and have a proper regard for His laws,
which, as the natural subjects of the kingdom,
they were able to do. If they did this they
would escape the death penalty, that is, the
death of the body, in inflicting which, God as
their king declared he had no pleasure. As
regards the spiritual Israel of a future day, the

language of Jehovah is very different, for He speaks thus : " A new heart also will I give you and a new spirit will I put within you ; and I will take away the stony heart out of your flesh, and I will give you an heart of flesh" (Ezek. xi. 16–20, xxxvi. 24–28).

The children of Israel eventually became tired of having no visible king as their head, and, therefore, asked to have a man for a king (1 Sam. viii. 4–7 ; see also xii. 12). They did not intend to reject Jehovah as their God, but as their king—the political Head of the nation. Although their request was granted, and visible kings were given to them, yet Jehovah never gave up the reins of political government into other hands. Their kings were His vicegerents, and no political act of consequence could they do, such as going to war or making peace, without His consent. They were not allowed to alter their political laws nor add to them, as other nations could and did do, and are continually doing. They had their laws direct from Jehovah their rightful King, and He permitted no addition or alteration by any one but Himself. The laws that governed them in David's time were the only true laws for their government a thousand years after, when our Lord came into their midst, notwithstanding the traditions of men and the false additions of their rabbis.

There were three ways by which Jehovah communicated His will to their kings as their political Head; by dreams, by Urim, and by prophets, and it was an evidence that Jehovah had ceased to acknowledge Saul as His servant when He refused to answer him in either of these ways (1 Sam. xxviii. 6).

The Jews wanted a man for their king. Alas, when Jehovah Himself came to them as a man —as the true Messiah, the true King of the Jews—in the person of Jesus of Nazareth, they scorned and rejected Him just as they had done of old. "How often would I have gathered thy children together, even as a hen gathereth her chickens under her wings, and ye would not" (Matt. xxiii. 37-39). This was the mournful language of Jehovah-Jesus, their rightful King. How similar, too, His mournful utterances of old—"They have turned unto Me the back, and not the face, though I taught them, rising up early and teaching them, yet they have not hearkened to receive instruction" (Jer. xxxii. 33). How similar, also, the sorrowful utterances in Deut. xxxii. 28, 29, to the sorrowful language of their rejected King when He wept over Jerusalem (Luke xix. 41-43). Then, "He came unto His own (rightful possessions), and His own (people) received Him not" (John i. 11). But the day is approaching when He will a second time come to His rightful possessions, and when, as He Himself said even in His hour of sadness, His own people would say, "Blessed be He that cometh in the name of the Lord" (Matt. xxiii. 39). Yes, the day of Zion's glory is coming, when Zion shall rejoice in her rightful King, Jehovah-Jesus—true man, yet true God (Jer. xxiii. 5, 6, xxxi. 31–34 ; Ezek. xxxvii. 21–28 ; Micah iv. 1–7).

Until that day the Lord is gathering in a chosen people from all nations ; a people given to Him by His Father before the world was ; a people—over none of whom will He ever have cause to weep because of their rejection of Him as their Saviour and Lord, inasmuch as His Father who gave them to Him will also draw them to Him by the quickening grace of the Holy Spirit (John vi. 37, 44, 45, x. 11, 16 ; Eph. ii. 1–9). His own faithfulness and omnipotence are also engaged on their behalf, so that they can never perish (John vi. 39, 40, x. 27–29). As their Shepherd He will never lose a single sheep for whom He laid down His life. As their Saviour, their Surety, their Covenant-Head, He will never lose one of those for whom, as substitute, He died, and for whom, in so doing, He fully and for ever satisfied the claims which Divine justice had against them.

In studying God's word it is necessary to distinguish between (1.) The people of the one nation of the past dispensation—the Jews—in relation to Jehovah, their God and King; (2.) The spiritual people of the present dispensation—chosen out of all nations—in relation to Jesus their Saviour, and to His Father and their Father; and (3.) The one nation of spiritual people of a future dispensation—the restored kingdom of the Jews—in relation to Jehovah-Jesus, their God-man King, reigning in Zion amongst His earthly but then truly spiritual people.

A right understanding of these things will be a key to explain many passages, both in the Old and New Testament Scriptures, which, otherwise, it would be impossible rightly to comprehend.

Fifth Part.

BRIEF THOUGHTS AND COUNSELS, WITH
SPECIAL PORTIONS OF SCRIPTURE FOR
THE SPIRITUAL LIFE IN THE DAILY PATH.

FIRST DIVISION. I.—XXXI.

I.

*" But this man, after he had offered one sacrifice
for sins for ever, sat down on the right hand
of God."*—Heb. x. 12.

"THIS MAN." How the heart bounds with joy
at the remembrance that the exalted and Holy
One, who is now seated in the place of power,
"the right hand of God," ruling throughout all
creation, is a real man, possessing a humanity
like our own—body, soul, and mind. How
much more real, more human, more tangible,
heavenly things are, when we are conscious that
at the head of all is "this Man," Jesus; and
that the Being whom angels worship and adore,

and before whom they bow in loving submission,
is the very one who dwelt a lowly one amongst
men. "This Man," so loving, so gentle, so
gracious, so kind, so humble-hearted, so tender
in His sympathy, and faithful in His love, is
ours—still our Shepherd, Friend, and Guide,
our ever-gracious Sympathiser and ever-ready
Helper.

When He undertook the burden of His people's
guilt, their sins became His own—not His own
practically, but His own judicially—they, therefore, stood in the way between Himself and the
"right hand of God." He cleared them out of
the way by becoming the " one sacrifice for sins,"
and then "sat down on the right hand of God "
—sure token that we who trust in Him ; we
whose sins He thus made His own, shall with
Him also sit down "on the right hand of
God."

One with the Father as God, yet is He ever
"this Man." Little do we know how wonderfully His humanity was fashioned and mellowed
by His many sufferings, and weaknesses, and
sorrows, and pains, and persecutions ; in order
that He might the better sympathise with His
people, and be the more consciously and really
like unto His tried and suffering ones. Of this,
however, we are sure, that He who lived as man

on earth is still "this Man, . . . on the right hand of God;" and of this, also, we are sure, that the "right hand of God" is our eternal home, for where He is, there shall we be also.

II.

" Thy gentleness hath made me great."
—Ps. xviii. 35.

God's hand is a gentle one, though it be a mighty one, for, to us, it is the once pierced hand of Jesus. The gentleness of Jesus is as much a feature of His character as His love, and it is because He loves so much, He is so gentle in His dealings with His people. No mother can lead her darling child so gently, or watch its path so carefully, or stoop to do such lowly acts for its well-being, as our Jesus leads, and watches over, and works for His people.

Adversity often finds rough voices and unfriendly conduct where least expected, but it always meets with gentleness in Jesus. They whose eyes are often blinded by affliction's tears best know how gently the gentle hand of the Lord Jesus can wipe sorrow's tears away. More glorious is omnipotence in wiping those tears away, than in the creation of a universe. It is the glory of omnipotence to be gentle. It is the sweetness of majesty to condescend. It is the beauty of love to walk in lowliness and uplift the fallen. Hearts wounded by disappointed hopes, by misplaced confidence, by harsh treatment, ever meet with sweet solace and soothing consolation in the gentleness of Jesus.

When the believer's feet have slipped and he has fallen into sin, fellow-Christians may speak harshly, and upbraid and condemn, but the returning wanderer always meets with gentleness in Jesus. "Thy gentleness hath made me great," for it hath raised me up from sin and shame, from sorrow and despair. Love never hesitates, and can never stoop too low to multiply the comforts and the joys of the beloved one. How low our Jesus stooped, let Bethlehem tell, and Gethsemane, Gabbatha, and Calvary. He still stoops low, for He comes down to our lowly walk and our little needs to be our daily companion, and to multiply our daily blessings; and when our lowly walk on earth is over, and from the light of glory we contemplate the path of our earthly pilgrimage, amongst the many manifestations of love then made clear, will be seen the gentleness of Jesus in His dealings with us every step of the way.

III.

" God, willing more abundantly to shew unto the
heirs of promise the immutability of His
counsel, confirmed it by an oath; that by
two immutable things, in which it was im-
possible for God to lie, we might have a
strong consolation (or " encouragement ")
who have fled for refuge to lay hold upon
the hope set before us " (Heb. vi. 17, 18).

ONE of the most comforting assurances of this
word is, that all the good promised is not to those
who have any good in themselves, but to those
who, filled with fear because of the bad which is
theirs, have fled for refuge, out of themselves and
away from themselves, to the hope of the Gospel
—that is, to a crucified Saviour—in order that
they may obtain the salvation assured to all who
trust in Him.

In the words which characterise this people
it is implied that there was peculiar to them,
—a fear about future and deserved judgment—a
conscious helplessness and hopelessness as far as
regards self or any other human help—a satisfaction with the provision made ready for them
—and a laying hold of this provision in the
manner of a fugitive fleeing to a refuge.

This fleeing for refuge is a frequently recurring experience with many a true believer who has long known the only sure hope of salvation. At the beginning of his Christian life, when, under deep conviction of guilt and pursued by an accusing conscience, a condemning law, and a sense of coming judgment, he first looked to Christ, it was as one fleeing to a place of refuge ; and often very often in after days, when, from the power of unbelief and the enmity of his evil nature, his experience becomes one of darkness and doubt, he finds no light, no rest, until he again flees to the old and only refuge, Jesus Himself—Jesus as lifted up crucified for sinners. So that many a believer all through life is best known to himself, as one who has fled, and continually flees for refuge to Christ.

Here then is the comfort of this word—those who have thus fled for refuge are called " the heirs of promise," and their eternal safety is assured by the immutability of God's counsel, and the sacredness of God's oath.

IV.

*And of His fulness have all we received, and
grace for grace."*—John i. 16.

IF then we have not, the cause of our not having
is in ourselves, not in the Lord.   He is still the
same, and in Him is all fulness for all our need
—fulness of strength, for our weakness—fulness
of wisdom, for our ignorance—fulness of joy, for
our sorrow—fulness of knowledge, for our perplexity ; yea, a fulness of grace, for every duty,
every trial, and every affliction.

The reason of so much spiritual weakness and
soul-deadness is, because there is such a lack of a
receiving disposition.   " Of His fulness have all
we received."

We may be very busy here and there, engaged
in multiplied religious activities, giving time,
physical strength, and mental energy ; but is it
always well with the soul of the busy worker ?
Liberal givers should be large receivers.   Those
who actively work in the Lord's service should
know how patiently and quietly to wait upon
the Lord Himself, else the doing will but bring
barrenness of soul.   Alas ! how many, through
being the self-constituted keepers of others' vine-
yards, have neglected their own.

He who gives and labours beyond his receiving of the Lord, and his calling of the Lord, gives and labours without warrant, and without real soul-blessing, and his works are of the flesh, and not of the Spirit, even though the gospel be taught, and good works be accomplished, and there be much joy experienced in the labour.

Sweetest fruits are usually found on the best cultivated trees.

The most refreshing streams come from the deepest springs, and thus are ever living, and ever renewed.

It is more easy, and more in accordance with the pride of our fallen nature, to be active workers, and influential givers, rather than humble receivers, and quiet, patient, waiting ones ; moreover, the natural buoyancy and stimulus manifested in, and encouraged by increased activities, are too often mistaken for spiritual vigour.

God works through the fulness of Christ ; if, therefore, we are not receivers from that fulness —receiving multiplied grace—grace constantly renewed—" grace for grace "—we are not working according to God's order. Oh for the humble, childlike, receiving heart, which, out of " His fulness "—the fulness of our Lord Jesus— is continually receiving " grace for grace."

V.

" That night they caught nothing."—John xxi. 3.

"THAT night they caught nothing." And it was well. The Lord Jesus knew it—knew their failure—ordered that it should be so—but why? even that He might have a fuller opportunity to show His love and watchful care.

Failure is sometimes blessing; and when the believer is led into the holy and gracious habit of looking at all things from the side of the Lord Jesus, he will praise Him for failure, as well as for success; for both are the result of a love and wisdom that ceaselessly watches for the good of the well-beloved ones.

They toiled much, and caught nothing. It was not the right time, the Lord's time; but when that time came, and they obeyed the word, then they toiled little, and caught much. So is it ever. When the Lord's time has fully arrived, His people behold their hopes more than realised; their path cleared and difficulties removed with an ease and completeness that shows the work is the Lord's; and constrains them to acknowledge with gratitude His faithfulness and loving-kindness, and that He was better to them than all they could have thought or hoped.

VI.

" For even Christ pleased not Himself."
—Rom. **xv.** 3.

BLESSED Jesus, how complete Thy self-denial!
How perfect Thy servitude! To live, and labour,
and suffer for our salvation was not a path pleasing to self, yet a path Thou didst willingly choose,
and with a patient endurance, a loving heart, and
a lowly spirit, didst meekly tread!

" He pleased not Himself,"—therefore, though
often weary and worn and fasting, He still
taught and laboured for the comfort and good of
others. " He pleased not Himself,"—therefore
did He "endure the contradiction of sinners
against Himself," as it is written, " the reproaches
of them that reproached thee, fell on Me." " He
pleased not Himself,"—therefore was His soul
" exceeding sorrowful even unto death," that He
might be able to say, " Father, I have finished
the work Thou gavest Me to do." " He pleased
not Himself,"—hence Gethsemane and Calvary
—hence the agony and bloody sweat—the cross
—the curse—the death.

Blessed Jesus, Thou didst not please Thyself,
therefore Thou didst count no price too precious,
no weariness too exhausting, no effort too great,

no servitude too humiliating, no heart-wounding too keen, no shame too deep, no self-denial too complete, to show Thy great affection for us. O Lord Jesus, how little are we like Thee! Lord Jesus, teach us this lesson, so little understood, and so slowly learned, that in pleasing not ourselves, we often become the greatest blessing to others; and that in knowing the fellowship of Thy sufferings, we shall more fully realise the power of Thy resurrection, and more fully share the glory of Thy kingdom and Thy crown.

"And in the fourth watch of the night Jesus went unto them walking on the sea."— Matt. xiv. 25.

Just at the right time Jesus always shows Himself; never too soon, never too late. Impatience or unbelief may think He has forsaken His tried one, because He cometh not in the third watch; but He always has His own time. Let our hearts say—Lord, Thy time be it,—we will wait the fourth watch!

VII.

" Rooted in Him."—Col. ii. 7.

THE spiritual growth and fruitfulness of the believer on earth results from spiritual rooting by faith in Christ, now living at the right hand of God in heaven. The more vigorous and uninterrupted the rooting, the more fair and abundant will be the fruit.

To be more rooted by faith in Christ as the life and strength of His people, will result in receiving more life and strength from Christ, and in more decided living for Christ. To be more rooted by faith in the love of Christ, will result in more of the fruit of love to Him and His. To be more rooted by faith in the faithfulness and all-sufficiency of Christ, will result in more of the fruit of heart-rest and consolation in the midst of all the trials, afflictions, and sorrows of life.

Every day should the believer be consciously rooting into Christ, that he may receive refreshing and strengthening grace for every day's need, and that he may grow exceedingly and bear increasing fruit to the honour and glory of Christ Jesus his Lord.

" Built up in Him."—Col. ii. 7.

Herein is the stability and firmness of the believer : " Built up in Him "—not in self—not in experiences—but in Him—Christ Jesus. He, the foundation of every gift and every grace— Knowledge built up in, and always resting on Him—Faith built up in, and always resting on Him—Love built up in, and always resting on Him—Joy built up in, and always resting on Him—Patience built up in, and always resting on Him ;—and thus grace after grace—each grace being a distinct portion of the one great building, with Christ always as the foundation. The higher a building is raised, the more weight rests on the foundation ; so the higher the walls of grace are built, the more the soul is leaning upon Jesus than it did before—more consciously realising His power and love, because more " built up in Him." Oh ! my soul, be thou a steady, a patient, and persevering builder ; and be thou careful, not only as regards salvation, but as regards every following gift and grace, that Jesus, and not self, be the foundation all through.

VIII.

"I pray not for the world, but for them which Thou hast given Me, for they are Thine, and all Mine are Thine, and Thine are Mine."
—John xvii. 9.

It is very comforting to think how peculiarly and wonderfully precious believers are to the Father and to the Son. We belong to the Father, and we belong to Jesus. The Father gave us to Jesus in covenant love, ere He drew us to Jesus by constraining grace. He gave us to Jesus that we might be redeemed from eternal misery. He gave us to Jesus that we might be separated from the world. He gave us to Jesus that we might be preserved from the power of the evil one, and from the dominion of sin. He gave us to Jesus that we might be brought safely home at last, and presented unto Himself pure and beauteous in His own image—even like unto Him who is the First-born among many brethren.

Jesus loved the Father's gift and received it joyfully at His hands, and undertook all responsibility for its full salvation, and for its well-being here, and glory hereafter; but, oh! at what a mighty cost, His lowly birth, His laborious life, His shameful death do testify.

How wonderful that the deep eternal love of the Father, Son, and Holy Ghost, should be fixed on such as we are! No gift the Father could have bestowed was so much prized, so longed for by the Son, as the gift to Him of those for whom He died. Oh, then, with such a Jesus, and such a Father, all must be well, and all the experiences of time are but the secret whisperings of a love without beginning and without end.

IX.

" Behold, I stand at the door and knock: if any man hear My voice and open the door, I will come in to him, and will sup with him, and he with Me."—Rev. iii. 20.

ALAS! how sad! the Lord Jesus outside the heart of the believer—outside His own dwelling-place—and the door shut! Nevertheless, the loving One goeth not away. He knocks! He stands and knocks! He stands, for his resting-place is inside. He stands, for He wants to be admitted. He lifts up His voice, for He wants to come in. He will not force an entrance. When at first He took possession for salvation, He entered without knocking, but when he wants to enter for communion and rest, He would have the door willingly opened for His admittance ; therefore He stands, and knocks, and speaks, lifting up His voice. But why is He kept waiting outside so long? Why is His voice not heard? Alas! because another is lording it in His place—not Satan, he is cast out for ever, but self, which, making the will its slave, rules triumphantly, filling the heart with pride, because satisfied—or with turmoil, because dissatisfied ; so that there is no heed to the knocking, no hearkening to the voice outside. But the Lord stands patiently, and still knocks. He will not take the apparent denial, He stands and knocks. Oh, believer, no longer keep out thy Lord, no longer be in confederation with that usurper, self. Art thou not weary of its rule? weary of its tyranny? Then open the door of thy heart at once, and receive the Heavenly One, not as a transient guest, but as the rightful Lord and owner of thyself and all that thou hast.

" Behold, I stand at the door and knock : if any man hear My voice, and open the door, I will come in to him, and sup with him, and he with Me." That heart is indeed a pleasant, joyous, yet quiet banqueting-house, where the Lord is ruler of the feast.

X.

" Why weepest Thou ? "—John xx. 13–15.

BEFORE we weep let us be quite sure there is true
cause for sorrow.   That which may at first sight
seem to be the overturning of all our hopes, may
really prove to be the foundation of our brightest
joys ; for God's ways are not as our ways.   God
plants, and because thorns first show themselves,
the heart often thinks that there will be nothing
else but thorns ;—yet, at the right time, the blossoms always appear, and the fruit follows.

" Why weepest thou ? "   There appeared much
cause for weeping.   There was the cross—the
death—the empty grave ; and that empty grave
seemed to be the consummation of her sorrow.
Yet this was the way God's plant of renown was
growing—true, the thorns came first, they often
do, but the blossoms quickly followed, and the
fruit—oh, how abundant that has been ! and
although nearly two thousand years have passed
away since Mary wept at the empty tomb of
her loving Lord, the fruit is still abundant.

Let us then, before we weep, be quite sure
that there is just cause for tears, or we may find
ourselves rebuking the very hand that lovingly
and patiently is working out our highest good
and our brightest joy.

" *For the wind was contrary.*" " *The sea arose by reason of a great wind that blew.*" " *And He arose and rebuked the wind.*"—Matt. xiv. 24 ; John vi. 18 ; Luke viii. 24.

" Stormy wind fulfilling His word." When the Lord intends fuller revelation of Himself, He brings man into circumstances which more completely empty him of self. When the Lord means deeper love-tokens, He shows man more deeply his unworthiness.

Opposing powers in the path of duty are sure to be the means of increased blessing to that child of God who trusts, and waits, and perseveres. The great wind blew that the disciples might more fully know their great need, and the great love that watched over them.

XI.

"And he dreamed, and behold a ladder set up on the earth, and the top reached to heaven, and behold the angels of God ascending and descending on it, and behold the Lord stood above it. . . . And he called the name of that place Bethel, but the name of that city was called Luz at the first."—Gen. xxviii. 12, 13, 19.

SIN made this world a Luz, or "place of separation" from God, but grace can make a Bethel or "house of God" anywhere. What Jacob once saw in vision, is always the reality in the believer's pilgrimage. There is in every incident of the journey, and in every step of the way home, "a ladder" between the believer and heaven; and whether it be the ladder of providence or grace, it is always the ladder of love, and the same Lord stands above it, as in Jacob's vision—even the Lord Jesus Himself—now the real man, then only appearing as a man, even the same as appeared to Abraham on the plains of Mamre, and the same, ages afterwards, whom Stephen saw "standing on the right hand of God." The earthly end of this ladder is wherever the believer may be; at the heavenly end is Jesus, ever sending down covenant blessings.

Oh, to walk in the power of this Heavenly association, and everywhere and in everything to realise the "ladder" of love and grace, with the Lord Jesus "standing above it!"

Blessed be His name for the angels He sends as ministering servants, but infinitely blessed be His name in that he Himself always stands above, watching and working with changeless love.

" Many, O Lord my God, are Thy thoughts which are to usward."—Ps. xl. 5.

The thoughts of the Lord are ever in a very special manner towards His tried ones—thoughts of love—thoughts of wisdom—thoughts of gentleness—thoughts of tenderness—thoughts of blessing. The believer's thoughts may often wander from Him, but the Lord's thoughts never wander from the believer. They are fixed thoughts, for He thinks always and with a loving remembrance of every need.

His thoughts towards them are many, reaching to the very least thing which has any relation to their well-being. God forgets the sins of His people, but He never forgets them, nor their sorrows. Why then should the child of God be anxious, or perplexed, or burdened, or disquieted, or cast down, when the Lord—so gracious, so tender-hearted, and so mighty—has so many and such loving thoughts towards Him ?

XII.

*" Most gladly therefore will I rather glory
('boast') in my infirmities (' weaknesses')
that the power of Christ may rest upon
me."—*2 Cor. xii. 9.

How often the believer makes his weakness the excuse for non-success in resisting temptations and overcoming evil, for breaking down under trial and difficulty, or drawing back from active duty, or shrinking from the solitary path of suffering : whereas it is only through conscious weakness he can succeed in anything, because human weakness is the channel through which divine power delights to manifest itself.

If believers were consciously weaker, they would be really stronger ; even as the Apostle Paul saith :—" when I am weak, then am I strong." "I can do all things through Christ which strengtheneth me." If he had not realised his own weakness, he would never have realised Christ as his strength, therefore he boasted in his infirmities, that Christ's power might more fully rest upon him, and thus Christ's name and grace be exalted.

The power of Christ rests upon weak ones, and rests most upon those who are most weak, and who, wisely knowing their weakness, look to Him.

"I can do nothing," says the believer, thinking of himself. "I can do all things," says the believer, looking unto Jesus.

Thus the path of conscious weakness is to the soul that trusts in Jesus the path of omnipotence.

XIII.

" God is faithful, by whom ye were called unto the fellowship of His Son Jesus Christ our Lord."—1 Cor. i. 9.

THE hand that led the weary soul to Jesus never loosens its hold. That soul is ever in the hand of the Father, as well as in the hand of the Son. The Father is faithful to His children, for He is God, and He will fulfil His word. He will perform His promises. He is faithful also to His Son, in giving Him the reward of His toil, and in permitting Him fully to see of the travail of His soul—for this He promised, and will perform.

In His providence He is faithful in giving,

and no less so in withholding. In sending sorrow, as well as in causing joy. In pulling down, as in building up. In every way He is faithful. He manifests His faithfulness in placing the fulness of every blessing in His beloved Son, for the supply of His needy ones. All that His faithfulness gives (and His faithfulness gives all) the trusting heart receives as need arises; but all is in His Son. The faith of the believer ever proves the faithfulness of his God and Father in the fulness and fellowship of His Son.

The word "fellowship" means "partnership" —God has called believers into partnership with Christ, in all He is and has, as "the first-born among many brethren"—heirs of God, joint-heirs with Jesus Christ; and He who calls to this, is faithful to carry out His purposes of love. "God is faithful."

XIV.

" He took the blind man by the hand, and led him out of the town."—Mark viii. 23.

THE Lord Jesus doeth His divine wonders after the manner of a man, and a brother. See Him, the mighty God, as the gentle, true-hearted man,

walking hand-in-hand along the streets of Bethsaida, with this poor blind fellow-man. Giving
sight to him was not so wonderful a thing as
the condescending familiarity of that public
walk. Verily He is not ashamed to call us
brethren, or to show Himself a brother. He is
still the same—all that He works for us as God,
He doeth as a man, that we may, in holy confidence and affection, walk in fellowship with Him.

What matters it if we cannot see our way,
so that Jesus holds our hand. We shall see in
His own good time, and He will give sight in
His own wise and loving way. Sometimes it is
better not to see, not to know, and then His
loving-kindness keeps us in the dark.

" Bethsaida " means " the house of snares."
The Lord Jesus suffered the man to remain
blind while in Bethsaida, but He left him not
alone there. He himself became his guide, and
when outside the town, the same hand that
guided him opened his eyes.

Sometimes a child of God is walking in a
" Bethsaida " path, and through love and grace is
permitted not to see until the end of the way is
reached. The blindness that hides the way,
hides the snares ; but there is safety, for it is
Jesus takes him by the hand.

When our " Bethsaida " way is passed, and

our opened eyes contemplate the dangers and
snares of the road He hath led us, we are glad
and thankful we remained in ignorance of all
that we had escaped, until all was passed for
ever.   Oh ! 'tis blessed not to know, if He wills
it.   " He took the blind man by the hand, and
led him out of the town."

XV.

" Peter then denied again."—John xviii. 7.

AND yet Peter was truly sincere when he said
to Jesus, " If I should die with Thee, I will not
deny Thee in any wise "—but alas ! Peter knew
not himself when he thus spake.   If, instead of
this self-confident language, he had sought help
from his Lord and Master to enable him to stand
firm in the hour of temptation, he would not
have left such a sad instance of the depth of un-
faithfulness and falsehood to which a disciple of
Christ may fall, when left to endure temptation
in his own strength.

What a warning is this for all believers, and
how mistaken is he, who, conscious of integrity,
declares that it is impossible that he could ever
be guilty of the viler, the fouler sins, the worst
of the ungodly practice.   Let such an one take

heed, for he speaks as did Peter, and with a heart like Peter's; and it may be, if this self-confidence continue, that the Lord will permit him, in chastisement and for discipline, to fall in the very way he thought the most impossible, even as He did with Peter.

How little the believer knows the depth of evil within him. The Lord Jesus knows it all, and yet it alters not His love, for that love has provided a sure remedy, and that remedy is Himself.

He walks most safely who walks conscious that there is no evil into which he would not fall, but for the preserving grace of Christ. He only is truly strong who is strong in the grace that is in Christ Jesus. "Let him that thinketh he standeth take heed lest he fall." "In me, that is in my flesh, dwelleth no good thing." "Without Me ye can do nothing,"—and so, O Lord! my prayer to Thee is, "Hold Thou me up, and I shall be safe."

XVI.

*" God even our Father which hath . . . given us
good hope through grace."*—2 Thess. ii. 16.

WHAT a blessing it is to have always the consciousness of " a good hope through grace "—a
good hope of eternal life, that is—a hope well
grounded and fully assured, and which nothing
can shake.

For sinners to have such a hope as this, it
must indeed be " through grace,"—grace that lays
the foundation of it, grace that gives the assurance of it, and grace that makes the assurance
abiding and unchangeable.

The God of grace has provided for all this in
His covenant arrangements made known in His
Holy Word, where we learn that this " good
hope " has for its foundation the everlasting
love of God the Father ; the perfected salvation
for sinners wrought out through the shed blood
and perfect obedience of the Lord Jesus as the
sinner's substitute ; and the unerring testimony
of the Holy Spirit.

It is, however, one thing to have this hope
assured generally to the children of God in
covenant arrangements ; and another thing to
have it assured personally to the individual con-

sciousness of the awakened sinner. Yet, without this there can be no abiding consolation.

This personal assurance comes through believing—believing in the Lord Jesus as the way of salvation through His atoning death, and trusting to the promise of God that all who thus believe shall never perish, but have everlasting life.

A true sense of need, however, always precedes this believing on Jesus ; and a sense of need accompanied with real earnestness of mind and heart, such as only true need truly realised will cause. An earnestness which nothing earthly can extinguish, because, through the grace of the Holy Spirit, it is the earnestness of a soul that wants to escape from the wrath to come, and which can find no rest until fully assured of having escaped for ever. It is an earnestness which puts all temporal things in a very secondary and subordinate place, and which, however hindered by indwelling sin, or outward seducing, or opposing influences, returns yet again and again as the unalterable manifestation of the newly quickened life of grace in the soul, until finding rest in the finished work of Christ, the soul rejoices in the assurance of being, indeed, the possessor of a " good hope through grace."

XVII.

" In the world ye shall have tribulation ; but be
of good cheer, I have overcome the world."
—John xvi. 33.

STERN conflict makes the experienced warrior.
It is the battle alone that produces the conqueror. The believer's path is one of warfare, because he is walking through an opposing world,
but it is also one of victory, if therein he walks
with Jesus. So much depends upon the soul's
position in faith. If from the midst of worldly
associations it views Jesus afar off, it will be
often overcome, but if it views the world and its
associations from a walk of close fellowship with
Him, it will always conquer, for it is ever in the
place of victory. To such, the world's tribulations but make Jesus, who is Heaven's hiding-
place for earth-worn souls, more welcome and
more precious ; for here on earth the Lord
Jesus is best known by the help He affords,
and the joy He gives to His needy and tempted
ones.

The conscious need of the believer is one of
his highest claims upon his Lord's omnipotence.
It is that experience of soul which most pre-
vails with Jesus, and moves Him to send forth
His choicest covenant blessings.

Oh, my soul, be not thou cast down though tribulations multiply; for thy Jesus is ever near. Look thou to Him, walk thou closer with Him, listening to His words of love and grace, " Be of good cheer, I have overcome the world," and thou too shalt be conqueror, yea, more than conqueror through Him who loveth thee.

XVIII.

" Whom He did predestinate, them He also called."—Rom. viii. 30.

EFFECTUAL calling is of God Himself, in the omnipotence of His power, and in the accomplishment of His purposes of grace and love. It is different from the mere outward call through the ministry of the word, concerning which it is said, that "many are called, but few are chosen ;" for it awakens the hearer to a true sense of his condition, and effectually influences him to render a suitable response, and is therefore called "effectual ; " whereas the mere outward call, however it may influence the hearers for a time, leaves them still unawakened.

This effectual call is an inward and creative act by the Holy Spirit, whereby an ear is given which hears, a mind which understands, and a heart which is made willing in this the day of God's power.

It is a call to spiritual light : but this light is given with the call, as surely as physical light followed the word when God said, " Let there be light." It is a call to spiritual life ; but this life is given with the call, as surely as physical life was given to the dead body of Lazarus when the Lord Jesus said, " Lazarus, come forth."

It is a call to partake of good provided, but it creates a desire for it, so that now the soul is not satisfied unless it partakes of the good to which it is called. It is a call to a peace made ready, but this peace becomes the desire of the soul. It is a call to Christ and His salvation, but now Christ and His salvation become the soul's deepest need.

The consciously needy sinner is indeed the effectually called sinner, and he is called to see his need fully met in Christ.

How much cause for thankfulness and praise have all who are thus effectually called of God to see their need as guilty ones, and to look for salvation in Christ alone, for this effectual calling is an assurance that all else of covenant good is theirs, both of the past, present, and future : for " Whom He did predestinate, them He also called ; and whom He called, them He also justified; and whom He justified, them He also glorified."

XIX.

"*Fear thou not; for I am with thee. . . . I will strengthen thee; yea, I will help thee; yea, I will uphold thee.*"—Isa. xli. 10.

TRUE, the path is strange and trying, and thou art weak and weary and canst not see one step before thee, but Jesus is with thee. Look to Him; fear not—the path is not strange to Him —He knows it well, and He is with thee in it. Dost thou say it is a lonely one? but remember He is with thee, therefore thou canst never be alone, for He will never leave thee. He knows that thou art weary, but He is with thee; lean on Him—His arm is thy support; lean on it— lean hard—thou canst never weary Him, He is thy everlasting strength.

Thou meetest with none that truly understand thee, none fully to sympathise with thee; but He is with thee. He understands thee, He knows thee,—He knew thee of old; before He created the world and all that is therein, thy name was written in His book of life : He knows

thee and He knows the way thou takest; He
fashioned thee, He called thee His own, and
planned this way that thou shouldst walk with
Him therein, and learn how deep is His sympathy and love.

Dost thou look around, and do thoughts cause
thy tears to flow? But look to Him; He is with
thee, thy joy, thy light, thy peace; be thou of
good cheer, "let not your heart be troubled."
Remember, too, thou art going home; every step
shortens the homeward journey; a little, a very
little while, and 'tis home—home with Jesus—
home for ever. Thou art now a traveller, a pilgrim, but thou art going home,—that where He
is, there thou mayest be, and behold and share
His glory for ever and ever. Then fear thou
not, for Jesus says, "I am with thee, I will
strengthen thee; yea, I will help thee; yea,
I will uphold thee."

XX.

" *Who shall deliver me from the body of this
death? I thank God, through Jesus Christ
my Lord.*"—Rom. vii. 24, 25.

TRUE believers are a peculiar people in many
ways. One of their most marked peculiarities is

the constant presence of two opposing influences within them. One of these influences moves them to desire earthly good as the chief end of life. The other moves them to seek those things which are above, and to find the chief end of life in a growing intimacy with Christ, and in the consecration to Him of all they are or have.

In every step in the inner life of grace the believer is sure to find a hindering influence in the consciousness and longings of his carnal and earthly nature. But if he be looking unto the Lord Jesus for strength, crying unto Him for help against the foe, while no encouragement is willingly allowed to it, he will find that grace is given according to his need, and that the opposing influence of the earthly nature is not only overcome, but that it is overruled to work for his good, in bringing him nearer to Christ, and teaching him, more than ever, the all-sufficiency of His grace, and His readiness to help.

XXI.

*" Now the God of hope fill you with all joy and
peace in believing, that ye may abound in
hope, through the power of the Holy Ghost."*
—Rom. xv. 13.

" In believing ; " — it is all " in believing."
" The just shall live by faith." " The life I now
live, I live by the faith of the Son of God." To
seek joy and peace, apart from faith in the Lord
Jesus, whether by prayer or service, will end in
failure, for the Lord has so closely connected
them with faith, that the increase of true joy
and true peace can only be realised by an increase of faith. Joy in the Lord Jesus, and peace
which the Lord Jesus gives, are the result of that
faith which looks always to Him, and trusts in
Him, and thinks only of Him, and not of the joy
or peace.

Believing in the Lord Jesus as the Saviour,
brings the joy and peace of salvation. Believing
in the same Lord as an ever-present friend and
sure helper, brings the joy and peace of fellowship. This results in a sure hope of full deliverance from every evil, and a quiet waiting for
the Lord's time and way.

The Holy Spirit is ever working within, when
the thoughts are quietly and trustfully fixed on

Jesus. A believing and trusting heart is to the
Holy Spirit a palace of delight, where He rejoices
to heap up His hid treasures, and unfold his
deeper secrets ; and these treasures, these secrets
are all in Christ Jesus. Yes, it is all "in believing," believing and trusting as a little child.
"In believing"—your sorrow shall be turned
into joy. "In believing"—your disquieted spirit
shall be hushed, and rest and peace be your portion, and your hope of a brighter future will
grow more firm and abiding. Yes—it is all
"in believing."

XXII.

" He goeth before them."—John x. 4.

CHILD of God, that path is not untrodden into
which your sometimes reluctant feet are guided.
The good Shepherd goeth before thee. Jesus,
the Father's Shepherd over the Father's sheep,
knoweth every step. He seeth every danger—
the end as well as the beginning is marked out
by Him—therefore in that path, however trying
and unexpected, all is, all will be well.

"He goeth before them,"—then looking to
Him they cannot go wrong. The path of duty
is where He leads in His providence, and directs

by His word, for in His providence He gives the opportunities for action, and in His word He gives the principles by which to act.

The path of duty is ever the path of safety, for there—and there only—" He goeth before them." Why should the disciple fear and be dismayed, why be doubtful, and wavering, and discouraged? The path He points out, judged by sense and not by faith, may seem more difficult and more uncertain in its issues, and be more opposed to his own wishes, and the expressed desire of friends; but if it be the path of duty, it matters not how sure and desirable other ways may appear to be; in this and this only can it be said, " He goeth before," and therefore in no other way but this can blessing be experienced, and blessing be the issue.

The path may be dark and trying at the beginning, but it will be light and joyful at the end; whereas, however light and joyful other ways may appear to be at the outset, there will be darkness and sorrow at the end, with the knowledge of time lost, and the right way to be sought at last amidst increasing difficulties. But even then the right way is well sought, though late and amidst increasing difficulties; for being at last the right one, He now goeth before, and all is well.

It is better, however, never to go out of His way, so shall our joy abound, and our path ever be as the ways of pleasantness, and the paths of peace—for " He goeth before."

XXIII.

" But grow in grace."—2 Pet. iii. 18.

BELIEVERS can judge as to their growth by comparing their present experience with that of years ago, and considering whether the Lord Jesus is more a reality to them as their refuge, their friend, their helper, and their Lord; and whether there is a growing distaste for those things that hinder fellowship with Him, and a more ardent desire after whatever has been found helpful to growth in the knowledge of Him, and likeness to Him ; also, whether they are more self-distrustful, and more Christ-trustful, and more content with Him and His providential disposal of things concerning them.

Spiritual growth, like physical growth, results from living upon suitable food, and avoiding whatever is injurious to health. To live to the pleasing of the flesh is always injurious to spiritual health ; whereas, to live daily a life of faith upon Christ, seeking continually to be strong in the grace that is in Him, and to act in all things according to His word, is the sure way to promote spiritual health and growth.

Growth downward into a deeper experience of spiritual things, in close heart-walk with the Lord Jesus, will result in a fuller manifestation of healthy fruit. A superficial rooting can never produce a very prosperous tree, though it may make a very showy appearance for a time.

In the Lord's garden no two plants are alike: so many things exist to make each a special object with Him, that it is never well to judge ourselves in comparison with others.

XXIV.

" He maketh ('equalleth') *my feet like hinds' feet, and setteth me upon my high places."* —2 Samuel xxii. 34.

IF a believer, forgetting his high and heavenly calling, seeks by his own plans to climb into the "high places" of earthly honour and authority amongst his fellowmen, he will learn, sooner or later, that such are indeed slippery places, and possess no firm standing for his feet either in safety or in honour, as a child of God.

If, however, the Lord Himself setteth the believer upon "high places" which were unsought by him, the same Lord will make his feet "like hinds' feet," so that in such high places he shall not stumble nor be ashamed, but shall be as safe and as much at rest as in the more lowly and less dangerous walks of life; for as the hind is enabled to pursue her way in safety and with ease over the high and rocky declivities, by instinctively equalling her feet to the unevenness of the ground, so the Lord equalleth the feet of His saints to the path along which He leads them. Thus they find the high places, which they may probably have dreaded, are safe places, and that the dangers are not so terrible, nor the difficulties so insurmountable as they imagined they would be, when thinking of the way, before they walked therein. Then fear not, believer, for if the Lord setteth thee upon thy high places He will surely make thy feet like hinds' feet.

" The Lord is gracious and full of compassion."
　　　　　—Psalm cxlv. 8.

These streams never cease flowing, for Jehovah
is the fountain whence they spring, and Jesus
the channel in which they run, and needy hearts
are the vessels they fill.

XXV.

" Content with such things as ye have, for He
　hath said, I will never leave thee nor forsake
　thee." More literally: " Content with the
　things that are present, for He hath said,
　No, I will not leave thee, neither forsake
　thee, no, not at all."—Heb. xiii. 5.

THE Lord Jesus never leaves His people.
Whether they realise His presence or not, it does
not alter the fact, for He is ever with them as
their loving and sympathising friend and helper
—true God, yet always true man.

" I will never leave thee,"—there is the assurance of His gracious presence. " Nor forsake
thee,"—there is the assurance of His watchful
care and changeless love. It is possible for a
person to have much of the company of one by
whom he is forsaken in heart affection. The

Lord Jesus deals not thus with His people. His language means—" My presence shall ever go with thee, My heart shall ever be towards thee, and My hand shall ever hold thee." There is nothing in the darkest and most trying path in which a believer can possibly be placed, that need prevent him constantly realising the presence and love of His Lord, and quietly resting in Him. Fully, however, to realise the Lord's presence and love, and quietly rest in Him, there must not only be looking up, and trusting, and waiting, but the heart must also be content with the pro· vidential path below.

If a believer would walk in loving fellowship with the Lord Jesus, when in the path of trial, there must be a quiet, contented, patient abiding in that path where the Lord has placed him ; for there, and there only, will the Lord Jesus meet with him. Discontentment with the path shows that the heart is not walking in it as the appointed place of meeting with Jesus, however the feet may be compelled to tread it. The heart therefore misses Him by leaving the place of meeting. The heart of the believer must quietly come down to the circumstances of the path, so as to be in agreement with them, before he can fully realise the presence of the Lord Jesus, and rest wholly in Him. Disagreement with the path is disagreement with Him who ordained it.

There should be not only abiding with the Lord as the source of rest and comfort, but abiding in the path as the way of His appointment in love. The want of this patient abiding is the reason why so many believers have such a joyless, anxious, troubled, barren experience. " Content with the things that are present, for He hath said, No, I will not leave thee, neither forsake thee ; no, not at all."

XXVI.

" Putting on the breastplate of faith and love."
—1 Thess. v. 8.

Faith in the Lord Jesus, and love to the Lord Jesus, form the double breastplate of those who are more than conquerors.

Faith singles out the promises and faithfulness of Christ, and rests there. Love singles out the person of Christ, and rests only in Himself.

Faith gives courage in service and thinks of its responsibilities. Love gives pleasure in service and thinks of its privileges.

Faith believes all is for the best, knowing the

Lord ruleth. Love accepts all as the best, knowing the Lord loveth.

Faith trusts in darkness, knowing that all is light to Jesus. Love is content in darkness, knowing that Jesus is always near.

Faith waits the Lord's time and giveth patience. Love would have no other time, and is happy while waiting.

Faith gives way to no fear, saying, " I can do all things through Christ." Love gives way to no weariness, saying, " I can suffer all things for Christ."

Faith leans on the arm of Jesus, and is strong in the Lord. Love leans on the bosom of Jesus, and rejoices in the Lord.

Faith would be valiant for Jesus and fight. Love would please Jesus and obey.

Faith exultant cries " Victory ! " for it overcometh the world. Love gently whispers " Satisfied," for it can say, " I am my Beloved's, and my Beloved is mine."

" Putting on the breastplate of faith and love," the believer can either quietly wait, or bravely fight, or patiently suffer, or steadily and peacefully walk in darkness or in light, even as the Lord shall call.

XXVII.

" I am He that liveth, and was dead ; and, behold, I am alive for evermore."—Rev. i. 18.

THEN be not cast down, O child of God ! if Jesus lives, all must be well. What though friends prove faithless ?—the Lord Jesus liveth, and His friendship never ceaseth. What though all around misunderstand and misrepresent thee ?— Jesus lives and Jesus knows. What though circumstances prove adverse, and no earthly helpers are near ?—the Lord liveth, and He is always with thee, a sure help in time of trouble. What though the evil within be too mighty for thee ?—the Lord liveth, and it is not too mighty for Him. What though thou standest alone, uncared for amidst thy fellows ?—thou canst not be alone nor uncared for, since thy Jesus lives, and lives for evermore !

He "once was dead" — mark that : these words mean much,—they tell thee that He as a man trod the path of earthly life, experiencing its trials, its weaknesses, its necessities, its sorrows, its sympathies, its affections, its loneliness, its sufferings, and then—He died. Oh, how well He understands what human life is, and how well able to sympathise with and succour thee, for remember He now lives—and lives for evermore,—the sympathising, ever-loving Man, the gracious, ever-loving God, in one person.

Be then of good cheer,—nought can do thee harm since Jesus liveth, for He is thine, and thou art His.

XXVIII.

" But we have the mind of Christ."
—1 Cor. ii. 16.

To have the mind of Christ is to look at all things from the side of Christ, and judge of them as He judges of them. This should be the position and experience of all believers ; but, alas! how many look at things from a merely human point of view, and judge of them after the manner of a worldly mind, to the encouragement of worldly principles and worldly plans, which ever result in fears and sorrows, inconsistencies and failures.

To have " the mind of Christ," brings quietness and assurance in every circumstance of life. To one who judges with the mind of Christ, what a different aspect have trials and afflictions, than when judged by a worldly mind. To have the mind of Christ, gives such a different view of the world, and the things of the world, its strifes, its glories, its favours, or its persecutions.

How powerful for preservation from unbelieving fears and murmurings it is to have the mind of Christ! How powerful too for separation from evil within, and without! What an incentive also to patient endurance, to God-honouring service, to lowly self-denial! How great too the victory over self, and how great the blessing on the daily path to have the mind of the meek and lowly Jesus! Mine, then, be the aim henceforth, to look at all things with "the mind of Christ," and to walk through life as one who ever walks with Jesus, and thinks with Jesus.

"*The Lord trieth the righteous.*"—Psalm xi. 5.

Just as a mother trieth the affection of her little one by putting it to the proof in many ways, and finding it stand the test, rejoices greatly in her child—so the Lord trieth His children by putting to the proof their faith, and patience, and meekness, and gentleness, and hope, and love; and finding them stand the test, His heart is increasingly glad over them, and He rejoices to do them good.

XXIX.

" For we walk by faith, not by sight."
—2 Cor. v. 7.

AND yet how many believers are walking for
the most part by sight and not by faith, very
much to the discomfort of their souls, and to the
hindrance of their growth in spiritual life and
spiritual understanding.

Some walk by the sight of the evil within—
they are frequently examining it—they see much
of it, and it has this peculiarity, that the more it
is looked at, the more there is to look at, and the
result is, they often walk in doubt and fear ; but
if, instead of walking by sight, they walked by
faith in Christ, contemplating their position as
complete in Him before the Father, they would
walk more joyfully, and would more readily
overcome the evil within.

Others walk by the sight of their frames and
feelings, and as these are always changing, so is
their comfort; but if they walked by faith in
Christ, by faith in His unchanging love for them,
and His perfect work on their behalf, they would,
by casting off all gloom, better recommend to
others the gospel they profess.

Others walk by the sight of trying providences,

and increasing difficulties, and the result is they are often almost overwhelmed; but if they walked by faith in Christ, by faith in His watchful and constant care for them, and in the assurance that nothing can befall them but what His love and grace ordains, and did by faith walk with Him in the path He appoints, their hearts would be filled with confidence and peace.

Others again walk by the sight of their own weakness, and so tremble at every step; but if they walked by faith in Christ, by faith in His constant presence and power, ever looking away to Him, they would better understand the experience of the Apostle (because themselves realising it) when he says, "I can do all things through Christ which strengtheneth me."

What the Lord wants in His service is men and women who will not only "walk by faith and not by sight," but regardless of sight when sight seems to contradict the word of Him, whose word never fails.

XXX.

" My meditation of Him shall be sweet."
—Psalm civ. 34.

A BELIEVER never need be without pleasant thoughts, and sweet, if the Lord Jesus be the subject of his meditation. How sweet to meditate on His love—so wonderful, so fervent, so pure, so changeless. How sweet to meditate on His faithfulness amidst all the changeful circumstances of life, and the too frequent changefulness of earthly friends. How sweet to meditate on His life on earth, so gentle, so kind, so holy, so self-denying, so perfect as a servant in carrying out his Father's eternal purposes of love in bringing many sons unto glory. How sweet to meditate on His constant presence with His people as "the first-born amongst many brethren," who laid down His life for them, and who watches over their every step, with a care and an interest far beyond that of a mother for her only child. How sweet to meditate on His second coming, when we shall see Him, and be made like unto Him, and realise the blessedness of being "together with the Lord." How sweet to meditate on His eternal presence in the midst of the eternally loved family, in the glorious family home above—its leader, its teacher, its joy for ever.   Verily my meditation of Him is sweet.

XXXI.

" So shall we ever be with the Lord."
—1 Thess. iv. 17.

WE wait for that bright and happy day—that eternal morning without a cloud.   It will come, and come soon, though to our longing souls it seems to tarry.

We are not to expect freedom from sorrow and sighing here.   The brightest day may have clouds ere sunset.   Wayside greetings are but the prelude to wayside partings.

Sorrow, and tears, and sighing are not necessarily the result of unbelief, neither are they necessarily un-Christ like, for Jesus groaned in spirit, and "Jesus wept."   The Apostle Paul also sorrowed as well as rejoiced.   We too rejoice in the Lord, but that joy makes us not as Stoics— makes us not tearless when thorns pierce ; but influences us to weep as though we wept not, and to sorrow, but not as those without hope.   But oh! for the coming day when " we shall see Him as He is," and when " we shall be like Him," and "there shall be no more death, neither sorrow nor crying, neither shall there be any more pain, for the former things are passed away." " So shall we ever be with the Lord."

Let us then show our gratitude by seeking, while here, to love Him more, and walk in closer fellowship with Him, and to have our hearts more in unison with His. We seem to have nothing of Him compared to what we want. Let us press on. Let us exhort and encourage each other in this ; and let us together emulate the noble example of the Apostle when he says :— "This one thing I do, forgetting those things which are behind, and reaching forth unto those things which are before, I press toward the mark for the prize of the high calling of God in Christ Jesus."

Sometimes we seem to have a thirsting after Him, which, when satisfied, is but increased. Then, again, there are seasons when the spiritual energies are so quiescent, that the soul knows not its own thirst, or knowing it, cannot drink so deeply as was its wont. Sometimes there are seasons when the soul, bowed down under a deep sense of great weakness and great need, is being prepared for a more earnest pressing on than ever, and for a fuller realisation of the fact that the strength of the Lord Jesus is made perfect in weakness.

Still, then, though amidst weariness and perplexities, foes without and foes within, still let us press on ; for greater is He that is for us, than all they that can be against us.   Leaning on Him, looking to Him, and walking with Him in conscious need, and conscious fellowship, our path will be as the morning light which shineth more and more to the perfect day.   That perfect day, that long-looked-for day, when we shall "ever be with the Lord!"

I.

"*And it was now dark and Jesus was not come to them, and the sea arose by reason of a great wind that blew. So when they had rowed about twenty-five or thirty furlongs, they see Jesus walking on the sea and drawing nigh unto the ship.*"—John vi. 17–21.

"*Therefore will the Lord wait that He may be gracious unto you.*"—Isa. xxx. 18.

THE Lord Jesus is never in a hurry. However much unbelief may desire to hasten His hand, He still abides His own time. Omnipotence can afford to wait, because it is always sure of success; and when that omnipotence is combined with infinite love and wisdom, the right thing is sure to be done at the right time, and in the right way.

Sometimes the Lord waits until it is quite

evening time before He breaks forth in refreshing
and delivering and directing light and grace.
The dusk becomes more gloomy, and yet He waits.
He waits to be gracious. He waits His own
opportunity; and then, when twilight has ceased
and it is quite eventide, when all plans are frustrated, all hopes disappointed, no help seems near,
and darkness thickens, then He shines forth
suddenly and gloriously, and there is light abundant. The deliverance is complete and the way
made plain to the end.

So, believer, be encouraged. Whatever may be
the path of service clearly appointed you by the
Lord, continue therein notwithstanding all present
difficulties, and your Lord will appear in His own
time for your help. Remember that although it
was dark and the sea rose high by reason of a
great wind that blew, the disciples still continued
rowing. It was all they could do, and it was all
that was required of them. In a little while the
Lord appeared, and at once their purpose was
accomplished, and the ship was at the land
whither they went.

Thus it is that patient perseverance in the path
of duty, amidst many and great difficulties, often
results through the Lord's grace in more complete
and unexpected success than could otherwise have
been accomplished. Therefore, believer, do what

you can—still continue rowing, and when the right time comes the Lord's hand will be manifest, for He doth " wait that He may be gracious unto you."

II.

" *Christ liveth in me, and the life I now live in the flesh, I live by the faith of the Son of God.*"—Gal. ii. 20.

" CHRIST liveth in me." Blessed experience, indeed. Christ liveth at the right hand of God ; but, the Apostle also saith, " Christ liveth in me." In one sense this is true concerning every believer, for the Holy Spirit engrafts the soul into Christ by His quickening power, and makes that soul vitally one with Christ, which was ever one with Him in God's purpose, and love, and covenant engagements. In this sense of vital union, Christ liveth in every true believer. But the word "liveth," implies here something more than that, even a living with power and dominion—a living in peace and rest—self dethroned and cast down, and another taking the place of power, even Christ. That is indeed a peaceful, restful, joyful heart, where Christ liveth in power, and which is made the dwelling-place, as well as the kingly throne, of the Lord Jesus.

But this is all through faith, for Christ is in the heart, experimentally, just what faith understands and receives Him to be. Little faith has little experience of Christ, and consequently little power. Much faith has much experience of Christ, and consequently much power. Oh! why should we make our hearts a place of unrest for Jesus, by allowing self to mar the quietude of His home? The Lord Jesus has a place of rest in His Father's love, and another place of rest in His redeemed Church, as one with Himself, and still another place of rest in a believing, trusting heart, where self no longer rules. Let us, then, no longer allow self to step in, and with unruly hand, and noisy clamour, disturb the quietness of our Master's earthly abode, for where in the whole world can He find rest if not in a believer's heart? A life of faith in "the Son of God" is Christ's highest glory on earth, and the believer's highest comfort and joy.

III.

"And this is the Father's will which hath sent Me,
that of all which He hath given Me I should
lose nothing, but should raise it up again at
the last day."—John vi. 39.

FULL and complete salvation you, as a believer,
can never lose, however feeble and dim may be
your spiritual experience, for your salvation is .
secured by covenant engagements sealed by the
precious blood of Jesus Christ. You may however, from various causes, lose the assurance of
your salvation, and therewith your peace and joy.
It is therefore well that you be settled in the
consciousness of your full salvation, by the remembrance of what has been done on your behalf.

It is not what you have done yourself in
sorrowing for sin, in seeking salvation, in believing in Jesus, in praying for grace, that is
the foundation of your assurance of salvation;
but in what has already been done for you in
the past, and is already engaged to be done for
you in the future by your covenant God and
Father, and by His Son Jesus Christ our Lord.

It is your Heavenly Father who, by giving
you the Holy Spirit, has made you an awakened
soul. It is your Heavenly Father who has shown
you your sinfulness, and who has led you to see

that you are by nature without anything good or acceptable before God. It is your Heavenly Father who has shown you that there is nothing in yourself or in your works, however religious they may now be, to bring you salvation or help you in any way thereto. It is your Heavenly Father who has led you to see in Christ crucified your only way of deliverance from deserved wrath (John vi. 37, 44, 45, 65). It is your Heavenly Father who has condescended to bind Himself to you by promise and oath for the confirmation of your faith (Heb. vi. 17, 18).

By these things you are assured that you are evermore the object of His covenant grace and love (John x. 29) ; and that you are a child of His, and that full satisfaction for all your sins has been provided by Him on your behalf, and that His beloved Son has engaged for your well-being and safety, as one given to Him by His Father before the world was.

IV.

" He that glorieth, let him glory in the Lord."
—1 Cor. i. 31.

THERE we rest. There begins and ends our glorying — " in the Lord." True, in a lower

sense, the Apostle gloried in his infirmities (weaknesses), but only that in a higher sense he might
more fully glory in the Lord, who made His servant's conscious weakness the marked opportunity of increased and abundant grace ; for the
more conscious the Apostle was of weakness, the
more prepared was he to receive power from the
Lord Jesus, and the more able to glory in the
Lord, through more fully realising that all power
was from Him alone.

Those most glory in the Lord Jesus who most
make Him their all, for such find Him to be
what they make Him, namely, their all. Glorying
in the Lord comes not from a mere intellectual
knowledge of Him, but from a heart experience
of constant need continually and abundantly met
by the fulness which is in Christ Jesus.

Out of the abundance of the heart the mouth
speaketh, and that heart which is filled with Christ
will give forth, as from a living fountain, praise and
glory to His most holy name. Whatever hinders
this glorying in the Lord is of the flesh ; and no
greater hindrance is there than being occupied
with self in any of its various forms, such as self-
vileness or self-righteousness, self-feeling or self-
hardness, self-pleasing or self-hating.

To a heart full of Christ, self is never a subject
of consideration. Such an one is occupied with

Christ, and looks at all things from the side of Christ, and evermore glories in Him, whatever be the path of providence into which He may lead His beloved one. " He that glorieth, let him glory in the Lord."

V.

" Putting on . . . for an helmet, the hope of salvation."—1 Thess. v. 8.

" THE hope of salvation." This points to a future day, and implies that there are evils from which no present deliverance is to be expected. But the Apostle exhorts believers to put on " for an helmet the hope of salvation," and this implies that although there is no present deliverance from such evils, the hope of full salvation—of full deliverance at a future day—should be a source of comfort to the believer, and should enable him to lift up his head fearlessly and cheerily and hopefully, while still pressing on in the trying path, fighting the good fight of faith, looking unto Jesus, though amidst evils of every kind—moral, spiritual, social, domestic, political, or physical—evils without and evils within.

The Lord Jesus takes care that the evils do

not overwhelm and eternally destroy His believing ones, for He has engaged to do this, both in His free promises to them and in His covenant engagements to the Father; but oh! how often the heart sighs and longs to be away from the presence of these evils; for though they cannot destroy, they have, alas! great power to hinder and depress.

When the believer is too much occupied in the contemplation of the evils around—the sins, the miseries, the selfishness, the heartlessness, and the absence of the good and the holy, and the true and the Christlike; or when too much occupied in looking into his own heart, and beholding the more than counterpart of every evil there, so that of all demons, to him, no demon seems so frightful as sinful self—old, evil self—fallen, corrupt self—the self of sin and death. Oh, then, how the head hangs mournfully! How the steps tread heavily, and the eyes see dimly because of tears, and the heart becomes depressed and burdened. Then comes the exhortation—" putting on as an helmet the hope of salvation "—teaching us that it will not last long—a little while and the conqueror's song will be ours—a little while and full salvation will be realised, and with such joyous shoutings as only those can utter who have had such an experience of evils as ours.

Let us therefore "put on the helmet." Let us lift up our heads, for the deliverance is at hand, and the Deliverer is nigh. Blessed and welcome will be the deliverance, but infinitely more blessed and welcome will be the Deliverer Himself.

VI.

" She hath wrought a good work on me. . . . She hath done what she could."—Mark xiv. 6, 8.

OFTEN in the activities of benevolence, there is danger lest the doers be led to act from a sense of self-satisfaction in the doing and in its manifest results, rather than with a direct view to the glory of the Lord Jesus Himself.

Again, with those who are busy workers amongst the poor, always active in going hither and thither, there is sometimes danger of too readily judging and condemning others who are not also actively engaged in the same work, though to their mind they appear to have as much opportunity and ability for it as themselves.

The apostles' judgment of this woman shows that they fell into both these snares. But how different was the Lord's judgment,—" She hath wrought a good work on Me." Yes, He Himself was her all. Love to Him was the all-absorbing and impulsive power which moved her. Had the apostles wisely judged, they would not have charged her with extravagance and inhumanity; for that heart which is ever moved by love to Jesus can never go wrong in any relationship in life.

"She hath done what she could," He further said. Others might not think so. It was not a great work in the eyes of her fellows. It was to them nothing like raising the dead, or healing the sick, or feeding the hungry multitude. These were to them great works indeed. But the Lord was her judge. "She hath done what she could;" and above all she did it for Him—therefore her memorial should descend to all generations.

May it ever be our aim to do what we can, and to do it for Jesus; knowing that whatever may be the judgment of our fellows, our memorial is with the Lord.

VII.

" For I know that this shall turn to my salvation through your prayer."—Phil. i. 19.

THINGS the most untoward, and the most contrary, are made in the overruling hands of the

Lord Jesus to serve the best interests of His tried ones. How often when difficulties and trials have multiplied, and darkness has increased, and friends have become fewer, and earthly ground for hope has been removed how often has the Lord made these circumstances work out the highest good for His tried one! Such times are times for patient waiting, and for believing prayer—not for complaining and sadness. Such too are times for Christian sympathy, and for united supplication.

The greatest earthly helper a believer can have at any time, and especially in such times as these, is an earnest, loving-hearted, praying friend. If however he have none such, let him still take courage, for Jesus is with him and He is ever faithful, and He ever liveth to make intercession for him. At the right time He will either send full deliverance, or grace so abounding that his heart confidence and joy shall be far beyond that which even full deliverance would have brought him (2 Tim. iv. 16-18).

VIII.

*"I called upon the Lord in distress, the Lord
answered me, and set me in a large place,"*
OR, *"from the strait place I called the
Lord, the Lord answered me in a broad
place."*—Psalm cxviii. 5.

THE Lord Jesus sometimes leads the believer into
a strait place, where there are nothing but
thorns on either side, and no way of turning, no
prospect of deliverance, and where there are no
earthly helpers, no loving friends to comfort. It
is a very strait and narrow way, with darkness
on before. The believer looks around, but all
is cheerless—light only is above; and now he
begins to look up as he never did previously; he
learns to live looking up.

Before he entered the strait place he lived
too much looking around—too little looking up;
now look up he must, for light is only found in
so doing. If tempted to look around, he staggers
against the thorns, and is wounded; but looking
up, his steps are steady, and though the thorns
are always near, they do not pierce—and here, it
is well not to be anxious—it is well not to be in
haste—haste often causes a false step and a fall
—haste brings hurt—brings a wound—it is best

to walk patiently, and learn the lesson His love would teach, the lesson of always looking up.

When this is fully learned, the cry is answered, the way suddenly opens, and the feet tread in a broad place. Then through the teaching of the past the believer better knows the safety and the joy of living always looking up, and not looking around, whether the feet tread in the strait way or the broad place.

It is a comfort to know that the Lord Jesus is the light in the strait way, and the guide into the broad place, and that His leading is ever the leading of unchanging love.

IX.

" We love Him, because He first loved us."
—1 John iv. 19.

BELIEVER in Jesus, to forget you, Jesus must first forget Himself. To cease to love you, He must cease to live, for that love and that life are one.

You see some of the tokens of His love in His drawing you to Himself, and thus showing you, that in Himself alone can your truest joy be found, and that in Himself alone can you realise a sufficiency for every need, both for time and eternity.

You are as much a necessity to His joy, as He is to yours. He finds a heart-rest in His thoughts of love for you, and He in love has shown you that you can only find heart-rest in thoughts of that love of His, and what it has wrought for you.

In your heart-desires after the Lord Jesus, though such desires may not have reached their full realisation, yet in these desires, and your heart-sorrows because of desires unrealised, you see sure evidences of your love for Him.

You would not long after that for which you had no liking. The very longing shows the love. You would not look for rest and peace and joy to one in whom you did not believe, and in whom you had no confidence. The fact of looking only to Jesus for rest and peace and joy, evidences a faith not born of earth, a faith of Heaven's own gift, and the true outflow of that new nature which nothing but Christ can satisfy.

Sometimes a child of God cannot go beyond the language of Isaiah xxvi. 8—"The desire of our soul is toward Thy name." It is joy indeed when the soul can say as in Cant. vii. 10, "I am my Beloved's, and His desire is toward me." This you can truly say; for your desire toward Him is really the result of His desire being first toward you. How emphatic are the more literal words, "We—we love Him, because He first, He loved us."

X.

" Weep not ; she is not dead, but sleepeth."
—Luke viii. 52.

IT certainly did seem to be a hopeless case, but yet it was not really so. It only seemed to be. Onlookers saw no ray of light amidst the surrounding gloom ; but that was because they knew not Him who was so near. They knew not His love, His grace, His power, and so the words of cheer even from His lips seemed like mockery to them. Alas! so is it now too frequently even with those who know somewhat of the power and love of Jesus. If trials continue and increase, and help and deliverance are not soon afforded, tears flow, gloom and despondency prevail. This, however, should not be. Jesus still lives; Jesus still loves ; Jesus is still mighty to deliver, and He is ever nigh. Let then the believer say : "Why art thou cast down, O my soul, and why art thou disquieted within me?" What though "deep calleth unto deep" at His command ? I will still hope and quietly wait for His appearing on my behalf, for I shall yet praise

Him for His delivering grace, for "He is the
health of my countenance,"—"my Lord and my
God."

XI.

" I follow after, if that I may apprehend that
for which also I am apprehended of Christ
Jesus."—Phil. iii. 12.

THERE are many believers who are saved "so as
by fire." There are others who, through much
and continued hungering and thirsting after
Christ here, have an abundant entrance into the
kingdom of glory, and a greater measure of glory
hereafter, as the Lord's more specially prepared
vessels made more capable of receiving a greater
fulness of glory than others, though all will have
a fulness according to the measure of their
capacity.

Christ more closely followed here; Christ more
longed for here; Christ more looked to here;
Christ made the object and end of life here; Christ
made continually the soul's joy and strength here;
this enlarges the soul's capacity while on earth,
and makes it more capable of receiving a larger
measure of glory, through an enlarged capacity
for enjoying more of Christ hereafter.

Alas! how much believers are losing by not making much of Christ. How unlike the untiring earnestness of the Apostle Paul. Oh, to be able with him to say, "I follow after, if that I may apprehend that for which also I am apprehended of Christ Jesus."

XII.

"But the very hairs of your head are all numbered."—Matt. x. 30.

How well He knows us! How much He cares for us! Deep love creates deep interest in the very least things that pertain to the object loved. Oh, what love is His! How deep His interest in us when the very hairs of our head are all numbered. As the all-seeing God, He knoweth everything everywhere; but He knoweth us and everything pertaining to us in a special, and particular, and gracious, and Fatherly manner.

Two emphatic words here denote the particularity of the love, and the universality of its interest, "your" as distinct from those who are not His own ; "all," as showing that not even a little one is unnoticed. We, however, cease to wonder at our Father's special and watchful care for us in little things, when we remember that He gave for us His Son, His only-begotten Son; and if such minute things as the hairs of our head are a special object of thought to Him, how much more the varied things of daily life which have such an influence over our lives for good or evil. Let us then trust in Him at all times, and let our expectation be continually from Him.

XIII.

" Sorrowful, yet alway rejoicing."—2 Cor. vi. 10.

"SORROWFUL," because there is so much power for evil in the world. " Sorrowful," because error increases, and spiritual truth is less and less relished. " Sorrowful," because of so little fellowship amongst true believers. " Sorrowful," because Christ is so little known, so little loved, so little honoured. And sorrowful, oh! how sorrowful, because of a heart prone to wander,— because of an evil nature within, that so constantly wars against the new and the better.

"Yet alway rejoicing," for Jesus giveth grace, and giveth victory, and in Him the believer is evermore complete and changelessly perfect before God. " Alway rejoicing," because the Lord Jesus liveth and reigneth, and His purposes are sure of accomplishment. " Alway rejoicing" because greater is He that is with His people, than all they that can be against them. " Alway rejoicing," because the Lord's love for His people is ever the same, and His presence ever abides with them. " Alway rejoicing," because the Lord is coming " to be glorified in His saints and to be admired in all them that believe." " Alway rejoicing," for the Lord is near, and full redemption draweth nigh. " Alway rejoicing," because of a glorious future in a bright and happy home with Jesus.

Let this " alway rejoicing" be ours; for 'tis the earnest of the joys of heaven, the foretaste of that home experience in which the " sorrowful " no more doth mingle, for there it is everlasting joy, and sorrow and sighing have for ever fled away.

XIV.

" These things have I spoken unto you that in Me ye might have peace."—John xvi. 33.

YESTERDAY on the mount, to-day in the deep valley, is ofttimes the pilgrim's experience. Nevertheless we are daily nearing home, and still Jesus continues everything to His people; willingly so Himself, and appointed to be so by our Father. Therefore let us use Him as such in our need always.

When the tongue of man in falsehood, and enmity rises against us, then—Jesus is our defence. When evil pursues us from without or within, then—Jesus is our refuge. When duty calls and the heart trembles, then—Jesus is our help. When the spirit is weary, and worn, and sad, then—Jesus is our rest.

The Christian pilgrim, like an ordinary traveller, needs a resting-place, where, for a season, he can stay in quiet before he starts again on his way. Sometimes the mind becomes so fagged and weary that it is not so much help to walk that is sought for, but rather a place of rest for a little season, because so weary. Such a resting-place is Jesus—a quiet resting-place to His weary ones.

The varied vicissitudes and experiences of the Christian life only bring out more fully the variety of blessing there is in Him, and cause us to prize Him more. Water is most prized by the thirsty. Help by the weak. Medicine by the sick. Food by the hungry, and rest by the weary. So Jesus is most prized by those who most feel their need of Him. His heart-healing love is best known by those who have had most heart-wounds. The deeper realisation of His presence is oftener found in deep-water experiences (Isa. xliii. 1, 2).

XV.

" Thy will be done."—Matt. xxvi. 42.

BELIEVERS often plead, " Lord, take away all that
would prevent me saying without reserve, Thy
will be done." This pleading must however be
accompanied by wise dealing with self. Our
physical and mental powers are servants, ready
when in health to do our bidding at all times,
whether for good or evil, according as they are
made the servants of the old nature or the new.

Whatever hinders a perfect acquiescence in the
will of the Lord is of the old nature; but this
old nature makes the mind its servant in this
hindering work. We cannot alter this old nature,
though its powers may be weakened greatly by
disuse, and by grace. A very efficacious way to
prevent its doing mischief is to take out of its
hands the instruments it uses for evil. Now,
whenever the mind is much occupied with the
troubles, and difficulties, and burdens of the way,
the old nature is using it, and is gaining strength
thereby for further activity and mischief; soon
depression follows, and then discontent and
unbelief. Therefore make a firm stand against
the use of the mind by the old nature, and bring
it into the service of the new nature. That

would at once refer everything to Jesus; that would lead the mind to think much of Him; and only of the trial as making Jesus more needful, and the heart more hopeful and trustful in Him. However heavily the matter may press; still ever be thinking of Jesus in His love, and faithfulness, and presence, and power, and grace. The mind being thus exercised on Him, the heart is preserved from being overwhelmed, and can humbly say, " Thy will be done."

XVI.

" When my soul fainted within me I remembered the Lord."— Jonah ii. 7.

WHAT experience of our physical frailness we are continually having! What intimations that we must soon put off our mortal body! Under the full consciousness of this the mind can only be stayed and the heart comforted by remembering the full deliverance from condemnation and the complete acceptance in Christ, provided by the covenant of grace and love.

We need to live much by faith, seeing that the visible gives us no assurance of permanent consolation. Experiences too, what poor helpers they are! How often fear arises when courage should abound. How often when we desire the good, evil makes itself manifest. How often to our sorrow, there is more of the unspiritual, the temporal, the worldly influencing us, rather than the spiritual and the heavenly. How often the believer is tossed upon a sea of varied experiences, from not one of which can he derive any comfort or any assurance that the end will be well.

What a relief it is under such circumstances to remember the everlasting love of our Heavenly Father, and of our gracious Lord and Saviour; and to remember their own complete and changeless arrangements for our present and eternal safety. Arrangements made in full view of all the evil and incompetency we mourn over. Nay, undertaken for us because of that evil and incompetency, and kept in hands that are able to work out to a successful issue all the purposes and plans of infinite love. "When my soul fainted within me, I remembered the Lord." So if we would have full peace and strong consolation we must, like Jonah, remember the Lord, and what a God of love and grace He is, in making such a rich provision in Christ His Son for our eternal well-being.

XVII.

" This Man doeth many miracles."—John xi. 47.

TRUE witness, though it came out of the mouth
of His enemies—and *" this man"* is *man* still,
though ascended into the heavens, and seated on
the throne of power and glory—and still He
doeth "many miracles," both in providence and
grace. Still He manifests His miraculous grace
in quickening dead souls. Still He manifests
His miraculous providences in opening out a
way of deliverance to the perplexed, of succour
to the needy, of peace to the troubled; and this
too, when all human endeavours have failed, and
men have ceased even to hope. Yes, for His
perplexed ones He maketh " a way in the wilderness;" and for His weary ones, "rivers in the
desert," leaving them still in the wilderness and
in the desert, that by contrast they may more
fully see " this man " still " doeth many miracles."

Sometimes in chastisement He makes a fruitful
place a wilderness, but again in His tender mercies and loving-kindnesses He rewardeth patient
endurance by causing the desert to rejoice and
blossom as the rose ; yea, to blossom abundantly,
and rejoice with joy and singing. Wherefore,
let those that are of a fearful heart be strong and

fear not, for "this man" is Jesus, the same evermore—God and man—and He yet "doeth many
miracles." Happy is the soul that trusteth only
in Him.

XVIII.

*" Thou hast enlarged my steps under me, so that
my feet did not slip."*—Ps. xviii. 36.

SOMETIMES the Lord Jesus, in leading His people,
suits their feet to the rough and dangerous path.
Then He makes their feet like hinds' feet, so that
they walk evenly in uneven places, or He maketh
their shoes iron and brass, so that they walk un-
injured over a rough and thorny road.

At other times He alters the path to suit
their feet. Then the language of the believer
is—" Thou hast set my feet in a large room "
(Ps. xxxi. 8); "Thou hast enlarged my steps
under me, so that my feet did not slip."

How often a timid, trembling child of God has
dreaded the path in prospect, and has suffered
much in the anticipation of sore trial apparently
unavoidable ; but the dreaded time arrives, and
lo ! it is a way of peace—the clouds disperse, the
threatened tempest arises not, the difficulties are
as nothing, and the deliverance is so fully wrought

that the trembling one gratefully can say, " He
brought me forth into a large place" (Ps. cxviii. 5).

So true it is that those who trust in the Lord
Jesus shall not want any good thing. " He that
believeth in Him shall not be confounded."

XIX.

" I will rejoice in the Lord."—Hab. iii. 18.

JOY, even joy in the Lord of a deeply emotional
character, long continued, would be more than our
physical nature could at present bear. There is,
however, a quiet trustful joy that makes the soul
calm and peaceful and happy in Jesus at all times.
This joy is not strongly emotional in its manifestations, but is deeply real and stable, and much
more to be desired than the strongly emotional.
The latter is like the intense joy experienced
when much-loved friends meet for the first time
after a long separation. The other is the calm,
happy feeling they experience in each other's
company, and in the consciousness of each other's
love. A feeling that is very deep down in the
heart, and which finds its truest expression in a
look of satisfied affection and pleasure, and
which finds its strongest manifestation in quiet,

self-forgetting services. Oh! to be frequently
during the day sending such a look upward to
Him who is ever looking down upon us with a
look of unutterable affection. Oh! for grace to
show our love more continuously by quiet, self-
forgetting service, seeking in all things to please
Him who loved us and gave Himself for us.

A truly deep affection is more of the quiet
than of the emotionally demonstrative character,
because it is so much a part of our very being.
The very demonstrative is often but the ebullition
of an evanescent and easily awakened feeling.
The other is so much a part of our being, that if
it were possible that the object of our affection
could be annihilated, it would not be so much
that our feelings would be wounded, as that a
part, and the chief part, of our very being would
seem to be gone for ever.

Blessed be the name of our gracious Lord
Jesus for evermore, we shall never lose Him—
neither will He ever lose us; for the language of
His heart is—" Because I live, ye shall live also."
"Father, I will that they also whom Thou hast
given Me be with Me where I am." Therefore
will we in restful assurance "rejoice in the Lord
alway," and quietly wait the time when He will
come again to receive us to Himself, that where
He is, there we may be also.

XX.

" Whatsoever ye do, do all to the glory of God."
—I Cor. x. 31.

How slow we are in following Christ! What
glory the Father had in Him! No glory in all
else compared with what He had in Christ. The
more we are like Christ in doing and disposition,
the more shall we give glory to God. But oh!
how impossible it sometimes seems to overcome
that natural unlikeness to Christ which we still
possess. How difficult to avoid doing all things
to please self, to exalt self—self with its lean-
ings, and longings, and gratifications, and plans,
and dislikes. Nevertheless, all things to which
we are called, are possible to us when strengthened
from above. The Lord never calls to a duty
without providing all that we need to enable us
to do it. In Him is our help found.

How encouraging is the word, "As thy day
so shall thy strength be." "Thy day" and "thy
strength" go together; because the Lord Jesus
who appoints the day well knows the require-
ments of the day, and He is Himself the strength
for the day to all who look to Him. "Strength
of Israel" was His name of old. It is still
and ever the same, so that every believer can

truly say — " I can do all things through Christ which strengtheneth me." " Do all things"—then, through Christ, whatsoever we do, we can " do all to the glory of God."

XXI.

" And they that weep, as though they wept not."
—1 Cor. vii. 30.
" That ye sorrow not, even as others which have no hope."—1 Thess. iv. 13.

CLOSER still to Jesus, not only includes wider separation from everything that would draw us away from Him, but often an acquaintance with those things that make this world still more a wilderness than before.

When Jesus, however, really becomes all to the believer, life is such a very different thing. Then all earthly things, and earthly joys, even the most innocent and desirable, are held with a loose grasp, so that when it pleases Him to remove them, the already loosened grasp makes it easier to let them go, and if the tear does fall, it is soon wiped away by His loving and gentle hand ; if the heart does feel a wound, it is soon alleviated by Him who delights to comfort those

that mourn, and to lift up those that be bowed
down.

Earth's fairest flowers should ever have Christ
for their root. Severed from Him they soon lose
their fragrance, and the tighter they are grasped the
sooner they wither and perish, leaving nothing
but thorns behind.

Truly the flowers of earthly friendship and
earthly love bloom most brightly and shed forth
a sweeter, richer fragrance when planted in the
garden of the Lord, with the "rose of Sharon"
in the midst. Such friendships—associations so
endeared—know no lasting severance ; for when
removed from the garden of the Lord here, it is
that they may be transplanted to the heavenly
Paradise, there to shed forth a richer, sweeter
fragrance for evermore.

In the consciousness of this, when our tears
flow through being called to part for a season
from loved ones, we can indeed be of the number
of those who weep " as though they wept not,"
and who " sorrow not, even as others which have
no hope."

XXII.

"All things work together for good to them that
love God, to them who are the called accord-
ing to His purpose."—Rom. viii. 28.

"To them that love God, to them who are the
called according to His purpose." "According to
His purpose"—for He had purposed before the
world was who His called ones should be, and also
purposed that all things should work for their
good.   The doings of His grace in time are ever
the result of the purposes of His grace before the
foundation of the world (Rom. viii. 30).

"Them who are the called according to His
purpose"—"called" to know themselves as guilty
before God and deserving of eternal condemnation — "called" to know the all-sufficiency of
Christ to save—"called" to trust in His atoning
death as their only hope of salvation—"called"
out of the world ; no longer to revel in its
gaieties, to enjoy its fellowships, or be swayed by
its principles—"called" to be followers of the
Lord Jesus through evil report or good report.
This is the calling which distinguishes those who
love God, and for whose good it is said "all
things work together."

Yes—"all things work together." It is not

said that they work singly or alone, but in relationship to one another—they " work together." One little thing which we cannot at all understand, or see the reason of, the Lord sees is necessary to make several other things properly work for our good. Without that one thing— that one very unpleasant thing—all the rest would not be for our benefit.

We are too apt to look at things singly, and therefore the mind often becomes perplexed. A single thread is not of much importance in itself, but if left out in the weaving, the pattern in the loom would be rendered imperfect.

These " all things " are so many shuttles running to and fro, weaving the web of goodness and blessing for the children of God. The hand that throws the shuttles is the hand of Jesus. In the web He weaves no thread will be found misplaced, when the weaving is over.

Therefore let us leave all things in the hands of Jesus, who has the whole plan of the life of each believer always before Him, and who in His infinite wisdom understands how to put one thing to another, so as to produce the best results and accomplish all His purposes of love.

Let us trust in Him at all times, even when our expectations of earthly things are disappointed and our plans frustrated, or when darkness sur-

rounds our path, and trials and affliction are our
portion ; being assured that when we have attained a keener vision and a fuller understanding
than our pilgrim state affords us, we shall see that
"all things " did but work together for our good,
whilst they also testified to the wisdom, power,
and love of Him who " doeth all things well."

XXIII.

"In My Father's house are many mansions."
—John xiv. 2.

WHAT an up-and-down life is the life of the
present, especially for a believer ! Such experiences, as so often are his portion here, ought to
make the prospect of the rest of his eternal home
a very desirable one.

"In My Father's house are many mansions."
No earth-born cares are there, no pain nor weariness, no perplexities nor hindrances. Yet the
many things, little and great, which at times
come one upon another like the waves of the sea,
so often distract the mind of the believer that,
for the time being, he loses all thought of his high
and heavenly calling and of the bright home prepared for him above by a Saviour's love and care.

What poor, weak, failing creatures we are! How often, when we aim to be at our best, a deeply humbling lesson is taught us in our being permitted to be at our worst. Yet the Lord's loving-kindness changes not. The Christ-denying Peter is as much an object of changeless love and watchful care, as when upon the mount with his Lord.

We often learn more of the exceeding greatness of our Lord's love by learning more of the exceeding greatness of our unworthiness and sinfulness. His love seems to shine the brighter from the blackness of the contrast. The full and complete knowledge of that love we can never attain unto, for it is infinite. We shall however more fully understand it, and see more of its height and depth and length and breadth, when we reach our "Father's house" above, where, in the "many mansions," Jesus Himself will be our visible companion and teacher, and our joy, world without end.

XXIV.

*" I dwell with him that is of a contrite and
humble spirit."*—Isa. lvii. 15.
*" I will come again and receive you unto Myself;
that where I am, there ye may be also."*
—John xiv. 3.

IT is Christ we want more of. Nothing but
Christ can satisfy a quickened soul. The Christ-
nature and the Christ-life within long after Christ
Himself; and the more healthy the inner life,
the more is Christ thus longed for.

There is a twofold experience of soul very
necessary, if we would enjoy a greater fulness of
Christ within. It is to lie low and to lie still.
The former the result of our consciousness of self-
vileness, the latter the consciousness of our self-
helplessness. Then lying low and still in soul
before Him, He comes most surely and graciously
to be that soul's life and joy. All His dealings
in the way of discipline are but to teach us that
lesson more effectually.

What a precious friend is the Lord Jesus!
How comforting is the full assurance of the hope
of our future in Him and with Him. How
wonderful that His eternal happiness should be
bound up with the eternal happiness of His people,

and that heaven without them would be no place
of happiness for Him; and that part of the glory
given Him by the Father consists in having them
with Him hereafter, so that where He is, there
they may be also. It is wonderful, but it is
true.

"Because I live ye shall live also," is His
language to His people, and why? Because
(amongst other reasons) it is He in them and they
in Him. His life is their life. His glory is their
glory. His eternity is their eternity. They
stand together—for ever one in grace, and love,
and glory.

XXV.

" *When I sit in darkness, the Lord shall be a
light unto me.*"—Micah vii. 8.

THE light of earthly friendship is sweet; the
light of communion between loving hearts is
precious; the light of family and social joys is
cheering. But friendship's light may grow dim;
the communion of loving hearts must one day, to
the survivor, be but a thing of memory until the
dawning of the eternal day; the light from family
and social joys must also cease to be. But Jesus

never dies, Jesus never changes, Jesus is never far away.   That light never grows dim in its shining. The waves of tribulation may quench every other light, but they can never quench that.   The sure changes produced by the passage of time can never alter that.

The light of all that is earthly is a fading light; one light only maintains its shining as ages pass, and that light is Jesus Himself.   The light of this world is but the light of a dying spark; the light of life, the light of eternal day, is only found in Jesus.

Amidst the vicissitudes of life, believers too often turn for light to earthly sources, but he looks not high enough for light to guide his steps, and light to gladden his heart, who looks lower than Jesus.   All things earthly are but for a season, but the light of heaven never ceases shining, for that light is "Jesus Christ, the same yesterday, and to-day, and for ever."

XXVI.

" Now the Lord of peace Himself, give you peace always by all means."—2 Thess. iii. 16.

" By all means,"—that is not only by likely, but by most unlikely means, and such as to sense and unbelief would only cause trouble, anxiety, and distress; and would appear rather to hinder every good, and encourage every evil. Nevertheless by such means, yea, by all means, the Lord of peace can and does give peace to the trusting heart.

"Always by all means," or, more literally, "always in every way" (or "turning"); so that in whatsoever path the child of God is called to walk, and however new and strange may be the incidents, the duties, and the trials of that path, the Lord gives peace always to those who look to Him.

The path for a season may be sunny, and smooth, and pleasant—the traveller anticipates no change; but suddenly he reaches an unexpected "turning," where he finds the path gloomy, and rough, and dangerous. He has daily and hourly to face difficulties, oppositions, and persecutions, to which he had hitherto been a stranger. Inexperienced and weak, he would soon be overwhelmed, but looking to the Lord Jesus, the Lord of peace, he finds that He gives peace, and gives it always, and "in every turning," however gloomy and unexpected; so that the heart and mind are kept and guarded by "the peace of God which passeth all understanding."

XXVII.

*" God is our refuge and strength, a very pre-
    sent help in trouble.   Therefore will not we
    fear, though the earth be removed, and
    though the mountains be carried into the
    midst of the sea."*—Ps. xlvi. 1, 2.
*" For in Him dwelleth all the fulness of the God-
    head bodily."*—Col. ii. 9.

In the path of special trial and perplexity it is
well sometimes to look at the worst, and calmly
to expect the most unfavourable issue, as men
express it, not with mere philosophic or moral
effort, or with physical energy and a determined
will, as men of the world can do, but with a
Christian calmness, resignation, and assurance,
which only those know who take all things
from the hand of Christ, and who, because of the
burden these things produce, take them back
again to Him, to seek in Him their strength and
comfort amidst all.

If the Lord leads the believer into rough and
troubled waters, He is ever with him ; and He
leads him there that he may learn special lessons of grace, and enjoy special fellowship with
Himself; lessons which could not so well have
been learned, and fellowship that could not have
been so fully realised elsewhere.

The child of God never walks alone in any path where the Lord may place him; though he may often walk lonely therein, through his mind being so occupied with its difficulties and trials, that he loses all thought of the Friend who walks with him, and who desires to make it the place of heavenly joys in loving manifestations of Himself to the soul.

Heart-experience is the result of believing thought, therefore that which most occupies our minds will have most influence on our hearts, either for hope or fear, joy or sorrow, peace or trouble, good or evil. Seeing then that, as a believer in Jesus, all hope and joy, all grace, all good of every kind, even all the fulness of God is centred in Christ for you; and that all is placed there by God your Father for your use; it follows that the sure way of full deliverance from and prevention of heart-trouble and distressing fears, is to look to Him as "a very present help in trouble" and to think of Him, and to think much of Him, and of His love for you, and of His ever-faithful and ever-watchful care over you, and make Him always your "refuge and strength."

Remember it is He Himself who says—" Let not your heart be troubled; ye believe in God, believe also in Me."

XXVIII.

" I am with you alway."—Matt. xxviii. 20.

SOME are continually seeking to realise the life of Christ within them, making that the chief object of their thoughts ; but that is not the way to live happily. Others are continually trying to realise the presence of Christ as near to them wherever they may be ; but this too is a mistake, and is not the right way to order our thoughts concerning Him.

Our thoughts should be engaged about Him as the man who ascended to heaven, and who is now there at the right hand of God. True God and yet always true man, and always the friend and the guide of His people. It is not Jesus within us, or Jesus about us, but Jesus in heaven who is the object of faith (Acts iii. 21 ; Col. iii. 1 ; Heb. i. 3, viii. 1, x. 12, xii. 2). He is ever there as the object for worship and fellowship ; ever there as the source of consolation and joy.

We should not make the joy of Christ's presence the chief object of desire, for this would turn our thoughts more to the desired experience than to Jesus Himself. We should rest content with the declaration of His word—" I am with

you alway." By relying upon this continually
the experience of peace and joy will follow in
due course. The realisation of Christ's presence, however desirable, will never be attained
if the realisation itself be the prominent object
of thought.

The fact of Christ's presence, believed in
because of His own word, and made the leading
thought in the mind daily, will always result
in the joyful realisation of His presence.

XXIX.

" Return unto thy rest, O my soul."—Ps. cxvi. 7.

So great is the power of the body over the mind
that great bodily weakness often unfits the mind
for the calm realisation of spiritual things.
Sometimes again the mind is quickly disturbed
by unpleasant or unexpected occurrences, or by
its compelled attendance to the little and constantly recurring, but needful matters of daily
life, often when very unfitted for them, so that
the believer is unable peacefully to realise those
blessings and privileges which are his in Christ
Jesus, and even for a time forgets all his privileges and blessings in Christ.

This should not, however, be allowed to discourage the soul and hinder it from beginning again its dealings in need with an ever-present, ever-helpful Christ. Ceaseless forgettings must of necessity be followed by ceaseless beginnings again. Indeed, the believer needs often, in one sense, to be beginning again, and yet not beginning as with a new friend, but with one known and proved. The Lord Jesus never reproaches us, He never becomes weary of us, He never turns His face from us. We cannot ourselves decide what is best for our ultimate good, and it is therefore a comfort to know we are in the hands of One who is as able as He is willing to decide for us.

It is certain that all His dealings with His people are but to make Himself more a necessity and a reality to them. This result is produced when physical weakness and perplexing circumstances make us more fully conscious of our complete incapacity for anything good.

Christ likes to be to His people a Christ to lean upon. Not merely a Christ to be worshipped, a Christ to be followed, a Christ to be preached, but especially a Christ to be leaned upon. A Christ for weary and needy souls. This is His glory, and this is our blessing. Whatever therefore brings us nearer to Him as a helpful Christ, is a messenger of love.

When the Lord deals very specially with any child of His, bringing that child very low, He means that the result shall be special blessing. The voice of all His dealings is—" Come nearer to Me." Did He not love us He would not desire this.

XXX.

" I will go down with thee into Egypt."
—Gen. xlvi. 4.

INTO Egypt—the place of spiritual darkness; yet the place to which His providence had appointed they should go and tarry for a season. But He would go with them, and be found of them that looked for Him. A true sanctuary would He there be to His trusting ones; so that they might have Bethel experiences even in the land of Egypt.

Believer in Jesus, you may in providence be guided by the Lord into a place of spiritual barrenness and darkness—a very Egypt in its surroundings; and may have to make it your place of abode for a season. Nevertheless, He will Himself be with you, and it will be your own fault if you do not enjoy spiritual prosperity even there.

How often the children of God cast upon their Egyptian surroundings the blame of their spiritual sloth and deadness, instead of upon themselves; forgetting that when the Lord removes a believer from earthly sources of spiritual instruction and fellowship, He is ever in an especial manner with that believer in the place of barrenness; ready to more than make up by His grace and love in direct fellowship and guidance, through the believer's more close and personal dealing with Himself, what he has lost by change of place.

Sometimes the Lord's special object in removing a believer from pleasant spiritual surroundings and pleasant spiritual fellowships, either by affliction or change of abode, may be that He intends more than ever to be the all of that believer, through enforced closer personal dealings with Himself.

Again, the Lord may lead a believer into Egyptian surroundings for some special service there, and to bear faithful testimony for His name in the midst of the surrounding darkness.

At other times, it may be that in faithfulness and love to His disciple, and for his spiritual good, the Lord leads him away; for not a few have permitted their pleasant spiritual surroundings so to absorb their affections and attentions, that the Lord Jesus Himself has seemed to have often but a subordinate place in their regard. When spiritual surroundings thus become the foundation of comfort and joy instead of the Lord Himself, no wonder that the Lord in loving-kindness either removes that foundation from the believer, or the believer from that foundation, to prevent greater spiritual injury, and promote spiritual health.

Whatever may be the secondary causes of our removal, it is well in all to see the hand of the Lord ; and to know of a truth that His object is ever the truest good of His beloved ones, and that He will never fail them in any place whither they may go, for He hath said : "I am with thee, and will keep thee in all places whither thou goest" (Genesis xxviii. 15).

The Lord's arm is not shorter or weaker in Egypt than it is in Canaan ; and when He leads into Egypt, saying, "I will go down with thee," it is implied that in Egypt only shall the true blessing be found ; and that if the believer refuse to go down there, even the Canaan in which he delights shall be to him a place of snares, a place of darkness and barrenness, and sore trouble to his soul.

XXXI.

*" Willing rather to be absent from the body, and
to be present with the Lord."*—2 Cor. v. 8.

JESUS is indeed a real friend; and His presence
when realised makes heaven and earth seem so
near together that we feel we should see Him
instantly, if the soul were outside the body only
for a moment; for we feel the body to be a dark
veil upon the spirit's keener vision.

No one understands us so thoroughly as Jesus
does. No one can have such love for us as He
has, and no one takes such an interest in us, for
He is interested in even the most trifling things
of our daily life: where we are, what we are
doing, what we are saying, what we feel either of
physical pain or heart emotion, what causes us
sorrow or joy, and what we are thinking about;
all—all are intensely interesting to Him.

In every step of the journey He is with us.
He is with us by night and by day, in our down-
sitting and our uprising, in our going out and
coming in. And He is leading us daily nearer
home. Ah! that word "home," how it makes us
feel that we are indeed pilgrims and strangers
here. "Home,"—it is not here, for we cannot see
Him. We cannot feel at home until we see Him,

and are made fully like unto Him. Association, not place, makes our true home. Were the universe without our ever-loving Lord Jesus, it matters not though the universe were a paradise, our restless footsteps wandering hither and thither, index of a restless heart, would find no rest—no home for us. Where He is, is our home. "In my Father's house are many mansions. I go to prepare a place for you; and if I go and prepare a place for you, I will come again and receive you unto myself, that where I am, there ye may be also."

I.

*" It is good that a man should both hope and
quietly wait for the salvation of the Lord."*
—Lam. iii. 26.

STEADINESS of mind and strength of heart come
through quietly, restfully trusting. There may
be much monotony in standing still, but it is often
the way in which men see the salvation, the providential salvation they long for. In God's ways
to man and man's need, hurry on the part of the
latter often hinders, while patient, quiet, hopeful
waiting greatly helps.

" The Lord lifteth up the meek."—Ps. cxlvii. 6.

Himself the meek One—He placeth meek ones
near His side.

" Even so, Father, for so it seemed good in Thy sight."—Matt. xi. 26.

These words of the Lord Jesus express the acquiescence of faith, and the satisfaction of love.

Let us behold in Him the pattern for our faith and love; and whether in the more manifest doings of His hand in the temporal and providential path, or in the more hidden doings of His grace in spiritual and eternal things, relating to ourselves or to others, let our language ever be : "Even so, Father, for so it seemed good in Thy sight."

II.

" Nevertheless, I am continually with thee."
—Ps. lxxiii. 23.

THIS is the utterance of a faith which triumphs over contradictory circumstances and contradictory experiences.

Believer in Jesus, bear in mind that this "nevertheless" stands firm for you also, whatever may be the "although" of adverse circumstances and experiences you put before it.

Because of the covenant faithfulness of Him in

whose hand of grace and love you are, you can truly say :

Although I am weak and helpless, "nevertheless I am continually with Thee."

Although I am vile and undeserving, "nevertheless I am continually with Thee."

Although I am so foolish and prone to wander, "nevertheless I am continually with Thee."

Although trials and afflictions beset me, "nevertheless I am continually with Thee."

Although all forsake me, "nevertheless I am continually with Thee."

Although I cannot realise Thy presence, "nevertheless I am continually with Thee."

Thus, whatever may be your "although," let the "nevertheless" of your faith always triumph, for the grasp of Christ's hand never slackens, the power of Christ's arm never fails, the love of Christ's heart never changes.

III.

" He that believeth shall not make haste."
—Isa. xxviii. 16.

THERE is such a thing as being over-earnest, and so missing what we aim at. There is such a thing as a fearful, anxious, restless energy that wants it scarcely knows what, that longs for what it has not, simply because it has it not, that sometimes sees a goal before it that may be reached and yet reaches it not, because in so great a haste.

It is well to remember that "the race is not to the swift, nor the battle to the strong," and that in the spiritual race he often is the conqueror who best knows how to " wait." He often is successful who understands how to " be still."

The firmer the faith the quieter will be the spirit, and the surer, if slower, the step. " He that believeth shall not make haste."

" *And David was greatly distressed, for the people spake of stoning him, but David encouraged himself in the Lord his God.*" —1 Sam. xxx. 6.

HERE is the source of true courage, and patience, and victory. David was nothing, but David's God was everything.

Jesus, " My Lord and my God," Thou changest not, and Thou hast said, " I will never leave thee nor forsake thee" (Heb. xiii. 5). " My grace is sufficient for thee" (2 Cor. xii. 9). Help me, therefore, ever to encourage myself in Thee, and to trust in Thee and not be afraid.

IV.

" I am the bread of life."—John vi. 35.

FOOD always seasonable, always nourishing, always needed, always free, always at hand, and always plentiful.

The great want is—not the bread, but the spiritual appetite. He gives bread to "whosoever will." He gives more bread to "whosoever will." He gives most bread to "whosoever will."

"I am come that they might have life, and that they might have it more abundantly" (John x. 10).

If then we are spiritually weak; if our spiritual life lacks vigour and stability; it is not from want of an abundant provision of spiritual food, for Jesus ever abides, and He is ever the same.

Oh, for a more vigorous spiritual appetite! Oh, for grace to make each day a royal feast day, that we may grow exceedingly; so that by a more vigorous spiritual life, our "profiting may appear unto all."

" *Whom having not seen, ye love.*"—1 Pet. i. 8.

Both the person and the work of Christ are the true objects of faith ; although faith is often fixed mostly upon His work and its result. It is, however, the person of Christ alone that is the true object of love.

Faith produces satisfaction with Christ's work on the soul's behalf ; but love is not satisfied with that, because it is not love's true object. Love wants a greater nearness to Christ. Love wants more fellowship with Christ. Love wants to see Christ in everything. Love wants Christ Himself.

V.

" *Jesus Christ the same.*"—Heb. xiii. 8.

BELIEVER in Jesus, always remember that all grace, and light, and joy is for you in a Person, and that Person is Jesus. Jesus your Saviour —your Friend, and Helper, and your constant companion. The Lord Jesus never places anything between your heart's need and Himself. The path is always open and always free. The more needy, the more welcome to Him.

Your weakness and need are your true capability to prove that He is the strong one ready to help. Fear not, for He never fails. Cease not to trust, for He ceases not to be trust worthy. He is always "Jesus Christ the same." What you have realised Him to be in your very best moments, He is the same in your worst moments. This Jesus is yours for evermore, and His love and life are bound up in you. Therefore rejoice in Him always, no matter what cause else for sorrow you may have in your providential path.

"Christ our Life."—Col. iii. 4.

Not merely the author of eternal life, through His death and resurrection to all who believe—that is true—but He Himself is our Life. " Our Life" for the spiritual experience of every day ; "our Life" for overcoming; "our Life" for labour; "our Life" for enjoyment ; "our Life" for learning ; " our Life" for suffering.

Christ is all this, and more; but where there is little of Christ in the heart, there is but little life for these things; but little spiritual success against evil—but little spiritual labour—but little spiritual patience in suffering—but little spiritual enjoyment. Self becomes active, and the believer gradually ceases to live in the power of Christ, and, alas! often tries to mend the matter by increased energies in the flesh—wrestling, struggling, groaning, expostulating with God, murmuring—with the usual result, confusion, darkness, deadness, defeat. But, oh! what a change when self is given up, and the believer ceases from the flesh, and the Lord again reigns. The weak one becomes strong indeed; strong and full of vigour both in heart and life; but this renewal, this revival, begins in the heart; there must Christ first be Lord of all, and then, as Lord of life, He is Himself " our Life," henceforth for all.

VI.

" And went and told Jesus."—Matt. xiv. 12.

THE best earthly friends cannot rightly understand the heart's need and the heart's longing; but the Lord Jesus can. The best of earthly friends cannot be trusted always with everything; but it is so different with the Lord Jesus. The heart longs for true friendship here on earth, but nothing can fully satisfy save the realised friendship of Jesus. In Him the heart ever finds a full satisfaction for all its longings—a rich supply for all its needs. Earthly disappointments but make Him the more precious, causing the heart to rest in Him where no disappointment ever follows. He is the sure Friend. He is more than Brother. He is ever a true sympathiser, ever the strength of the weak, the guide of the perplexed, the joy of the sorrowing, the healer of the wounded heart. In all this He never fails.

"One in Christ Jesus."—Gal. iii. 28.

Blessed bond of union ! Friendships formed on this foundation and, with God's blessing, continued and cultivated in this relationship, are bright flowers on earth's lowly pathway, which no storm can destroy—no blight can wither—no enemy pluck up; but which, when ceasing to bloom here, are transplanted to a heavenly paradise, there to send forth a richer, fresher fragrance for evermore. Blessed bond indeed. " One in Christ Jesus." Alas ! when believers seek a lower bond of union than this.

VII.

" Casting all your care upon Him, for He careth for you."—1 Peter v. 7.

CHILD of God, care is a thing too heavy for you to carry, but remember, Jesus desires you to cast it on Himself, therefore bring the care and the cause of it to Him. No matter what the cause of your care and anxiety may be, leave it with Jesus, who is always thinking about you. Put the cause into His hands without reserve, and all trouble about it will cease.

Be content to live only in the day that is present, and for which alone grace is promised.

Whatever be your circumstances of trial, always remember that you belong to the Lord Jesus, and that He is pledged to care for you to the end of your pilgrimage; therefore tell Him everything that weighs upon your mind. By thus doing you make such things in a very special manner His concern and care; and be assured that He will never refuse the responsibility, nor let go the matter you have thus brought to Him, whatever may be your fears to the contrary. It more concerns Him than it concerns you, much as you may think it concerns you only.

The more literal rendering of the passage is—

" Casting off upon Him all your anxious care ; for it is a matter of concern to Him about you."
Then, child of God, leave it all with Jesus.

" *He opened the rock, and waters gushed out.*"
—Ps. cv. 41.

God often sends His choicest blessings through the most unlikely means. Trying providences become channels of sweet comfort. The wilderness path is often the way of blissful experience.

Believers sometimes look for the Lord in pleasant meads, when His way is in the stormy waters.

Wells of water are to be desired, but the Lord more frequently gives marked testimonies of His favour in unfavourable circumstances. " He opened the rock."

VIII.

" *He knoweth the way that I take.*"—Job xxiii. 10.
" *The Lord is on my side.*"—Ps. cxviii. 6.

THE heart may wonder, what next ? But the reply is—" He knows." There you leave it. You will trust and not be afraid.

In the way of His appointment He will hold your hand, and thus guide you that you do not wander. He will keep your feet, and thus sustain you that you do not stumble. He will strengthen your heart, and thus encourage you that you do not fear. He will be your light, and thus cheer you that you do not doubt. He will be your strong tower, and thus defend you that you be not overcome. Indeed, He will be all to you that you need, so that you may truly and continually say—" The Lord is on my side, I will not fear." "He knoweth the way that I take."

" *The Lord is good, a stronghold in the day of trouble, and He knoweth them that trust in Him.*"—Nahum i. 7.

To trust the Lord in darkness gives Him more glory than to trust Him in the light; to such He gives brighter joys in the end, and more manifest tokens of His favour. " He knoweth them that trust in Him."

IX.

" The night is far spent: the day is at hand."
—Rom. xiii. 12.

YES, it is night, for we see not Him whom our souls love. It is night, for there is much darkness of evil within, over which we mourn. It is night, for difficulties and dangers of every kind surround us. It is night, for we see at the best but as in a glass darkly. It is night, for it doth not yet appear what we shall be.

Let us however be of good cheer. "The day is at hand"—that endless day, when no night of adverse circumstances, no night of dark experiences, no night of evil or of ignorance, shall throw its deep shadow across our path. "The day is at hand" —the day of full light and liberty, the day of endless joy and glory, the day of manifested likeness unto Him, and oneness with Him, in the glorious home of light and joy above. Yes, we will comfort ourselves, and comfort one another with the thought that "the night is far spent, the day is at hand"—it may be very close at hand. A day without a cloud—a day that shall never know an eventide.

" *To depart, and to be with Christ; which is far better.*"—Phil. i. 23.

The soul has its glory change now, the body its glory change hereafter. Death is the body's sleep, but the soul's rising. Travellers usually awake and take their departure, but here the traveller falls asleep and departs to his home to be with Jesus.

The mortal body is the soul's fading earthly robe. The grave is the receptacle of the soul's worn-out garment. "With Christ" is the soul's joyous resting-place.

The risen body is the soul's glorified raiment, all fair and beauteous, like unto that of the risen Lord Himself. Verily "to depart and to be with Christ is far better."

X.

" *Let patience have her perfect work.*"—James i. 4.

MORE literally, "Let endurance (or 'patient endurance') have a perfect work." The word translated "endurance" means primarily "a remaining behind" after others have gone, after friends and helpers have departed. It implies a remaining behind because conscious of being in the path of duty. It also implies a willingness to await the attack of the enemy and the consciousness of a sustaining power, though unseen and unknown by others. It implies also a determination to persevere to the end.

Thus the full meaning of the word indicates that a perfect work of patience is a complete victory over the opposition of self, and over all other opposing influences in the path of daily service.

The Lord Jesus, in opening out the way for patience to have her perfect work, often places the believer where there is increased and increasing need for patience, because every prospect is so unpromising, and every association is so uncongenial. Then, indeed, does the believer find that the perfect work of patience and its resulting victory is only accomplished through a perfect rest in Jesus, and in quiet waiting upon Him, and for Him, in each circumstance of the daily path.

XI.

" *For ye were as sheep going astray, but are now returned unto the Shepherd and Bishop of your souls.*"—1 Pet. ii. 25.

" YE were as sheep going astray ; " how distinctly this shows that those sinners who trust in the Lord Jesus for salvation, were already His sheep when as yet they had not been brought to know their need of the great salvation accomplished for them by their "good Shepherd."

" Ye are now returned unto the Shepherd and Bishop of your souls ; " how distinctly this shows the sure results of grace through the quickening work of the Holy Spirit. As the result of that work the Lord Jesus possesses the chiefest attraction for them. " My sheep hear My voice . . . and they follow Me." They now seek no other place of refuge, no other guide but Himself. They may possess but little comfort. They may have but a very faint assurance of their interest in His love. Great may be the depths of inbred evil over which they mourn ; yet withal they can truly say that their eyes are towards Him, and the desire of their hearts is after Him. The sure evidence this, that His eyes were previously towards them, and His desire first after them, and that His voice has effectually called them to Himself. "Them also I must bring, and they shall hear My voice." How emphatic! How certain is the Shepherd's language! "I *must* bring"—"they *shall* hear."

How complete are the arrangements of the everlasting covenant! How irresistible are the workings of sovereign, electing grace! So is it always. He begins the work in the soul of His beloved; and it is He who carries on that work unto the end. Both the beginning and the end shall evermore be to the glory of His matchless, free, and unmerited grace.

XII.

"I will trust and not be afraid."—Isa. xii. 2.

CIRCUMSTANCES are the Lord's opportunities and the Lord's servants, for preparing the hearts of His people for a fuller revelation of Himself, and for fashioning them as special instruments for special service here or hereafter.

That future service will reveal how necessary was the previous training, and how needful was the rough east wind in its day, as well as the gentle south wind : and that even when He led

His chosen ones through deep waters and through the fires, it was for a fashioning which nothing else could accomplish.

Moreover He always does it Himself; His own loving hand is always engaged in the work, therefore all must be well; and though ofttimes the believer may be perplexed, yet the language of his heart should ever be, " I will trust and not be afraid," for the Lord is always deserving of the heart's unreserved trust, even when to sense it may appear as if all things were against the believer's progress and well-being.

In the darkest path, faith knows there is an eye watching that never slumbers; a hand working that never wearies; a heart loving that never changes; and that both eye, and hand, and heart are, through sovereign grace, engaged in completing the work that grace began.

XIII.

"Ye are Christ's; and Christ is God's."
—1 Cor. iii. 23.

WHAT a privilege, what an honour it is to belong to Jesus, and to be one with Him in the Father's love, in the Father's joy, in the Father's home.

Chosen together, loved together, justified together, sanctified together, glorified together. Oh! what a bond is that of the heavenly family! It is indissoluble. It is eternal.

He is ours, and we are His. We belong to Jesus. We can, therefore, well wait with confident and restful hearts until He comes to take us home. We are as safe here as at home, though not as happy. As safe, for He is with us always; not as happy, for we see Him not; as safe, for He guards us as "the apple of His eye;" not as happy, because we are still pilgrims and strangers in a strange country; as safe, for we are one with Him, and because He lives we shall live also; but not as happy, for we are not yet "made like unto Him."

We wait then for going-home time to see Him, to be with Him, to be like Him for ever and ever.

" To comfort all that mourn."—Isa. lxi. 2.

One of the sweetest and most blessed features in the character and work of the Lord Jesus was the fact that He came "to comfort all that mourn." His people are to be conformed to His image; and many of the consolations He affords His tried ones are sent through earthly channels. Thus, comforters of one another are we.

No more God-like errand can man have, than, as Heaven's messenger, to wipe away the tears of the mourner, and " speak comfortably " (Isa. xl. 2) to the sorrowing; and those are, through the Lord's grace, most able to comfort others, who have had unusual need of comfort themselves (2 Cor. i. 4, 5).

XIV.

" He endured, as seeing Him who is invisible."
—Heb. xi. 27.

THE salvation which the Lord Jesus has purchased is indeed a great and infinite blessing, but salvation does not satisfy those longings which the Holy Spirit has enkindled in the heart of the believer. Salvation is not Jesus Himself; it is Himself alone that satisfies. Salvation is the first taste of His love. Salvation is the first draught out of that fountain from which we want to drink more and more.

We need not wait until we reach heaven to have much of heavenly joy and heavenly rest. That which will make heaven a heaven to the

believer, is the fact that he will then see the Lord
Jesus and be wholly like unto Him. This will
produce perfect rest and joy ; but this joy and
rest may be attained here in a measure far beyond
what most believers think possible. True, we
cannot see Him face to face as we shall then, but
we may so walk as seeing Him who is invisible,
so walk in continued consciousness of His personal
presence and watchful love, that His presence
will be more realised by us than that of those
around us whom our eyes behold, and He Himself
be more our joy than any earthly being whatever.

We may so rest in Him by faith here, that in
Him every care shall find its cure, every sorrow
its solace, every difficulty its solution, and every
sin its defeat ; and although on earth, with this
body of sin and death to hinder, we can never
hope to be fully like unto Him, yet, thus walking
in communion, we cannot fail to grow more and
more like unto Him every day. Oh ! that we
who know the Lord did live more in accordance
with, and walk more conscious of, our position in
Christ—rejoicing in Him always.

What we want is a heart fixed on Christ—
intently fixed on Christ—and filled with Christ.
Then will the mind ever have thoughts of Him.
Then will the walk ever testify of Him.   Oh ! for

a heart steadfastly fixed on Him, whose heart is
so fixed in unchanging love on us.

XV.

" Rejoice in the Lord alway."—Phil. iv. 4.

THIS exhortation of the apostle does not imply
that every moment we are to be experiencing
conscious joy in the Lord Jesus, without inter-
ruption day after day, for this would certainly
prevent the fulfilment of many important duties
to which the believer is called, and which require
judicious thought, and such thought as, for the
time being, will prevent him having continuous
thoughts of Christ.

The object of the apostle is to teach us that
we should not have gloomy thoughts about the
Lord Jesus, nor hard thoughts, as if He were a
stern master, instead of a loving and ever-gracious
friend ; or as if He had forgotten us, or were
indifferent to our trials and need. He would
have us to be often thinking about Him ; and
whenever we do, always to think of Him as One
who is loving, gracious, faithful, gentle, and
wise ; and always to rejoice that we possess such
a friend ; or, in fewer words, he would teach us

that our fellowship with Christ in daily life is to
be always one of confidence, and thankfulness,
and peace, and gladness of heart.

XVI.

" *The Lord is able to give thee much more than
    this.*"—2 Chron. xxv. 9.
"*Is anything too hard for the Lord?* "—Gen.
    xviii. 14.
" *Able to do exceeding abundantly above all that
    we ask or think.*"—Eph. iii. 20.

WITH such a helper, such a provider, surely the
believer is well cared for, and may joyfully say,
" I will trust and not be afraid." If there be no
end to the believer's need, there is certainly no
end to the Lord's giving. However much a
believer may have received, or may now need, or
may have lost, or be likely to lose in the path of
faithful service, it is ever true, " The Lord is able
to give much more than this."

Though the difficulties in the path of duty
may seem insurmountable, the believer has
nothing to fear, for walking with the Lord in the
path of duty, the Lord walks with him in all
its difficulties, and, "Is anything too hard for
the Lord ?"

Moreover, what a liberal provider He is! The measure of His doing is not according to our conscious need; but He doeth "exceeding abundantly above all." Verily, we can say: "Who is like unto Thee, O Lord, who is like unto Thee, glorious in holiness, fearful in praises, doing wonders?"

XVII.

" That He might humble thee, and that He might prove thee, to do thee good at thy latter end."
—Deut. viii. 16.

WHEN the Lord prepares His children for future earthly blessings, it is sometimes by lessons hard to learn, and by discipline hard to bear. He would show them their folly that they may become wise, their sinfulness that they may become humble, and their emptiness that they may become more ready receivers. He would also show them the insufficiency of all that is of man, that they may more fully realise in the end that all good is of God. The Lord loves perfectly, therefore He loves wisely, and in view of the future.

To those who judge Him by sense, and not by faith, His dealings are often a perplexing maze, and the doings of His hand seem the hidings of His love rather than the manifestations thereof; but the trusting heart knows that however varied His providences may be, His love is still the same.

The Lord loves in view of the future. He sees the end of every path, and all His dealings with His children are for eventual good, "that He might do thee good at thy latter end." If the lessons are hard to learn, yet it is the once pierced hand of Jesus that appoints them, and His loving heart sympathises with the learner, both in the needed learning and in the needed discipline. Oh, for a patient heart! oh, for a meek and quiet spirit! not only to learn of Him, but to learn to be like Him.

Humbling times and trying times, rightly used, end in times of richer blessing to the children of God. The book of God's providence needs patient and quiet waiting spirits—such, and such only, learn the secrets of the Lord and always rejoice in Him. Before the Lord exalts much, He humbles much. Those who humbly walk with Him in lowly places shall joyfully walk with Him in high places, for "He that humbleth himself shall be exalted."

XVIII.

*" One thing have I desired of the Lord, that will
I seek after."*—Ps. xxvii. 4.

MANY believers purpose well, but their purposes
are seldom fully carried out, being so soon hindered
by opposing influences : they purpose over and
over again, but are always beaten back for want of
determination.   Others may be heard frequently
expressing earnest desires after the better way;
but desires are not all that is needed.

Many sigh, and long, and wish, and go no
further ; as if sighing, and longing, and wishing
would bring victory over spiritual foes, and
nerve the spirit for greater endurance, and make
the soul more spiritually-minded. Such sometimes even wonder why they are not different,
seeing they have such earnest desires for better
things ; whereas their great want is firmness of
will to act and persevere.

The Psalmist shows a better way when he
says, " One thing have I desired of the Lord "—
here was the good desire; but he did not stop
there, for he goes on to say, " that will I seek
after." Thus, praying, desiring, and determined
doing went together.   Wherever this is the case,
blessing is sure to follow in due time.

XIX.

" The way of the righteous is made plain."
—Prov. xv. 19.

THE Lord Himself who appoints the way also makes it plain. Waiting therefore on the Lord Jesus, walking step by step with Him, trusting in Him, the believer has no cause for anxiety or perplexity.

More literally, " The path of the righteous is raised up " (as a causeway). A causeway is a level road raised up high and dry through wet and marshy land, or over uneven rocky ground, so that the traveller goes on in a plain dry path, though there be bogs, and pits, or dangerous impediments on the right hand and on the left. So is it with " the righteous " (or " the upright ") ; his way is " raised up as a causeway ; " it is a plain path, a smooth path, a clean path, a safe path, a ready-made path, in which he is lifted up above all that would hinder his journey or cause him harm.

Sometimes the believer reaches a specially difficult part of his pilgrim path, and is like a traveller standing at the brink of a dark and dangerous morass which bars his further progress.

He knows not where to find safe footing.   He

is unable to take one step further by reason of
the dreaded dangers and of the gloomy mist
which almost shrouds him in darkness, when
suddenly the mist cloud arises—the light shines
—a plain, even, and safe path is discovered, and
he journeys on more rapidly and happily than
before. The same light that revealed the path
reveals also the dangers on the right hand and
left, and makes him the more grateful that he
has at last found a safe path for his feet.

Thus is it that "the way of the righteous is
made plain." Thus is it that the Lord Jesus
"preserveth the way of His saints."

XX.

*"In quietness and in confidence shall be your
strength."*—Isa. xxx. 15.

STRIVING and crying before the Lord for temporal
good in the providential path, or for pleasant
experiences in the heart, is often, in believers,
the result of self-love rather than of faith. Self
wants something for self-ease or self-satisfaction,
and this prompts to the crying and striving.
But it will never succeed. There must be a quiet
faith both as regards temporal things and plea-

sant experiences—a faith which seeks the Lord and His will, and trusts Him at all times. The soul's strength is in quietness, not striving—in the assurance of the Lord's loving-kindness, and not in having the mind most filled with desires for temporal good, or desires after pleasing experiences. Christ first, Christ always, and Christ only, should be the soul's desire, and this will also be the soul's consolation and strength, safety and joy.

In the quietness of a restful faith, and in a full confidence in the love and wisdom of a faithful God and Father, and of a gracious and loving Saviour, the soul is established as in a strong tower, and behind a sure wall of defence.

XXI.

" Jesus . . . lifted up His eyes to heaven."
—John xvii. 1.

THE Lord Jesus " lifted up His eyes to heaven," because His Father was there, and His home was there. We do the same, but we have Him there now as well as our Father, even Him who is " the first-born among many brethren," and One who is not ashamed to call us brethren.

Yes, we have Him there as well as our Father,

loving, watching over, and caring for us, and waiting for our coming home. Happy home! Happy travellers going to such a home. Happy, though often weary and much tried, yet happy still, because He who was made in all things like unto His brethren, even He is guiding us to that heavenly home and to that gracious Father who loves us as He loves His first-born. We, with the Lord Jesus, are His many sons, and Jesus, the first-born, among them, for we are all His children. "Thou hast loved them as Thou hast loved Me." So we too lift up our eyes to heaven seeking "those things which are above, where Christ sitteth on the right hand of God" (Col. iii. 1).

XXII.

"So Jotham became mighty, because he pre-pared his ways before the Lord his God."
—2 Chron. xxvii. 6.

OPEN dealings with the Lord Jesus, and the doing of all things as unto Him and not unto men, will bring power in the service, and confidence and peace in the heart, and blessing in the end. "Them that honour Me I will honour."

How many prepare their ways under the con-

sideration of what their fellow-men will see or
what their fellow-men will say, rather than under
the consideration of what the Lord will see or
what the Lord will say ; and thus they fall into
many a snare.

How often social position, the honour that
comes from man, the fear of losing caste, the
dread of seeming to be peculiar, and similar
influences, lead too many to plan and act as
before men rather than as before the Lord,
whom alone they should desire to please, whose
word alone should be their guide, and whose
glory alone should be their aim.

Oh ! for grace to be like the Apostle Paul, who
" counted all things but loss for the excellency
of the knowledge of Christ Jesus " his Lord ;
and to be like Jotham, who " became mighty,
because he prepared his ways before the Lord
his God."

XXIII.

" That they may be made perfect in one."
—John xvii. 23.

THIS is the only true perfection of believers in
all heavenly and earthly relationships. " Perfect
in one "—even Jesus. From His birth in Beth-

lehem to His ascension unto, and session at, the right hand of God, He was a representative Man, though always the true God.

In His righteous life the Father saw His people living in Him, and by His obedience made righteous ; and thus " made perfect in one." In His death the Father saw His people dying in Him, and in His death answering the penalty of a condemning law ; and thus " made perfect in one." In His resurrection and ascension and sitting on the right hand of God, His people's oneness with Him remained unchanged, as it is written,—" And hath raised us up together, and made us sit together in heavenly places in Christ Jesus,"—thus accepted before the Father as one mystical body complete in Christ the Head, and so " made perfect in one." At the great day of the consummation of all things, the glory the Father gave Him He will share with His people, so shall they be perfectly glorious and perfectly glorified, and thus manifestly "made perfect in one."

Their being " perfect in one " in the eternity to come, is but the outflow and full manifestation of their being " perfect in one " in the eternity that is past, in the Father's love and covenant arrangements, when He chose them in Christ Jesus before the world was.

XXIV.

" And when they came that were hired about the eleventh hour, they received every man a penny."—Matt. xx. 9.

THESE labourers had wrought but one hour, but no doubt they did that one hour's work to the best of their ability. They were only called to one hour's work, and they faithfully fulfilled the work to which they were called. It was probably no fault of theirs that they were left unhired all day, and thus constrained to stand idle. They were waiting to be hired. They were willing to work, but no man hired them. Probably they were the weakest-looking of all who sought to be hired. One may have borne the traces of a severe illness from which he had just recovered, and looked unfit for much labour. Another might be lame, and thus unable to do a hard day's work. A third might have some other manifest physical infirmity. All of them, no doubt, were the least likely labourers in the market, and therefore they were left unhired ; more robust-looking men being chosen instead.

At the eleventh hour they were called ; and their strength proved sufficient for the one hour's labour that awaited them. They did what

they could, and evidently they did it well, for
their master seemed satisfied, and gave them the
same remuneration as he gave to those who had
borne the heat and burden of the day.

It is well to know that the Lord Jesus never
calls to work for which the workman is unsuited.
As the strength is suited to the day, so the work
is suited to the workman and the workman to
the work.

In the eyes of men, those labourers in the field
of religious activities, who have borne the heat
and burden of the day, and whose names and
fame are in every man's mouth, are doubtless
considered the most praiseworthy and deserving
the greatest reward of grace. The Lord, however, sees and judges differently to men; and
His judgments are always right. At the great
day of manifestation, the labourer called but to
one hour's work, and who fulfilled his one hour
to the best of his ability, will receive from His
gracious Master approval and reward equal to
the all-day labourers; aye, and in comparison
far beyond, if the all-day labourers sat in judgment upon their less capable fellow-workers, and
thought more of themselves and their all-day work
than they ought.

The reward of grace for service is not according to the amount of work, or the success attend-

ing it, but according to our faithfulness to the
Lord Jesus in doing that work, be it little or
much, to which He calls us.

XXV.

" In whom, though now ye see Him not, yet be-
lieving, ye rejoice with joy unspeakable, and
full of glory."—1 Pet. i. 8.

IF the children of God have peculiar sorrows,
they have peculiar consolations. If they have
special trials, they have also special blessings.

The Lord does not give His brighter blessings
to all His children, but only to some of His
more favoured ones; and as a diamond shines
brighter in a black setting, so He often sends
His diamond blessings in the black setting of
affliction, trials, bereavements, losses, or persecutions; but oh! the brightness of the diamond
blessing! for it is Jesus Himself—Jesus more
vividly and continuously realised in His presence
and love; a joy in Him unspeakable and full of
glory.

It is indeed blessed to be made a partaker of
salvation-joy; the joy of assured deliverance
from the wrath to come. It is still more blessed

to be made a partaker of glory-joy while still a pilgrim here on earth :—" In whom though now ye see Him not, yet believing, ye rejoice with joy unspeakable, and full of glory."

XXVI.

" According to the good pleasure of His will, to the praise of the glory of His grace, wherein He hath made us accepted in the Beloved."—Eph. i. 5, 6.

IT is a great comfort to know that our standing in Christ, and acceptance in Him, are not according to the measure of our faith or of our spiritual experience, but " according to the good pleasure of His will, to the praise of the glory of His grace, wherein He hath made us accepted in the Beloved."

" Hath made us"—it is the Father's own doing, and it is already done, and so done, that no want of experience, or weakness of faith, or failure in testimony, or slowness of progress, or want of realisation, or consciousness of evil within, can possibly alter it in the least.

This is an unchangeable acceptance. We stand in Christ and as He stands. This, then, is a sure foundation for our hope, and a sure foundation for our joy, notwithstanding the fact that everything of our own is marred and worthless.

We rejoice in the Lord Jesus always, as our ground of acceptance, though often sorrowful because of increasing consciousness of our ill-desert. We rejoice also in the love and grace of our Father who has, because of that love and grace, "made us accepted in the Beloved."

XXVII.

" Gave Him to be the head over all things to the Church."—Eph. i. 22.

WE are altogether, and always, in the hands of the Lord Jesus. "In the hands of God," many would say, in an abstract and general view of divine appointments. The believer, however, should know that for him "divine appointments" are covenant arrangements; and that God is to him a loving Father who has put him, and all that concerns him, into the hands of the Lord Jesus; that in Him he might have not only an all-sufficient Saviour, but a sure friend, whose "appointments" are always guided by unerring wisdom and unchanging love.

"*His own sheep.*"—John x. 3

And how dear to Him let His own word declare—"I lay down my life for the sheep." How safely protected let His own words testify—"They shall never perish, neither shall any pluck them out of my hand." How honoured in companionship, for He says—"I am with you alway!" How glorious their position—"The glory Thou gavest Me I have given them!" How exalted their future—"That where I am, there ye may be also!" "But it doth not yet appear what we shall be, but we know that when He shall appear, we shall be like Him."

XXVIII.

"*Your Father.*"—Matt. v. 45.

O child of God, what a Father He is to you! It was "your Father" who chose you before the world was to be His child. It was "your Father" who loved you with an everlasting love. It was "your Father" who gave you to the Lord Jesus in His purpose of grace before the beginning of creation. It was "your Father" who gave the Lord Jesus to be your surety, your ransom, your Saviour. It was "your Father" who caused you to know and trust in that same Saviour, or you never would have known and trusted in Him. It is "your Father" who will receive you at the hands of Jesus, when you shall appear before Him with all the children "your Father" gave Him. It is "your Father" who is also the Father of your Lord, even Jesus, and thus the same Jesus is one of the family as well as Lord—"firstborn among many brethren," and Lord of Heaven and earth. "Your Father" made Him to be all to you that He is, and that He ever will be.

Oh! what a Father "your Father" is! He knoweth what things you need, and you are sure to receive every good thing at His hand, for the very best He had to give, He has not withheld, even the Son of His love. And oh! what a loving, obedient, trustful, humble-hearted child should you be towards such a Father as "your Father" is! Your life, your heart, your lips should praise and magnify that name which the Everlasting God has condescended in so endearing a manner to call Himself by, when, looking upon you, He calls Himself "your Father." And, oh! how pleasant, how joyful with the Lord Jesus as your companion and as the Firstborn among many brethren, to hear him say—" My

Father, and your Father." Happy day, when
this ceases to be a matter of faith, and becomes
a full realisation in that bright family home
above, which "your Father" has provided for
you and all His ransomed children.

XXIX.

" *And Jesus said, Let her alone, why trouble ye
her?* " Or rather, " *Why do ye occasion
her grief* " or " *vexation* " *?*—Mark xiv. 6.

SHE had made no complaint—she had expressed
no sorrow—but doubtless her countenance was
cast down with " grief" at the indignation and
false accusation of the disciples. The Lord saw
it, and at once took her part, and pronounced
her blessed, in expressing His approbation of
that act which others had condemned. Oh ! how
necessary it is to cease from man, and seek only
to commend ourselves to the Lord in all we do.
How readily man shows indignation, if matters
are not done according to his standard. How
readily man imputes wrong motives, when conscience is really void of offence toward God and
man. Well ! it is a comfort that the Lord—

the gracious, compassionate Lord Jesus is our Judge.

When therefore the heart beats quicker, and grief swells the bosom, because of the unjust judgment of our fellows, let this be our comfort, that the Lord knows all, and that He who so quickly and so firmly took Mary's part, is still the watchful friend and defender of His loved ones, and that He will, in His own time and way, according to His own word, bring forth their righteousness as the light, and their judgment as the noonday. Jesus said, "Let her alone, why trouble ye her ? "

XXX.

" Seek the Lord and His strength; seek His face evermore ! "—Ps. cv. 4.

THE more we " seek the Lord and His strength," the more shall we be consciously supported in seasons of weakness and need. The more we "seek His face," the more shall we walk in the light, wherever we may be called to walk. The sunshine of His countenance makes a wilderness to be a pleasant place. Without that the very garden of Eden itself would be but a barren desert to the child of God.

The " strength " of Jehovah is Jesus. The " face " of Jehovah is Jesus. Looking to Him, leaning on Him, walking with Him, will bring light, and joy, and strength to our spirit.

" In the multitude of my thoughts within me Thy comforts delight my soul."—Ps. xciv. 19.

" Thy comforts," O Jesus my Lord, even Thy constant presence, Thy changeless love and the sure word of Thy grace, even these shall be the stay and delight of my soul, when many and perplexing thoughts arise within to disturb its peace. " Why are ye troubled, and why do thoughts arise in your hearts? Behold My hands and My feet that it is I Myself " (Luke xxiv. 38, 39).

XXXI.

" *The world knoweth us not.*"—1 John iii. 1.

" *That the world may know that Thou hast sent me, and hast loved them as Thou hast loved me. Father, I will that they also whom Thou hast given me be with me where I am.*"—John xvii. 23, 24.

OH! what a high, what a privileged, what an honoured position is that of believers. The world knoweth us not, even as it knew not our Lord, but if worldly eyes were open, for ever so short a time, to behold, not indeed the glory that awaits believers hereafter, but the glory that surrounds them now, in their low estate—to see the bright angelic spirits that are ministering continually on their behalf (Heb. i. 14), to see how near and dear they are to the Father, and to the Son, and to the Holy Spirit; surely the humblest child of God would become to them an object of solemn awe, and dread, and amazement.

They will see and understand it all, when in a future day they know that as the Father has loved His Son, so has He loved, and with the same love, all those who trust in Him. Until then, we are the Lord's hidden ones, and the world knoweth us not, even as it knew Him not. His hidden ones now, but soon to be His manifested ones; for soon He cometh, and then we take our rightful place—that place eternally designed for us by the Father, and won and prepared for us by the Son.

Yet, after all, it is not the ministering servants we think of as we journey on, but of Him—even Jesus. Ah! angels are not members of His body, and of His flesh and of His bones (Eph. v. 30); "He took not on Him the nature of angels." And so He passed the angels by, having His heart set upon a richer treasure than they; and lo! that treasure, more precious to Him than unsinning angels, was found amongst the fallen sons of men. So " He took on Him the seed of Abraham." " Wherefore in all things it behoved Him to be made like unto His brethren." His brethren! what a relationship is ours! How wonderful! He would first be made like unto His brethren in lowliness and shame, then He makes His brethren like unto Himself in exaltation and glory.

It should be our joy to be always thinking of Him, always looking to Him, always living for Him, always glorying in Him. He will one day glory in each believer openly when He comes to be glorified in His saints.

Our Jesus—Yes, more can we claim Him ours
than the angels can. Our Jesus—in all things
like unto us. His people say, " The Lord is our
portion," and of Him it is written, " The Lord's
portion is His people." What a mutual affection
there is between them ! though sometimes it
seems as if the love were all on one side, even on
His—our regard for Him deserving not that
heavenly name of " love." By and by, however,
we will love Him with a perfected and unhindered affection when we " see Him as He is," and
are made fully like unto Him in our Father's
house above. Then will His own prayer be fully
answered—" Father, I will that they also whom
Thou hast given me be with me where I am."

INDEX OF TEXTS IN FIFTH PART.